FROM INDIA

TO

THE PLANET MARS

A STUDY OF A CASE OF SOMNAMBULISM

WITH GLOSSOLALIA

BY

TH. (Théodore) FLOURNOY

PROFESSOR OF PSYCHOLOGY AT THE UNIVERSITY OF GENEVA

TRANSLATED BY

DANIEL B. VERMILYE

First published in 1900

Published by Left of Brain Books

Copyright © 2023 Left of Brain Books

ISBN 978-1-396-32340-9

First Edition

All rights reserved. No part of this publication may be reproduced, distributed, or transmitted in any form or by any means, including photocopying, recording, or other electronic or mechanical methods, without the prior written permission of the publisher, except in the case of brief quotations permitted by copyright law. Left of Brain Books is a division of Left Of Brain Onboarding Pty Ltd.

PUBLISHER'S PREFACE

About the Book

"This is a skeptical inquiry into a remarkable 19th century French medium, here called Helene Smith. Her actual name was Catherine-Elise Muller (b. 1861 d. 1929). She popularized the concept of automatic writing, which earned her admiration from the latter-day Surrealists. And her interplanetary psychic visions are extremely similar to contactee accounts from the 1950s and 1960s.

Helene, at the hands of her bossy and controlling sprit guide 'Leopold,' visited remote times and places, particularly 15th century India (where she was a doomed princess), and 18th century France (where she was Marie Antoinette), and of greatest interest, Mars. This book documents the Martian language and writing, includes hand-drawn illustrations of scenes, and mysterious vignettes of life on another planet. Included are over forty short texts in 'Martian,' with translations in French (interlinear) and English.

Flournoy's book brought Helene fame, and the book is still in print over a hundred years later. However, she was not appreciative of his critical approach, and refused to work with him any further after the book was published."

(Quote from sacred-texts.com)

About the Author

"Theodore Flournoy (1854-1920) was a professor of psychology at the University of Geneva and author of books on spiritism and psychic phenomena. He is most known for his study of the medium Helen Smith (or Helene Smith - a pseudonym for Catherine Muller) who relayed information about past lives through a trance state, entitled From India To The Planet Mars (1899). He proposed this information as 'romances of the subliminal imagination', and a product of the unconscious mind (Stevens 1994). Flournoy was a contemporary of Freud, and his work influenced C.

G. Jung's study of another medium - his cousin Helene Preiswerk - which was turned into Jung's doctoral dissertation in 1902."

(Quote from wikipedia.org)

CONTENTS

PUBLISHER'S PREFACE
TRANSLATOR'S PREFACE 1
INTRODUCTION 10
   CHILDHOOD AND YOUTH OF MLLE. SMITH 19
   MLLE. SMITH SINCE HER INITIATION INTO SPIRITISM 32
   THE PERSONALITY OF LEOPOLD 58
   THE MARTIAN CYCLE 98
   THE MARTIAN CYCLE (CONTINUED)—THE MARTIAN LANGUAGE 137
   THE MARTIAN CYCLE (CONCLUDED).—THE ULTRA-MARTIAN 187
   THE HINDOO CYCLE 196
   THE ROYAL CYCLE 238
   SUPERNORMAL APPEARANCES 253
CONCLUSION 301

TRANSLATOR'S PREFACE

THE translation into English of *From India to the Planet Mars* has been undertaken in response to the demand created by the widespread and increasing interest which is manifesting itself both in Great Britain and the United States in the phenomena exhibited by its heroine—an interest which marks a new era in the progress of human knowledge.

Twenty—even ten—years ago the phenomena which Prof. Flournoy here describes in detail, and of which he offers a keen, skilful, psychological analysis, would have met with the sneers of popular science and the contempt of obscurantist orthodoxy; the book would have found few readers.

Times have greatly changed since the Society for Psychical Research was founded, eighteen years ago, by a few thoughtful men (included among them were those whose names would have conferred honor upon any body of men) interested in the investigation of abnormal mental or psychic phenomena.

In explaining their reasons for organizing that society, its founders made the following statement:

"From the recorded testimony of many competent witnesses, past and present, including observations accurately made by scientific men of eminence of various countries, there appears to be, among much illusion and deception, an important body of remarkable phenomena which are *prima facie* inexplicable on any generally recognized hypothesis, and which, if incontestably established, would be of the highest possible value."

The organization of this society constituted the first attempt in the world's history to investigate the phenomena of clairvoyance, automatic writing and speaking, trance conditions, second sight, apparitions of persons at the point of death, alleged spirit messages, etc., by a scientific body formed upon a broad basis.

As was to have been expected, the work and aims of the society were met by a storm of derision and ridicule, and by attacks which poured in from every quarter, the bitterest of which came from the always too numerous class of narrow-minded scientists, whose partisan prejudices, confining them to a narrow rut, hinder their seeing anything from a point of view other than that of their preconceived hypotheses, and prevent them from attaining that open-mindedness which is indispensable to and one of the first requisites of a true scientist in any field of investigation.

The interest shown to-day in the work of psychical research—among the evidences of which may be noted the reception accorded this work of Prof. Flournoy, which has, within a few months from the date of its publication, attained its third French edition—demonstrates the ultimate triumph of the founders of that society in their efforts to bring the thinking public to a realization of the supreme importance of a systematic scientific study of the mysterious psychic phenomena so long neglected by official science, but which are now beginning to assume their rightful place in the field of study and observation.

Men have come to realize that the facts proved by science have not thus far been adequate to satisfy the needs of mankind, and many are to-day asking whether the scientific investigation of psychic phenomena may not succeed in proving *the preamble of all religions*.

Already science has disclosed the existence of a hidden, subliminal world within each individual being, and it is the investigation of that part of the individuality of Hélène Smith which our author has undertaken in the following pages.

The importance of the subject and its intense interest lie in the fact that psychical research hints at a possible solution, by means of the same methods which science has been accustomed to use in the physical world, of the great problem of man's future destiny, of an answer to the question asked by Job four thousand years ago, "If a man die, shall he live again?" and which has been repeated in vain by every generation of men who have since inhabited the earth.

While, it is true, the great majority of men are still skeptical as to the ability of science ever to solve this problem, it is, however, a fact that a continually increasing number of thoughtful men are coming to believe that the hidden subliminal world within us may point to an unseen but spiritual world without, communication with which, if once established, would furnish us with the solution so ardently longed for.

Such men do not believe that it behooves them to be content with the passivity of pure Agnosticism are not willing that *Ignoramus et Ignorabimus* should be their only creed. They are beginning to search for new facts in the domain of the human mind, just as they have searched for and found them everywhere else they have looked for them.

Mr. F. W. H. Myers, the pioneer and leader of the psychical research movement, in an address recently delivered, says: "Starting from various stand-points, we endeavor to carry the newer, the intellectual virtues into regions where dispassionate tranquillity has seldom yet been known. . . . First, we adopt the ancient belief—implied in all monotheistic religion, and conspicuously confirmed by the progress of modern science—that the world as a whole, spiritual and material together, has in some way a systematic unity: and on this we base the novel presumption that there should be a unity of method in the investigation of all fact. We hold therefore that the attitude, the habits of mind, the methods by which physical science has grown deep and wide, should be applied also to the spiritual world. We endeavor to approach the problems of that world by careful collection, scrutiny, testing of particular facts; and we account no unexplained fact too trivial for our attention."

This is just what Prof. Flournoy has endeavored to do in regard to the strange phenomena manifested by Mlle. Helene Smith. No fact has been regarded by him as too trivial to escape his keen, careful scrutiny from a psychological point of view.

The first task which the investigators of these obscure mental phenomena set themselves was, naturally, that of separating and sifting the real, actually existent facts from the mass of fraud and deception in which mercenary charlatans, aided by the easy credulity of the simple-minded, had contrived so completely to bury from sight the true phenomena that for a long time the intelligent public refused utterly to believe in the existence of any real phenomena of the kind, but insisted that everything when fully probed would be found to be mere delusion, the result of trickery and fraud.

Probably no scientific fact since the dawn of modern science has required so great a weight of cumulative evidence in its favor to establish the reality of its existence in the popular mind than have the phenomena in question. The task, however, has been accomplished.

Prof. Flournoy's heroine, although she is a high-minded, honorable woman, regarded by all her neighbors and friends as wholly incapable of conscious fraud, has been subjected to the closest surveillance on the part of a number of eminent physicians and scientists of Geneva for more than five years past, while Mrs. Piper, the famous Boston medium, has been subjected to an even closer scrutiny by the Society for Psychical Research for the past fifteen years. In spite of the fact that this society has announced its willingness to become responsible for the entire absence of fraud in Mrs. Piper's case, and of a similar declaration on the part of Prof. Flournoy and his associates in regard to Mlle. Smith, there still remain a considerable number of ultra-skeptical persons who persist in asserting that fraud and deceit are at the bottom of, and account for, all this species of phenomena.

The well-known gentlemen who have investigated these crises have never been accused of easy credulity in other matters, and have cautiously and perseveringly continued, in their endeavor to satisfy skepticism, to pile Pelion upon Ossa in the way of cumulative proofs of the genuineness of the phenomena and to safeguard their investigations in every possible manner against all possibility of fraud, until they have finally come to feel that more than sufficient proof has been furnished to satisfy any honest, fair-minded, sensible doubt. They do not feel that they have the right to devote further time to the question of the genuineness of the facts observed by them—time which they believe might be better employed in endeavoring to discover the laws by which the phenomena are governed. They believe that those who are not satisfied with the evidence already offered will not be convinced by any amount of further testimony—that their skepticism is invincible. For persons so constituted this book will have no interest; its perusal will afford them no pleasure.

The endeavor to explain these mysterious phenomena by scientific investigators has resulted in their adoption of one or other of two hypotheses, viz.:

1. That the phenomena are the product of and originate in the subliminal consciousness of the medium; or,

2. That the phenomena are really of supernormal origin and emanate from the disincarnate spirits of the dead, who return to earth and take temporary possession of the organism of the medium, talking through her mouth, writing with her hand while she is in a somnambulistic state.

The first theory involves the crediting of the subliminal consciousness with almost miraculous powers of telepathy, since, on that hypothesis, it is necessary, in order to account for the knowledge possessed by the medium, to suppose that her subliminal consciousness is able to roam at will throughout the entire universe and read the mind of any being possessing the information sought for.

All open-minded investigators freely admit that either of the above hypotheses may be untrue; that very little is known by them as yet in regard to the nature of the phenomena; that the data are too slight to justify more than a provisional hypothesis, which the discovery of new facts may at any time entirely demolish. But, thus far, the hypotheses above given seem to be the only ones which will in any way rationally account for the facts: in which case, it is evident that each individual observer will be influenced in his choice of a hypothesis by his religious belief, which will greatly affect the point of view from which he approaches the subject, and also by his natural temperament, habits of thought, etc.

Prof. Flournoy states that he has endeavored to keep constantly in mind and to be guided by two propositions, which he designates respectively the "Principle of Hamlet" and the "Principle of La Place," the former being, "*All things are possible*," the latter, "*The weight of the evidence ought to be proportioned to the strangeness of the facts.*"

Guided by these two principles, Prof. Flournoy has come to the conclusion that Mlle. Smith really possesses the faculty of telekinesis—the ability to move ponderable objects situated at a distance, without contact and contrary to known natural laws. On the other hand, he does not believe the phenomena manifested by her to be of supernormal origin. The various alleged "spirit" messages, "incarnations," "gift of tongues," and all other apparently supernormal phenomena, in his opinion, spring from Mlle. Smith's subliminal consciousness, and he exercises great skill and ingenuity in his effort to trace the very wonderful and astonishing manifestations with which he has had to deal to natural sources.

Whether the individual reader adopts the author's views and theories, or finds in others a more natural explanation of the facts narrated by Prof. Flournoy, he cannot fail to admire the frankness, candor, and entire freedom from prejudice displayed by him. He evinces a true, open-minded, scientific spirit, never distorting facts in order to make them fit his hypotheses, and freely admitting the possibility of the discovery of new facts at any time, of a nature to compel him to adopt some other hypothesis than that which he has provisionally assumed to explain the phenomena.

A word on another subject before the reader goes on to the perusal of this narrative of strange facts:

One who is interested in Psychical Research,—when he has finally succeeded in convincing some obstinate skeptic of the genuineness of the phenomena—when the doubter has at last yielded to the weight of evidence, then, very frequently, the next question, which comes as a wet blanket to dampen the ardor of the enthusiastic devotee, is: "*Cui bono?* Admitting the truth of the facts, what useful purpose is subserved by their study? Science will never succeed in solving the problem of man's future destiny. It is all a waste of time and will end in nothing." And in a review of this very book, which recently appeared in one of our leading metropolitan newspapers, the reviewer asks, "What will science make of all this?" (referring to the phenomena manifested by Mlle. Smith); and then answers his own question by saying, "It is very unlikely that science will ever discover the nature of these mysterious phenomena or the laws which govern them."

From this conclusion the followers of Psychical Research emphatically dissent. It seems passing strange to them that such an opinion should be held by intelligent men at the present stage of development of human knowledge, in view of the mighty discoveries which have been wrested from nature by the laborious process of persevering observation of seemingly trivial facts. An eighteenth-century writer might with some show of reason have made a similar observation in regard to Dr. Franklin and his experiments with kite and key in a thunder-storm. It would indeed, at that epoch, have seemed unlikely that science would succeed in discovering the secret of the electric fluid by such means. But to-day, at the dawn of the twentieth century, with all the experience of the past to judge from, are not the probabilities all in favor of great results to science from repeated experiments by trained observers, such as Prof. Flournoy, upon cases similar to that of Mlle. Smith?

If the hypothesis that the world as a whole, spiritual and material together, has in some way a systematic unity, be true—and that is the hypothesis accepted by a majority of thinking men at the present time—then the importance of collecting and recording and analyzing such facts as those presented to us in the present narrative cannot be overestimated.

The scientific demonstration of a future life may be one of the great triumphs reserved for the science of the twentieth century to win, and Hélène Smith and Prof. Flournoy may ultimately appear to have contributed largely to its accomplishment.

To those who still persist in asking *Cui bono?* in reference to such work as that which Prof. Flournoy has here so ably performed, I beg leave to quote further from Mr. Myers the following:

"The faith to which Science is sworn is a faith in the uniformity, the coherence, the intelligibility of, at any rate, the material universe. Science herself is but the practical development of this mighty postulate. And if any phenomenon on which she chances on her onward way seems arbitrary, or incoherent, or unintelligible, she does not therefore suppose that she has come upon an unravelled end in the texture of things; but rather takes for granted that a rational answer to the new problem must somewhere exist—an answer which will be all the more instructive because it will involve facts of which that first question must have failed to take due account.

"This faith in the uniformity of material Nature formulates itself in two great dogmas—for such they are;—the dogma of the Conservation of Matter and the dogma of the Conservation of Energy. Of the Conservation of Matter, within earthly limits, we are fairly well assured; but of the Conservation of Energy the proof is far less complete, simply because Energy is a conception which does not belong to the material world alone. Life is to us the most important of all forms of activity—of energy, I would say—except that we cannot transform other energies into Life, nor measure in foot-pounds that directive force which has changed the face of the world. Life comes we know not whence; it vanishes we know not whither; it is interlocked with a moving system vaster than that we know. To grasp the whole of its manifestation, we should have to follow it into an unseen world. Yet scientific faith bids us believe that there, too, there is continuity; and that the past and the future of that force which we discern for a moment are still subject to universal Law.

"Out of the long Stone Age our race is awakening into consciousness of itself. We stand in the dawn of history. Behind us lies a vast and unrecorded waste—the mighty struggle *humanam condere gentem*. Since the times of that ignorance we have not yet gone far; a few thousand years, a few hundred thinkers, have barely started the human mind upon the great æons of its onward way. It is not yet the hour to sit down in our studies and try to eke out Tradition with Intuition—as one might be forced to do in a planet's senility, by the glimmer of a fading sun. *Daphni, quid antiquos signorum suspicis ortus?* The traditions, the intuitions of our race are themselves in their infancy; and before we abandon ourselves to brooding over them let us at least first try the upshot of a systematic search for actual facts. For what should hinder? If our inquiry lead us first through a jungle of fraud and folly, need that alarm us? As well might Columbus have yielded to the sailors' panic when he was entangled in the Sargasso Sea. If our first clear facts about the Unseen World seem small and trivial, should that deter us from the quest? As well might Columbus have sailed home again, with America in the offing, on the ground that it was not worth while to discover a continent which manifested itself only by dead logs."

It is deeply to be regretted that no appeals have availed to persuade Mlle. Smith to consent to the publication of her photograph, in connection with Prof. Flournoy's account of the phenomena manifested by her.

She shrinks from the publicity which her possession of these strange powers has thrust upon her. She dislikes extremely the notoriety given to her mysterious faculties, and refuses to be interviewed concerning them, or to discuss Prof. Flournoy's book.

The name Helene Smith is, as the reader will doubtless guess, merely a pseudonym. The individuality designated by that name, however, is held in highest esteem—in veneration even—by a very large circle of friends and acquaintances in the city on the shores of Lake Leman, in which she has passed her life from infancy, for whose benefit she is always ready to exercise her mysterious gifts and to give her services freely to such as seek her aid, refusing always to accept any pecuniary compensation for her services. Attaching, as she does, a religious significance to her powers, she would deem it a sacrilege to traffic in them.

DANIEL B. VERMILYE.

COLUMBIA UNIVERSITY, NEW YORK,
July, 1900.

INTRODUCTION

IN the month of December, 1894, I was invited by M. Aug. Lemaître, Professor of the College of Geneva, to attend some seances of a non-professional medium, receiving no compensation for her services, and of whose extraordinary gifts and apparently supernormal faculties I had frequently heard.

Having gladly accepted the invitation of my worthy colleague, I found the medium in question, whom I shall call Mlle. Hélène Smith, to be a beautiful woman about thirty years of age, tall, vigorous, of a fresh, healthy complexion, with hair and eyes almost black, of an open and intelligent countenance, which at once invoked sympathy. She evinced nothing of the emaciated or tragic aspect which one habitually ascribes to the sibyls of tradition, but wore an air of health, of physical and mental vigor, very pleasant to behold, and which, by-the-way, is not often encountered in those who are good mediums.

The number of those invited to take part in the seance being complete, we seated ourselves in a circle, with our hands resting upon the traditional round table of spiritistic circles. Mlle. Smith—who possesses a triple mediumship: visual, auditive, and typtological [1]—began, in the most natural manner, to describe the various apparitions which passed before her eyes in the partially darkened room. Suddenly she stops and listens; she hears a name spoken in her ear, which she repeats to us with astonishment; then brief sentences, the words of which are spelled out by raps on the table, explain the meaning of the vision. Speaking for myself alone (there were three of us to divide the honor of the seance), I was greatly surprised to recognize in scenes which passed before my eyes events which had transpired in my own family prior to my birth. Whence could the medium, whom I had never met before, have derived the knowledge of events belonging to a remote past, of a private nature, and utterly unknown to any living person?

---

[1] *I.e.*, Spirit-rapping—the faculty of obtaining responses by means of raps upon a table.

The astounding powers of Mrs. Piper, the famous Boston medium, whose wonderful intuition reads the latent memories of her visitors like an open book, recurred to my mind, and I went out from that seance with renewed hope of finding myself some day face to face with the "supernormal"—a true and genuine supernormal—telepathy, clairvoyance, spiritistic manifestations, it matters not by what name it be called, provided only that it be wholly out of the ordinary, and that it succeed in utterly demolishing the entire framework of established present-day science.

I was able at this time to obtain general information only concerning the past of Mlle. Smith, but it was all of a character favorable to her, and has since been fully confirmed.

Of modest bearing and an irreproachable moral character, she has for years earned an honorable living as an employée of a commercial house, in which her industry, her perseverance, and her high character have combined to secure her a very responsible and important position.

Some three years prior to the date of my introduction to her she had been initiated into a spiritistic group, where her remarkable psychic powers almost immediately manifested themselves; and she then became a member of various other spiritistic circles. From its commencement her mediumship manifested the complex type to which I have already alluded, and from which it has never deviated. Visions in a waking state, accompanied by typtological dictation and auditive hallucinations, alternately appeared. From the point of view of their content these messages had generally a bearing on past events usually unknown to the persons present, but which were always verified by referring to biographical dictionaries or to the traditions of the families interested. To these phenomena of retrocognition or of hypermnesia were joined occasionally, according to the environment, moral exhortations, communicated through the table, more frequently in poetry than in prose, addressed to the sitters; medical consultations, accompanied by prescriptions generally appropriate; communications from parents or friends recently deceased; or, finally, revelations as piquant as they were unverifiable concerning the *antériorités* (that is, the previous existences) of the sitters, almost all of whom, being profound believers in spiritism, would not have been at all surprised to learn that they were the reincarnations respectively of Coligny, of Vergniaud, of the Princess Lamballe, or of other notable personages. It is necessary, finally, to add that all these messages seemed to be more or less bound up with the mysterious presence of a "spirit" answering to the name of Leopold, who assumed to be the guide and protector of the medium.

I at once undertook to improve my acquaintance with Hélène Smith. She freely consented to give seances for my benefit, alternating with a series which she was giving M. Lemaître, and another for the benefit of Prof. Cuendet, vice-president of the Geneva Society (spiritistic) for Psychic Studies, all of which I was permitted to attend. In this way I have been able to be present at the greater part of Hélène's seances during the past five years. The personal observations that I have thus been able to make, reinforced by notes on sittings which I was unable to attend, kindly furnished me by MM. Lemaître and Cuendet, form the basis of the study which follows; to which must be added, however, certain letters of Mlle. Smith, as well as the numerous and very interesting conversations I have held with her either immediately preceding or following her seances, or at her home, where I also have had the advantage of being able to talk with her mother. Finally, various documents and accessory information, which will be cited in their respective time and place, have also been of assistance in enabling me partially to elucidate certain obscure points. Notwithstanding all these sources of information, however, I am still very far from being able to disentangle and satisfactory explain the complex phenomena which constitute Hélène's mediumship.

Dating from the period at which I made the acquaintance of Mlle. Smith (*i.e.*, from the winter of 1894-95), while most of her spiritistic communications have continued to present he same character as to form and content as before, a double and very important modification in her mediumship has been observed.

1. As to their psychological form.—While up to that time Hélène had experienced partial and limited automatisms only—visual, auditive, typtomotor hallucinations—compatible with the preservation to a certain extent of the waking state, and not involving noticeable loss of memory, from that time and with increasing frequency she has been subject to an entire loss of consciousness and a failure to retain, on returning to her normal state, any recollection of what has transpired during the seance. In physiological terms, the hemisomnambulism without amnesia, which had been her stopping-point up to that time, and which the sitters mistook for the ordinary waking state, was now transformed into total somnambulism with consecutive amnesia.

In spiritistic parlance, Mlle. Smith now became completely entranced, and having formerly been an ordinary visual and auditive medium, she now advanced to the higher plane of an "incarnating medium."

I fear that this change must in a great measure be attributed to my influence, since it followed almost immediately upon my introduction to Hélène's seances. Or, even if the total somnambulism would have inevitably been eventually developed by virtue of an organic predisposition and of a tendency favorable to hypnoid states, it is nevertheless probable that I aided in hastening its appearance by my presence as well as by a few experiments which I permitted myself to make upon Hélène.

As is well known, mediums are usually surrounded by a halo of veneration, which prevents any one from touching them during their trances The idea would never occur to any ordinary frequenter of spiritistic circles to endeavor to ascertain the condition of the medium's sensory and motor functions by feeling her hands, pinching the flesh, or pricking the skin with a pin. Silence and immobility are the strict rule, in order not to hinder the spontaneous production of the phenomena, and a few questions or brief observations on the receipt of a message is all that is permissible by way of conversation, and no one therefore would, under ordinary circumstances, dare to attempt any manipulation of the medium Mlle. Smith had always been surrounded by this respectful consideration, and during the first three seances I conformed myself strictly to the passive and purely contemplative attitude of the other sitters. But at the fourth sitting my discretion vanished. I could not resist a strong desire to ascertain the physiological condition of the charming seeress, and I made some vigorous elementary experiments upon her hands, which lay temptingly spread out opposite me on the table. These experiments, which I renewed and followed up at the succeeding seance (February 3, 1895), demonstrated that there is present in Mlle. Smith, *during her visions*, a large and varied assortment of sensory and motor disturbances which had hitherto escaped the notice of the sitters, and which are thoroughly identical with those that may be observed in cases of hysteria (where they are more permanent), and those that may be momentarily produced in hypnotic subjects by suggestion. This was not at all astonishing, and was to have been expected. But one consequence, which I had not foreseen, did occur when, four days after my second experimental seance, Mlle. Smith fell completely asleep for the first time at a sitting with M. Cuendet (February 7th), at which I was not present. The sitters were somewhat frightened, and, in trying to awaken her, discovered the rigidity of her arms, which were considerably contractured. Leopold however, communicating by means of the table upon which she was leaning, fully reassured them, and gave them to understand that such sleep was not at all prejudicial to the medium. After assuming various attitudes and indulging in some amusing mimicry, Mlle. Smith awoke in excellent spirits, retaining as a last recollection of her dream that of a kiss which Leopold had imprinted upon her forehead.

From that day on somnambulisms were the rule with Hélène, and the seances at which she did not fall completely asleep for at least a few moments formed rare exceptions to the course of events during the next four years. It is a great deprivation for Mlle. Smith that these slumbers ordinarily leave her no memory upon her awakening of what has transpired in her trance, and she longs for the seances of former times when the visions unfolded themselves before her eyes, furnishing her with a pleasing spectacle which was always unexpected, and which, continually being renewed, caused the seances to be to her a source of great delight. For the sitters, on the other hand, these scenes of somnambulism and incarnation, together with the various physiological phenomena of catalepsy, lethargy, contractures, etc., which accompanied them, added great variety and additional interest to Hélène Smith's remarkable and instructive triple mediumship.

The greater sometimes implies the less: simultaneously with the access of complete somnambulism came new forms and innumerable shades of hemisomnambulism. The triple form of automatism which distinguished the first years of Mlle. Smith's spiritistic experiences has been wonderfully developed since 1895, and it would now be difficult to name any principal forms of psychic mediumship of which she has not furnished curious specimens. I shall have occasion to cite several of them in the course of this work. Hélène constitutes the most remarkable medium I have ever met, and very nearly approaches the ideal of what might be called the polymorphous, or multiform, medium, in contradistinction to the uniform mediums, whose faculties only concern themselves with one kind of automatism.

2. A modification analogous to that which took place in the psychologic form of the messages consisting of a marked improvement in their depth and importance, was noticeable simultaneously in their content.

Alongside of the unimportant communications, complete at one sitting and independent one of another, which filled up a large part of each of Hélène's seances and in no wise differentiated her faculties from those of the majority of mediums, she manifested from the beginning a marked tendency. to a superior systematization and a more lofty chain of visions; communications were often continued through several seances, and reached their conclusion only at the end of several weeks. But from the period at which I made the acquaintance of Mlle. Smith this tendency towards unity began to assert itself still more strongly. Several long somnambulistic dreams began to appear and to develop, the events of which continued to be unfolded through months, even years, and indeed still continue; a species of romance of the subliminal imagination analogous to those "continued stories" which so many of our race tell themselves in their moments of *far niente*, or at times when their routine occupations offer only slight obstacles to day-dreaming, and of which they themselves are generally the heroes.

Mlle. Smith has no fewer than three distinct somnambulistic romances, and if to these is added the existence of that secondary personality to which I have already alluded, and which reveals itself under the name of Leopold, we find ourselves in the presence of four subconscious creations of vast extent, which have been evolved on parallel lines for several years, and which manifest themselves in irregular alternation during the course of different seances, or often even in the same seance.

All of these have undoubtedly a common origin in Hélène's subliminal consciousness; but in practice, at least, and to all appearance, these imaginative constructions present a relative independence and a diversity of content sufficiently great to render it necessary to study them separately. I shall confine myself at present to a general view of them.

Two of these romances are connected with the spiritistic idea of previous existences. It has, indeed, been revealed that Hélène Smith has already lived twice before on this globe. Five hundred years ago she was the daughter of an Arab sheik, and became, under the name of Simandini, the favorite wife of a Hindoo prince named Sivrouka Nayaka, who reigned over Kanara, and built in the year 1401 the fortress of Tchandraguiri. In the last century she reappeared in the person of the illustrious and unfortunate Marie Antoinette. Again reincarnated, as a punishment for her sins and the perfecting of her character, in the humble circumstances of Hélène Smith, she in certain somnambulistic states recovers the memory of her glorious avatars of old, and becomes again for the moment Hindoo princess or queen of France.

I will designate under the names of "Hindoo" or "Oriental" cycle and "Royal" cycle the whole of the automatic manifestations relative to these two previous existences. I shall call the third romance the " Martian" cycle, in which Mlle. Smith, by virtue of the mediumistic faculties, which are the appanage and the consolation of her present life, has been able to enter into relation with the people and affairs of the planet Mars, and to unveil their mysteries to us. It is in this astronomical somnambulism that the phenomenon of glossolalia, [1] appears, which consists of the fabrication and the use of an unknown language, and which is one of the principal objects of this study; we shall see, however, that analogous facts are likewise presented in the Hindoo cycle.

The personality of Leopold maintains very complex relations with the preceding creations. On the one hand, it is very closely connected with the Royal cycle, owing to the fact that the name of Leopold is only a pseudonym under which is concealed the illustrious Cagliostro, who, it appears, was madly infatuated with Queen Marie Antoinette, and who now, discarnate and floating in space, has constituted himself the guardian angel in some respects of Mlle. Smith, in whom after a long search he has again found the august object of his unhappy passion of a century ago.

On the other hand, this rôle of protector and spiritual guide which he assumes towards Hélène confers upon him a privileged place in her somnambulisms. He is more or less mixed up in the greater part of them; assists at them, watches over them, and perhaps in a measure directs them. He also occasionally appears in the midst of a Hindoo or a Martian scene, delivering his message by certain characteristic movements of the hand.

To sum up: sometimes revealing himself by raps upon the table, the taps of a finger, or by automatic writing; sometimes incarnating himself completely and speaking by the mouth of Mlle. Smith while entranced—Leopold fulfils in these seances the multiple and varied functions of spirit-guide,

---

[1] Glossolalia signifies the "gift of tongues," or the ability to speak foreign languages without having consciously acquired them.

giving good advice relative to the manner of acting towards the medium; of stage-manager hidden behind the scenes watching the performance and ready at any time to intervene; of benevolently disposed interpreter willing to furnish explanations of all that is obscure; of censor of morals sharply reprimanding the sitters when he deems it necessary; of sympathetic physician prompt at diagnosis and well versed in the pharmacopoeia, etc. He also appears under his own name of Cagliostro to the somnambulistic gaze of the resuscitated Marie Antoinette and answers her questions by means of auditive hallucinations. Nor is this all: to make our summary complete, it is necessary also to investigate the personal connection of Mlle. Smith with her invisible protector. She often invokes and questions Leopold at her own convenience, and while he remains sometimes for weeks without giving any sign of life, he at other times readily responds to her by means of voices or visions which surprise her while fully awake in the course of her daily duties, and in which he lavishes upon her in turn material or moral advice, useful information, or the encouragement and consolation of which she has need.

Although I have accused myself of perhaps having had much to do with the transformation of Hélène's hemisomnambulism into complete trances, I believe myself, however, altogether innocent of the origin, and therefore of the subsequent development, of the great subliminal creations of which I have spoken. The first, that of Leopold, is of very early date, even going back probably, as we shall see, prior to Mlle. Smith's initiation into spiritism. As to the three cycles, they did not, it is true, commence to display their full amplitude until after I had made Hélène's acquaintance; and since they start from the time when she first became subject to veritable trances, it would seem as though that supreme form of automatism is the only one capable of allowing the full expansion of productions so complex, and the only psychological *container* appropriate and adequate to such a *content*. But the first appearance of all three was clearly prior to my presence at the seances. The Hindoo dream, where I shall be found playing a rôle which I did not seek, evidently began (October 16, 1894) eight weeks before my admission to Mlle. Smith's seances. The Martian romance, which dates from the same period, is closely connected, as I shall also show, with an involuntary suggestion of M. Lemaître, who made the acquaintance of Hélène in the spring of 1894, nine months before my introduction to her. The Royal cycle, finally, had been roughly outlined at seances held at the home of M. Cuendet, in December, 1893. Nevertheless, I repeat, only since 1895 have the exuberant growth and magnificent flowering of that subliminal vegetation taken place under the stimulating and provocative influence, albeit wholly unintentional and altogether unsuspected at the time, of the varied environments of Mlle. Smith's seances.

As far as the indiscreet revelations in regard to my own family, which so much astonished me at my first meeting with Mlle. Smith, are concerned, as well as the innumerable extraordinary facts of the same kind with which her mediumship abounds, and to which she owes her immense reputation in spiritistic circles, it will suffice to return in the closing chapters of this book.

CHILDHOOD AND YOUTH OF MLLE. SMITH

THE psychological history of Mlle. Smith and her automatisms is naturally divided into two separate periods by the important fact of her initiation into spiritism at the beginning of 1892. Before that time, not suspecting the possibility of voluntary communication with the world of disincarnate spirits, she naturally manifested nothing more than a few spontaneous phenomena, the first flutterings of her mediumistic faculties which still lay dormant, the exact nature and progress of which it would be interesting to know in detail; unfortunately, in the absence of written documents concerning that pre-spiritistic period, we are confined to the statements of Hélène and her parents in regard to it, and the untrustworthiness of the memory in connection with events of a remote past is only too well known.

The spiritistic period, on the contrary, extending over the last seven years, and infinitely more fertile in artificially promoted (*e.g.*, the seances) as well as in spontaneous manifestations, is much better known to us; but in order to comprehend it intelligently, it is necessary first to pass in review the few facts which we have been able to gather relating to the pre-spiritistic period—that is to say, the childhood and youth of Mlle. Smith. That will be the subject of this chapter.

Mlle. Smith has lived in Geneva since her infancy. After attending school, she entered as an apprentice, at the age of fifteen, a large commercial house, where, as I have already stated, she still remains, and where, little by little, she has risen to a very responsible position. Her father, a merchant, was a Hungarian, and possessed a remarkable facility for languages, which is of interest to us in presence of the phenomena of glossolalia, a subject which will be discussed hereafter. Her mother is a Genevese. Both enjoyed excellent health and attained a venerable old age. Hélène had a younger sister who died in early childhood, and two brothers older than herself, who are now fathers of families and established abroad, where they have had successful business careers.

I am not aware that M. Smith, who was a man of positive character, ever displayed any phenomena of automatisms. Mme. Smith, however, as well as her grandmother, has experienced several thoroughly characteristic phenomena of that kind, and one, at least, of Hélène's brothers, it appears, could easily have become a good medium. This is another instance of the distinctly hereditary tendency of mediumistic faculties.

M. Smith, a man of active and enterprising character, died quite suddenly, probably of an embolism, at the age of seventy-five years. He had left Hungary in his youth, and finally established himself at Geneva, after having travelled extensively in Italy and Algiers, where he remained for several years. He spoke fluently Hungarian, German, French, Italian, and Spanish, understood English fairly well, and also knew Latin and a little Greek. It would seem that his daughter has inherited these linguistic aptitudes, but only in a latent and subliminal manner, for she has always detested the study of languages, and rebelled against learning German, in which she took lessons for three years.

Mme. Smith, who is a kind-hearted woman, with much good, practical sense, is sixty-seven years of age. Neither she nor her husband was ever a nervous or psychopathic subject, but both showed a marked tendency to broncho-pulmonary affections of a somewhat alarming type. Mme. Smith has, besides, suffered frequently from rheumatism. Hélène does not appear to have inherited these tendencies; she has always enjoyed robust health, and has not even had the slight diseases usually incidental to childhood.

Although both M. and Mme. Smith were Protestants, through a chain of peculiar circumstances their daughter was baptized a Catholic shortly after her birth, her name being inscribed some months later on the register of the Protestant church of Geneva. The memory of this unusual baptism has certainly not been lost by Hélène's subliminal imagination, and has duly contributed to the hypothesis of a mysterious origin. Of the years of childhood I know nothing specially interesting. At the intermediate school, at which she passed only a year, and where I have consulted the records of her class, she was not distinguished either for good or ill from the point of view of deportment, but she certainly did not reveal the full measure of her intelligence, since she failed to pass the examinations at the end of the year, a fact which decided her entrance upon an apprenticeship. On the other hand, the worthy pastor who gave her religious instruction somewhat later, and who has never lost sight of her since, has furnished me with most eulogistic testimonials as to her character; he remembers her as a young girl of serious disposition, intelligent, thoughtful, faithful in the discharge of her duties, and devoted to her family.

M. Smith never showed the least trace of mediumistic phenomena; from having been very indifferent, or even hostile, to spiritism until his daughter began to interest herself in it, he finally succumbed to her influence and became a believer in that doctrine towards the close of his life. Mme. Smith, on the contrary, has always been predisposed to it, and has experienced several phenomena of that nature in the course of her life. At the period of the epidemic of "table-tipping" which raged in our country about the middle of this century, she too experimented quite successfully for a while upon the table with her friends and acquaintances. Later, she had some sporadic visions. The following is one of the most typical. While her little daughter three years old was ill, Mme. Smith awoke in the middle of the night and saw an angel, of dazzling brightness, standing by the side of the little bed with its hands stretched out above the child; after some moments the apparition gradually dissolved. Mme. Smith awakened her husband and told him of the fatal significance which she attached to the vision, but he, unable to see anything, ridiculed her superstitious fears. As a matter of fact, the child died on the following day, to the great surprise of the physician attending her. This is a fine example of true maternal presentiment, subconsciously felt and transferring itself into the normal consciousness by a visual hallucination which borrowed for its symbolic content an appropriate popular image.

Mme. Smith never knew her mother, who died shortly after her birth; but she recalls and has related to me some characteristic visions of her grandmother, who brought her up; various phenomena connected with one of Hélène's brothers (hearing of steps in the night, etc.) have proved to her that one of her sons, at least, is a medium.

Hélène Smith was certainly predisposed, both by heredity and temperament, to become a medium, as soon as the outward opportunity—that is, the suggestions of spiritism—should present itself.

It is evident, indeed, from her recital of events, that she was more or less visionary from her infancy. It does not appear, however, that she ever manifested phenomena capable in themselves of attracting the attention of her family. I have not been able to discover any indication whatever of crises or attacks of an abnormal nature, not even of sleep-walking. Her automatisms have been always almost entirely con fined to the sensory or mental sphere, and it is only from her own narratives that other people have any knowledge of them. They assume the double form of reveries more or less conscious, and of hallucinations properly so called.

1. *Reveries.*—The habit of falling into reverie, of building castles in the air, of transporting one's self into other conditions of existence, or of telling one's self stories in which one plays the chief rôle, is more frequent among women than among men, and in childhood and youth than in mature years. This propensity seems to have always been extremely marked in the case of Mlle. Smith, since from her school-girl days she has shown herself to be of a sedentary and domestic temperament, preferring the quiet companionship of her mother to the games of her comrades, and her needle-work to out-door recreations. The fragments which have survived in Hélène's conscious memory are all that is known to us of the content of these reveries, but it suffices, nevertheless, to reveal to us the general tone of her fictions, and to show us that the images suddenly surging up before her mental vision had a peculiar, often very fantastic, character, and which enables us to see in them the beginnings of her later great somnambulistic romances. It is to be noticed also that the designs, embroideries, varied artistic works, which were always the favorite occupations of her moments of leisure and in which she excels, were almost always, from her infancy, not copies of exterior models, but the products of her own invention, marked with the bizarre and original stamp of her internal images. Moreover, these pieces of work grew under her fingers with an ease and rapidity that astonished herself. They made themselves, as it were.

She was always fond of indulging in day-dreams, and recalls many a half-hour passed motionless in an easy-chair, on which occasions she was accustomed to see all kinds of strange things, but, being of a very reticent nature, she seldom mentioned them to her parents for fear of not being understood. She used to see highly colored landscapes, a lion of stone with a mutilated head, fanciful objects on pedestals, etc. She does not remember the details, but does clearly recollect that they all bore a close resemblance to her Hindoo and Martian visions of later years.

These phantasmagoria also appeared to her in the night. She remembers, among other things, to have seen, when about fourteen or fifteen years old, a bright light thrown against the wall of her room, which then seemed to be filled with strange and unknown beings. She had the impression of being fully awake, but it suddenly occurred to her that she must have been dreaming, and it was only then that she comprehended that it was really a "vision" which she had experienced.

2. *Hallucinations.*—In the foregoing examples it would be difficult to say to exactly which category the psychologic facts belong, especially the nocturnal phenomena, and one may hesitate whether to regard them as simple dreams of a very vivid character, hypnagogic or hypnopompic [1] visions, or as veritable hallucinations. On the other hand, we undoubtedly have the right to give the latter designation to the numerous apparitions which Mlle. Smith has when in full possession of her senses in the daytime.

One day, for example, as she was playing out-of-doors with a friend, she saw some one following her, and mentioned the fact to her companion, who could not see any one. The imaginary individual, after having followed her around a tree for a moment, disappeared, and she was unable to find him again.

Of an entirely different order are the strange characters which she remembers having sometimes involuntarily substituted for French letters when writing to her friends, which must be regarded as graphomotor hallucinations. These were undoubtedly the same characters which at other times appeared to her in visual images.

This was the prelude to the phenomenon so frequently experienced by her in the last few years, and of which we shall hereafter see many examples—namely, automatic writing, mingling with her ordinary chirography in her waking state.

Alongside of hallucinations like these, which do not show any intentional or useful character and are only a capricious and fortuitous irruption into the normal consciousness, mere dreams or fancies filling up the sub-conscious strata, there are also manifested in Hélène's case some hallucinations of a

---

[1] This term is used to designate the visions which manifest themselves at the moment of awakening from sleep immediately prior to complete awakening, and which form a pendant to the well-known, much more frequent hypnagogic hallucinations, arising in the intermediate state between sleep and waking.

manifest utility, which have in consequence the sense of messages addressed by the subliminal consciousness of the subject to her normal consciousness, by way of warning and protection. It is to be noted that these hallucinations, which might be called teleological, have lately been claimed by Leopold, although he has no recollection of, and does not assert himself to be the author of, the earlier ones.

The following is a curious example: At about the age of seventeen or eighteen, Hélène was returning from the country one evening, carrying a fine bouquet of flowers. During the last minutes of the journey she heard behind her a peculiar cry of a bird, which seemed to her to warn her against some danger, and she hastened her steps without looking behind. On her arrival at home the cry followed her into her room without her having been able to see the creature from which it emanated. She went tired to bed, and in the middle of the night awoke in great pain, but was unable to cry out. At that moment she felt herself gently lifted, together with the pillow on which she lay, as if by two friendly hands, which enabled her to recover her voice and call her mother, who hastened to comfort her, and carried the flowers, which were too odorous, out of the room. Leopold, on being interrogated recently during a somnambulism of Hélène as to this incident, coming up again after so many years, has a very clear recollection of it and gives the following explanation.

It was not really the cry of a bird, but it was he, Leopold, who caused Hélène to hear a sort of whistle, hoping thereby to attract her attention to the danger lurking in the bouquet of flowers, in which was a great deal of garden-mint of powerful odor. Unfortunately Hélène did not understand, and retained the bouquet in her room. He adds that his failure to give a more clear and intelligible warning was due to the fact that it was at that time impossible for him to do so. The whistle which Hélène took for the cry of a bird was all that it was in his power to utter. It was again he who intervened at the moment of her nocturnal illness by raising her head in order to enable her to call for help.

I have no reason to doubt the substantial accuracy either of the account given by Hélène and her mother, or of the explanation recently furnished by Leopold. The incident belongs to the category of well-known cases where a danger of some sort not suspected by the normal personality, but which is subconsciously known or recognized, is warded off by a preservative hallucination, either sensory (as here—the cry of the bird) or motor (as in the lifting of the body). The subliminal consciousness is not always able to give a clear message; in the present case, the auditive automatism remained in a state of elementary hallucination, a simple whistle, without being able to elevate it to a distinct verbal hallucination. Its general warning sense, however, was understood by Hélène, thanks to the confused feeling of danger that she felt at the same time. Moreover, this confused feeling, which caused her to quicken her steps, it seems to me, ought not to be considered as the consequence of the whistle she heard, but rather as a parallel phenomenon; the appearance or the odor of the mint she was carrying, while not attracting her conscious attention, nevertheless dimly roused in her an idea of the danger lurking in the flowers, and that idea in turn affected her clear consciousness under the double form of a vague emotion of danger and a verbo-auditive translation which did not go so far as to formulate itself explicitly.

Under circumstances of a nature calculated to cause a strong emotional shock, and especially when the psychic sphere which involves the sentiment of modesty is strongly acted upon, Hélène has a visual hallucination of a man clothed in a long, brown robe, with a white cross on his breast, like a monk, who comes to her aid, and accompanies her in silence as long as the necessity for his presence continues. This unknown protector, always silent, each time appearing and disappearing in a sudden and mysterious manner, is no other than Leopold himself, according to the recent affirmations of the latter.

We should naturally expect that Hélène would have had in her youth many striking experiences of prevision, marvellous intuition, divination, etc., which are among the most diffuse forms of teleological automatism. Such, however, does not seem to have been the fact; neither she nor her mother has recounted to me anything remarkable of this nature, and they confine themselves to a general affirmation of frequent presentiments, which were subsequently justified as to the persons and events with which they were connected.

All the examples which I have above cited concur in bringing to light the strong penchant of Mlle. Smith towards automatism. But from the point of view of their meaning there is a notable difference between the teleological phenomena, presentiments or hallucinations of a manifest utility, and those which have none—mere reveries and other perturbations, which are altogether superfluous, if not actually detrimental, to Hélène's normal personality.

There are dreams and other automatisms absolutely useless which have insinuated themselves without rhyme or reason into Hélène's normal life. One does not know how or in what manner to interpret these phenomena, capricious and fortuitous as they seem to be, and they remain isolated, inconsiderable facts, without bearing and without interest, since they cannot be attached to any central principle, to one mother-idea or fundamental emotion.

We are, therefore, reduced to certain conjectures, the most reasonable of which is that these diverse fragments make part of some vast subconscious creation, in which all the being of Mlle. Smith, crushed and bruised by the conditions which the realities of life have imposed upon her, as is more or less the case with each one of us, gave free wing to the deep aspirations of its nature and expanded into the fiction of an existence more brilliant than her own. All that we know of Hélène's character, both as a child and as a young girl, shows us that her dominant emotional note was a sort of instinctive inward revolt against the modest environment in which it was her lot to be born, a profound feeling of dread and opposition, of inexplicable malaise, of bitter antagonism against the whole of her material and intellectual environment. While showing herself always very devoted to her parents and brothers, she had only feeble natural affinities for them. She felt like a stranger in her family and as one away from home. She had a feeling of isolation, of abandonment, of exile, which created a sort of gulf between her and her family. So strong were these feelings that she actually one day seriously asked her parents if it was absolutely certain that she was their daughter, or whether it was not possible that the nurse might some day by mistake have brought home another child from the daily walk.

This want of adaptation to her environment, this sort of mysterious homesickness for an unknown country, shows itself in a characteristic manner in the following fragment of narrative, in which Hélène, who has always attributed great importance to dreams, tells of one in which an isolated house figured. "To me this retired mansion, in which I lived alone, isolated, represents my life, which from my infancy has been neither happy nor gay. Even while very young I do not remember to have shared any of the tastes or any of the ideas of the members of my family. Thus during the whole of my childhood I was left in what I call a profound isolation of heart

And in spite of all, in spite of this complete want of sympathy, I could not make up my mind to marry, although I had several opportunities. A voice was always saying, 'Do not hurry: the time has not arrived; this is not the destiny for which you are reserved.' And I have listened to that voice, which has absolutely nothing to do with conscience, and I do not regret it, for since I have engaged in spiritism I have found myself so surrounded with sympathy and friendships that I have somewhat forgotten my sad lot."

This quotation speaks volumes in regard to the turn of mind and the emotional disposition which ruled Hélène as a little girl. It is surely, so to speak, the vulgar story and the common lot of all; many a child, many a youth, many an unrecognized genius, feel themselves suffocating in their too narrow environment when the latent energies of life begin to ferment. But there are differences in kind and in degree. With Mlle. Hélène Smith the sentiment of not having been made for her environment, and of belonging by nature to a higher sphere, was intense and lasting. Her mother always had the impression that Hélène was not happy, and wondered that she was so serious, so absorbed, so wanting in the exuberance of spirits natural to her age. Her father and her brothers, not comprehending the real reasons for this absence of gayety, taxed her very unjustly with pride and hauteur, and accused her sometimes of despising her humble surroundings. There are shades of feeling which can only be understood when they have been experienced. Hélène well knew that she really had no contempt for her material and social environment, which, on the contrary, inspired her with respect, but which simply was not congenial to her nature and temperament.

To this fundamental feeling of imprisonment in a too paltry sphere was joined, in Hélène's case, a timid disposition. Darkness, the least noise, the creaking of the furniture, made her tremble; by day, a person walking behind her, an unexpected movement, the ringing of the door-bell, gave her the impression that some one wishing to harm her had come to seize her and carry her off. On the whole, Hélène's tendency to be startled by everything and nothing constituted with her a grievous panophobia, a state of fear and insecurity which greatly strengthened her impression of want of union—of *mésalliance*—with an environment to which she was decidedly superior.

It is easy now to see the connection between that depressing emotionalism which was the attribute of Hélène's childhood and the slightly megalomaniac tone of her later subliminal romances. The idea intrudes itself that, in spite of—or by reason of—their apparent contrast, these two traits are not independent of each other, but bound by the tie of cause and effect. But this causal connection is in great danger of being interpreted in a precisely inverse sense by the empirical psychologist and the metaphysical occultist. The latter will explain Mlle. Smith's curious impression of strangeness and superiority to the base conditions of her actual existence, by her illustrious previous incarnations; the psychologist, on the contrary, will see in that sane impression the wholly natural origin of her grandiose somnambulistic personifications. In default of a complete understanding, always dubious, between these so different points of view, of which we shall speak later, it will be advisable to adopt at least a provisional *modus vivendi*, based on the party-wall of the native constitution or individual character of Mlle. Smith. On the farther side of that wall, *in eternity*, so to speak, *a parte ante* which precedes the arrival of Hélène into this life, the occultist will have full latitude to imagine such a succession of existences as it shall please him in order to explain the character she has had from her infancy. But on this side of the wall—that is to say, within the limits of her present life—the psychologist will have the right to ignore all these prenatal metempsychoses, and taking for his point of departure the innate constitution of Hélène, without troubling himself about anything she may have received by the accidents of heredity or preserved from her royal pre-existences, he will endeavor to explain by that same constitution, as it reveals itself in her daily life, the genesis of her subliminal creations under the action of occasional exterior influences. The occultist, then, can have the pleasure of regarding Mlle. Smith's characteristic trait as a child, that impression of solitude and wandering about in a world for which she was not made, as the effect of her real past greatnesses, while the psychologist will be permitted to see in it the cause of her future dreams of grandeur.

The emotional disposition which I have depicted, and which is one of the forms under which the mal-adaptation of the organism, physical and mental, to the hard conditions of the environment, betrays itself, seems therefore to me to have been the source and starting-point for all the dreamings of Hélène in her childhood. Thence came these visions, always warm, luminous, highly colored, exotic, bizarre; and these brilliant apparitions, superbly dressed, in which her antipathy for her insipid and unpleasant surroundings betrays itself, her weariness of ordinary, commonplace people, her disgust for prosaic occupations, for vulgar and disagreeable things, for the narrow house, the dirty streets, the cold winters, and the gray sky. Whether these images, very diverse, but of the same brilliant quality, were already existent in Hélène's subconscious thought while still a child or a young girl, we are unable to say. It is, however, probable that their systematization was far from attaining to such a degree of perfection as they have presented during the past few years under the influence of spiritism.

All the facts of automatism to which Hélène can assign a vaguely approximate date group themselves around her fifteenth year, and are all included between the limits of her ninth and twentieth years.

This evident connection with a phase of development of major importance has been confirmed to me by Leopold on various occasions, who says that he appeared to Hélène for the first time in her tenth year, on an exceptional occasion of extreme fright, but after that, not until about four years later, because the "physiological conditions" necessary to his apparition were not yet realized. The moment they were realized, he says, he began to manifest himself, and it is at the same period, according to him, that Hélène commenced to recover memories of her Hindoo existence, under the form of strange visions of which she comprehended neither the nature nor the origin.

After the age of about twenty years, without affirming or believing that her visions and apparitions ceased altogether, Mlle. Smith has no striking recollections of any, and she has not told me of any psychic phenomenon experienced by her in the series of years immediately preceding her entrance into spiritism. We may infer from this, with some reason, that the ebullitions of the imaginative subconscious life gradually became calm after the explosion of the period we have mentioned. They had been appeased. The conflict between Hélène's inner nature and the environment in which she was forced to live became less fierce. A certain equilibrium was established between the necessities of practical life and her inward aspirations. On the one hand, she resigned herself to the necessities of reality; and if her native pride could not yield to the point of condescending to a marriage, honorable undoubtedly, but for which she felt she was not intended, we must nevertheless pay homage to the perseverance, the fidelity, the devotion which she always brought to the fulfilment of her family and business duties. On the other hand, she did not permit the flame of the ideal to be extinguished in her, and it reacted upon her environment as strongly as possible, making its imprint upon her personality well marked.

She introduced a certain stamp of elegance into the modest home of her parents. She arranged for herself a small *salon*, coquettish and comfortable in its simplicity. She took lessons in music, and bought herself a piano. She hung some old engravings on her walls, secured some Japanese vases, a jardinière filled with plants, cut flowers in pretty vases, a hanging lamp with a beautiful shade of her own make, a table-cover which she had put together and embroidered herself, some photographs curiously framed according to her own design; and out of this harmonious whole, always beautifully kept, she evolved something original, bizarre, and delightful, conforming well to the general character of her fantastic subconsciousness.

At the same time that Mlle. Smith succeeded in accommodating herself to the conditions of her existence, the state of latent timidity in which she lived gradually diminished. She is still occasionally overcome by fear, but much less frequently than formerly, and never without a legitimate exterior cause.

Indeed, judging her by these latter years, I do not recognize in her the child or young girl of former days, always timid, trembling, and frightened, taciturn and morose, who has been depicted to me by herself and her mother.

It seems to me, then, that the wildness of the dreams and automatisms, which were symptoms of a tendency to mental disintegration, which marked the years of puberty, was succeeded by a progressive diminution of these troubles and a gradual gaining of wisdom on the part of the subliminal strata. We may presume that this harmonization, this reciprocal adaptation of the internal to the external, would in time have perfected itself, and that the whole personality of Mlle. Smith would have continued to consolidate and unify itself, if spiritism had not come all of a sudden to rekindle the fire which still slumbered under the ashes and to give a new start to the subliminal mechanism which was beginning to grow rusty.

The suppressed fictions aroused themselves, the reveries of former years resumed their sway, and the images of subliminal phantasy began to be more prolific than ever under the fertile suggestions of occult philosophy, rallying-points or centres of crystallization—such as the idea of former existences and reincarnations—around which they had only to group and organize themselves in order to give birth to the vast somnambulistic constructions the development of which we shall be obliged to follow.

MLLE. SMITH SINCE HER INITIATION INTO SPIRITISM

HAVING endeavored in the preceding chapter to reconstruct in its chief characteristics the history of Mlle. Smith up to the time when spiritism begins to be mixed up with it, I would have preferred in the present chapter to make a detailed study of her psychological life during these last years, without however, as yet, touching upon the content, properly so called, of her automatisms. Not having been able to accomplish this design to my satisfaction, for want of time and patience, I shall endeavor at least to systematize my notes somewhat by grouping them under four heads. I shall trace the birth of Hélène's mediumship as far as it is possible for me to do so from the meagre accounts I have been able to procure concerning a time at which I was not acquainted with her. Then, passing to facts with which I am more familiar, I will describe rapidly her normal state as I have been able to see it for the last five years. This would have been the place for a study of individual psychology, but I have been compelled to abandon the idea on account of multiple difficulties. Finally, I will offer a few remarks on the abnormal side of her existence, which it is convenient to divide into two groups, namely, *the spontaneous*—that is to say, springing up of themselves in the course of her ordinary life; or those *provoked* by the voluntary seeking for favorable circumstances, and which constitute the seances properly so called.

I. THE MEDIUMISTIC BEGINNINGS OF MLLE. SMITH

In the winter of 1891-92 Mlle. Smith heard spiritism spoken of by one of her acquaintances, Mme. Y., who lent her Denis's book, *Après la Mort*. The perusal of this work having vividly excited Hélène's curiosity, Mme. Y. agreed to accompany her to her friend, Mlle. Z., who was interested in the same questions, and who produced automatic writing. They then decided to form a circle for regular experimentation. I take from the notes which Mlle. Z. has had the kindness to furnish me, the account, unfortunately very brief, of the seances at which Hélène's mediumistic faculties first made their appearance.

"It was on the 10th of February, 1892, that I made the acquaintance of Mlle. Smith. She was introduced to me by Mme. Y., for the purpose of endeavoring to form a spiritistic group. She was then altogether a novice in spiritism, never having attempted anything, and did not suspect the faculties that have since developed themselves in her.

"February 20.—First reunion: We seat ourselves at the table; we succeed in making it oscillate. We regard Mme. Y. as the medium upon whom we can reckon. We try for writing. We receive through me encouragements to proceed.

"February 26.—Progress; the table moves itself considerably, salutes one by one all the members of the group, and gives us certain names, of which only one is recognized . . . Writing: Mlle. Smith, who tries for the first time, writes mechanically, her eyes closed, some phrases, of which we can decipher some words.

"March 11.—Nothing at this seance, except a communication written by myself.

"March 18.—Progress; clear communication by the table. Attempt to experiment in the darkness (which was not absolute, the hall outside having some incandescent lights which diffused a feeble light; we could distinguish each other with difficulty). Mlle. Smith sees a balloon, now luminous, now becoming dark: she has seen nothing up to this time. Writing: Mlle. Smith writes mechanically a quite long communication from the father of M. K. [a Bulgarian student present at the seance]; advice to him."

At this point the sitters became so numerous that they broke up into two groups, of which the one continuing to meet with Mlle. Z. does not concern us. Mlle. Smith became a member of the other, which met at the house of a lady named N., where weekly seances were held for a year and a half (up to the end of June, 1893). The records of these meetings, kept by Mme. N., are unfortunately very brief and obscure on many points of interest to the psychologist. Those of the first months are in the handwriting of Mlle. Smith, who acted as secretary of the group for thirty seances. As she only took down at the time the headings of the communications of the spirits and wrote out the remainder on the following day, we cannot rely very strongly on the objective accuracy of these accounts, which, however, have the advantage of presenting to us the mediumship of Hélène, as related by herself. She speaks of herself in the third person.

The following is a summary of the two first seances held in this new environment:

"March 25, 1892.—Eleven persons around a large and heavy dining-table of oak with two leaves. The table is set in motion, and several spirits come and give their names (by raps), and testify to the pleasure it gives them to find themselves among us. It is at this seance that Mlle. Smith begins to distinguish vague gleams with long white streamers moving from the floor to the ceiling, and then a magnificent star, which in the darkness appears to her alone throughout the whole of the seance. We augur from this that she will end by seeing things more distinctly and will possess the gift of clairvoyance.

"April 1.—Violent movements of the table, due to a spirit who calls himself David and announces himself as the spiritual guide of the group. Then he gives way to another spirit who says he is Victor Hugo, and the guide and protector of Mlle. Smith, who is very much surprised to be assisted by a person of such importance. He soon disappears. Mlle. Smith is very much agitated; she has fits of shivering, is very cold. She is very restless, and sees suddenly, balancing itself above the table, a grinning, very ill-favored face, with long red hair. She is so frightened that she demands that the lights be lit. She is calmed and reassured. The figure disappears. Afterwards she sees a magnificent bouquet of roses of different hues being placed on the table before one of the sitters, M. P. All at once she sees a small snake come out from underneath the bouquet, which, crawling quickly, perceives the flowers, looks at them, tries to reach the hand of M. P., withdraws for an instant, comes back slowly, and disappears in the interior of the bouquet. Then all is dissolved and three raps are given on the table, terminating the seance. [M. P. interprets the meaning of the vision of the bouquet and the serpent as a symbolic translation of an emotional impression experienced by Mlle. Smith]."

Such was the birth of Hélène's mediumship. Scarcely anything happened on the 10th of February, when the movements of the table were not attributed to her (although in all probability she caused them); in the following seances she appeared in two attempts at automatic writing (unfortunately lost) in imitation of the writing medium with whom she was sitting. The outcome of this second attempt leads us to suppose that Hélène's faculties would have developed rapidly in that direction if she had not abandoned it and changed her environment.

Her visual faculty, suggested by the experiments at obscure seances, shows itself on the 18th and 25th of March in the form of elementary hallucinations or vague figures having their point of departure probably in the simple entoptical phenomena, the retina's own light, consecutive images, etc. Then, encouraged by the predictions of the sitters, she attained on the 1st of April to visions properly so called, having a varied content and a real or symbolic signification. At the same time her typtological automatism was perfecting itself. We recognize it in the name of Victor Hugo, coming especially for Mlle. Smith, and suspect it to have been a name already given at the second seance.

Auditive hallucinations follow closely upon the visual, but it is impossible to know at just what date, as the records do not clearly indicate whether the messages recorded had that origin or were rapped out on the table. To these known forms of automatism must be added the frequent phenomena of emotion, shiverings, sadness, restlessness, fear, etc., which are experienced by Hélène without knowing why, and are afterwards found to be in perfect conformity to, and in evident connection with, the content of those emotional phenomena which they generally precede by a few moments.

Thus, in a half-dozen weekly seances, the mediumship of Mlle. Smith was invested with a complex psychological aspect, which from that time it preserved intact for three years, and of which I was a witness after I made her acquaintance. This rapidity of development is not at all unusual; but there is this peculiarity about Hélène, that her mediumistic faculties, after their first appearance, remained for a long time stationary, and then underwent all at once, in the spring of 1895, the enormous transformation and tremendous expansion which I have described in the first chapter, and to which I will not again refer.

II. MLLE. SMITH IN HER NORMAL STATE

I was about to say that in her normal state Mlle. Smith is normal. Certain scruples restrain me, and I correct myself by saying that in her ordinary state she seems just like anybody else. By this I mean that outside of the gaps which the seances and the spontaneous eruptions of automatism make in her life, no one would suspect, observing her performance of her various duties, or in talking with her on all sorts of subjects, all that she is capable of in her abnormal states, or the curious treasures which are concealed in her subliminal strata.

With a healthy and ruddy complexion, of good height, well proportioned, of regular and harmonious features, she breathes health in everything. She presents no visible stigmata of degeneration. As to psychic defects or anomalies, with the exception of her mediumship itself, I know of none, the timidity of her youth having entirely disappeared. Her physical strength is marvellous, as shown by the fact that she bears up under the strain of a business which demands nearly eleven hours of her time each day, nearly all of which she is compelled to stand on her feet, and from which she takes only one week's vacation in summer. Besides this confining work away from home, she assists her mother about the house morning and evening, in the housekeeping duties, and finds time besides to read a little, to practise at her piano, and to make the lovely handiwork, which she designs and executes herself with remarkable originality and good taste. To a life so full must be added, besides, the spiritistic seances which she is generally willing to give on Sunday, and sometimes on a weekday evening, very disinterestedly, to persons who are interested in psychic questions or who desire to consult Leopold on important subjects.

While hesitating to affirm that a person presenting phenomena so extraordinary as those of mediumship is perfectly normal in other respects, I am pleased to discover that as far as Mlle. Smith is concerned, through my conversations with her and as the result of my investigations concerning her, she does not present a single abnormality, physical, intellectual, or moral, between the periods of the irruptions of her automatisms. Her field of vision, which she has permitted me to measure with a Landolt perimeter, is normal for white as well as for colors, for which latter she has a very delicate perception. There is no trace of tactile anæsthesia in her hands. There is no known motor trouble. The tremor of the index-finger gives a line, of four oscillations per second on an average, differing not at all from the lines obtained from persons perfectly normal (see Fig. 2).

It cannot be expected that I should paint a full moral and intellectual portrait of Mlle. Smith, as I should be in danger of hurting her feelings in case my attempt should come to her notice. I can only touch on a few points. One of the most striking is her great native dignity; her bearing, her manners, her language are always perfect, and have a certain quality of noblesse and pride which accords well with her somnambulistic rôles. On occasion she shows a stately and regal hauteur. She is very impressionable, and feels little things very keenly. Her antipathies as well as her sympathies are quick, lively, and tenacious. She is energetic and persevering. She knows very well what she wants, and nothing passes her by unperceived, nor does she forget anything in the conduct of others towards her. "I see everything, nothing escapes me, and I forgive but never forget," she has often said to me. Perhaps a severe moralist would find in her a certain exaggeration of personal sensibility, but that sort of self-love is a very common characteristic of human nature, and is very natural in mediums who are continually exposed to public criticism.

She is very intelligent and highly gifted. In conversation she shows herself vivacious, sprightly, and sometimes sarcastic. Psychic problems, and all questions connected with mediumistic phenomena, of which she is herself so striking an example, occupy her mind a great deal and form the principal subject of her private thoughts and of her conversations with people in whom she is interested.

Her philosophical views are not wanting in originality or breadth. She does not believe in spiritism, in the generally accepted sense of the term, and has never consented, in spite of the advances which have been made to her, to become a member of the Geneva Society (spiritistic) for Psychic Studies, because, as she says, she has no fixed ideas on subjects so obscure, does not care for theories, and "does not work in the interest of any party." She investigates, she observes, she reflects and discusses, having adopted for her motto, "The truth in all things, for all things, and always."

There are two points in regard to which she is uncompromising—namely, the objective reality of Leopold, and the supernormal content of her automatisms. No one dares tell her that her great invisible protector is only an illusory apparition, another part of herself, a product of her subconscious imagination; nor that the strange peculiarities of her mediumistic communications—the Sanscrit, the recognizable signatures of deceased persons, the thousand correct revelations of facts unknown to her—are but old forgotten memories of things which she saw or heard in her childhood. Such suppositions being contrary to her inmost beliefs, and seemingly false in fact, easily irritate her, as being in defiance of good sense and an outrage on truth. But outside of these two subjects she will examine and discuss coolly any hypothesis one chooses. The idea that she should be the reincarnation of a Hindoo princess or of Marie Antoinette, that Leopold is really Cagliostro, that the visions called Martian are really from the planet Mars, etc., all seem to her to conform fully to the facts; but these beliefs are not indispensable to her, and she is ready, should they prove to be false, to change to other theories—as, for example, telepathy, a mixture of occult influences, a mysterious meeting in her of intuitions coming from some higher sphere, etc.

Undoubtedly the supposition of her pre-existences in India and on the throne of France seems to her to explain in a plausible manner the feeling, which has followed her from childhood, of belonging to a world higher than that in which the chance of birth has imprisoned her for this life; but she does not affirm a positive belief in that brilliant past, is not wholly convinced of it, and remains in a sensible state of expectancy of the true explanation of these ultimate mysteries of her life.

There is another subject, also, which is close to her heart. She has heard it said that in the eyes of scientists and physicians mediums are considered to be fools, hysterical subjects, or insane, or, in any event, abnormal, in the bad sense of the word. But, in the light of the experience of every day of her life, she protests vigorously against this odious insinuation. She declares emphatically that she is "perfectly sane in body and mind, not in the least unbalanced," and repels with indignation the idea there can be any serious abnormality or the least danger in mediumship such as she practises. "I am far from being abnormal," she wrote me recently, "and I have never been so clear of vision, so lucid, and so apt to judge correctly as since I have begun to develop as a medium."

Leopold, too, speaking through her voice during her trances, has more than once solemnly testified as to her perfect health. He has also returned to the subject by letter; we shall find farther on a very interesting certificate of mental equilibrium dictated by him and written by him with her hand, as if to give more weight to his declarations (see Fig. 8, p. 137.)

It is incontestable that Hélène has a very well-organized brain, as is evidenced by the admirable manner in which she manages the important and complicated department which is under her direction in the commercial establishment in which she is employed. To accuse her of being insane, simply because she is a medium, as some charitable souls (the world is full of them) do not hesitate to do sometimes, is, to say the least, a most inadmissible *petitio principii*.

The opinion which Mlle. Smith holds in her normal state concerning her automatic faculties is altogether optimistic; and there is nothing to prove her in the wrong. She regards her mediumship as a rare and precious privilege, with which nothing in the world would induce her to part. True, she also sees in it the reason for the malevolent and unjust judgments, the jealousies, the base suspicions, to which the ignorant multitude have in all ages subjected those who have succeeded in elevating themselves above it through the possession of faculties of this kind. But, on the whole, the disadvantages are more than counterbalanced by gains of a high order, and the inward satisfaction attached to such a gift. And here I desire to emphasize the statement, once for all, that Hélène does not belong to the class of professional mediums, nor to those who use their mediumship for the purpose of coining money. Mlle. Smith, who earns her living in the position which her intelligence and fitness have secured for her, and through which her family enjoys a modest ease, never accepts any pecuniary compensation for her seances or consultations. Such a traffic in faculties which have a sort of religious signification in her eyes would be absolutely repugnant to her feelings.

Hélène's spontaneous automatisms have often aided her in, without ever having interfered with, her daily occupations. There is, happily for her, a great difference in intensity between the phenomena of her seances and those which break in upon her habitual existence, the latter never having caused such disturbance of her personality as the former.

In her daily life she has only passing hallucinations limited to one or two of the senses, superficial hemisomnambulisms, compatible with a certain amount of self-possession—in short, ephemeral perturbations of no importance from a practical point of view. Taken as a whole, the interventions of the subliminal in her ordinary existence are more beneficial to her than otherwise, since they often bear the stamp of utility and appropriateness, which make them very serviceable.

Phenomena of hypermnesia, divination, lost objects mysteriously recovered, happy inspirations, true presentiments, correct intuitions—in a word, teleological automatisms of every sort—she possesses in so high a degree that this small coin of genius is more than sufficient to compensate for the inconveniences resulting from the distraction and momentary absence of mind with which the vision is accompanied.

In the seances, on the contrary, she presents the most grave functional alterations that one can imagine, and passes through accesses of lethargy, catalepsy, somnambulism, total change of personality, etc., the least of which would be a very disagreeable adventure for her if it should happen to occur in the street or at her office.

But here I am obliged to leave Hélène's ordinary state to enter upon the study of her automatisms.

III. SPONTANEOUS AUTOMATIC PHENOMENA

The automatisms which occur outside the seances in Mlle. Smith's everyday life, those, at least, which she is able to recall and narrate, are of a frequency very variable and utterly independent of any known circumstances; sometimes presenting themselves two or three times in the same day; at others, two or three weeks will elapse without a single one. Extremely diverse in their form and content, these phenomena may be divided into three categories, based upon their origin. The first proceed from impressions received by Hélène in moments of special suggestibility; the second are the fortuitous apparitions above the ordinary level of her consciousness, the romances in process of elaboration to which we are coming; the last, which differ from the two preceding species (which are always useless, if not detrimental) by their beneficial character and their adaptation to the needs of the moment, are roused by those teleological automatisms to which I have already called attention as having occurred in her childhood, and which have shared in the general recrudescence of her subconscious life under the lash of the spiritistic experiences.

Let us pass these different cases rapidly in review.

I. *Permanence of exterior suggestions.*—The spiritistic reunions are naturally their principal source. I do not mean that she has there been subjected to experiments in post-hypnotic suggestion. Justice to all those who have attended the seances compels the statement that they have never abused the suggestibility which she shows on such occasions, by suggesting ideas of such a nature as to cause her annoyance on the following days. The most that has been attempted has been the suggestion of some small matters by way of harmless experiment, to be executed by her a few moments after awaking from her trance. There is no need of intentional suggestions to influence her in a lasting manner; therefore we have avoided as far as possible everything that might leave disagreeable traces behind, and have suggested to her before the end of the seance that she have on the morrow no headache, fatigue, etc.; but it sometimes happens that certain incidents, often absolutely insignificant, are engraved on her memory in a most unlooked-for manner and assail her as inexplicable obsessions during the ensuing week. The following are some specimens of involuntary suggestion, which generally linger for three or four days, but may occasionally continue for twelve or fifteen.

Hélène told me one Sunday that she had been possessed several times during the day by the hallucinatory image of a straw hat, the inside of which was turned towards her, and-which remained vertically in the air about three or four feet in front of her, without being held by any one. She had the feeling that this hat belonged to me, and I happened finally to recollect that at the seance of the preceding Sunday I happened to fan myself with this very hat during her final trance, the image of which had been engraved on her mind in one of the flashes in which she opened her eyes and closed them again instantly before her final awaking. This obsession, said she, was very strong on Monday and the following day or two, but lessened somewhat towards the end of the week.

At another time she preserved during a whole week the sensation of the pressure of my thumb on her left eyebrow. (Compression of the external frontal and suborbital nerves is a means I often employ to hasten her awaking, after a hint given by Leopold.)

There happened to her also twice in the same day an auditive and visual hallucination of an aged person whom she did not recognize, but the extremely characteristic description of whom corresponds so well with that of a gentleman of Geneva who had been mentioned to her a few days previously, immediately before the commencement of a seance (when she was probably already in her state of suggestibility), that there is scarcely any doubt but that these apparitions were the consequence of that conversation.

'Following another seance where she had, at the beginning of a Hindoo scene, made vain efforts to detach a bracelet from her left wrist, she preserved for three days the feeling of something grasping that wrist, without understanding what it could be.

In the same way, various feelings of sadness, anger, a desire to laugh or to weep, etc., the cause of which she was unable to explain, have often followed her for a considerable length of time after the seances of which these feelings were the manifest emotional echo. This is often the effect of our dreams on our waking state: we forget the dreams, but their influence remains, and is often more marked in the dreams of a hypnotized person or a somnambulist than in those of ordinary sleep.

The seances are not the exclusive source of the involuntary suggestions which trouble Mlle. Smith in her daily life without any benefit to herself. It is evident that on every occasion when she finds herself in that particular condition of least resistance which we, in our ignorance of its intrinsic nature, designate by the convenient name of " suggestibility," she is exposed to impressions capable of returning to assail her in the course of her daily occupations. Fortunately this condition of suggestibility does not seem to develop itself readily in her outside of the spiritistic reunions.

2. *Irruptions of subliminal reveries.*—I shall have too many occasions to cite concrete examples of visions, voices, and other spontaneous outpourings of the work of imagination, which are continually going on under the ordinary consciousness of Mlle. Smith, to dwell long on this point. Some general remarks will suffice.

The connection which the unforeseen phenomena maintain with those of the seances themselves is very varied. Sometimes we are able to recognize them as reproductions, more or less incomplete, of episodes which occurred at the preceding seances, and consider them simple echoes or post-hypnotic repetitions of these last. Sometimes, on the contrary, it appears that we have to deal with preparatory rehearsals of scenes which will unfold themselves at length and will be continued at some later seance. Finally, sometimes it is a question of tableaux, having no connection with those which fill up the seances; they are like leaves, flying away never to return, romances which are continually being fabricated in the deep subliminal strata of Mlle. Smith's consciousness.

Hélène, in fact, does not long remember, nor in much detail, with a few exceptions, those visions which take place in her ordinary state, and which occur most frequently early in the morning, while she is still in bed, or just after she has arisen and while working by the light of her lamp; sometimes in the evening, or during the brief moments of rest in the middle of the day, and, much more rarely, while in the full activity of waking hours she is at her desk. If she had not long since, at my request, and with great good will, acquired the habit of noting in pencil the essential content of these apparitions, either during the apparition itself (which she is not always able to do) or else immediately afterwards, we should have still more deficiencies in the plot of her romances to deplore. Hélène's psychological state, during her spontaneous visions, is known to me only by her own descriptions. She is fortunately a very intelligent observer and a good psychologist.

Her narratives show that her visions are accompanied by a certain degree of obnubilation. For a few moments, for instance, the room, the light of the lamp, disappear from before her eyes; the noise of the wheels in the street ceases to be heard; she feels herself becoming inert and passive, while a feeling of bliss and ecstatic well-being permeates her entire individuality in the presence of the spectacle which appears to her; then the vision, to her great regret, slowly fades from her view, the lamp and the furniture reappear, the outside noises again make themselves heard, and she is astonished that the idea did not occur to her to put down in pencil the strange words she has heard, or that she did not touch or caress, for example, the beautiful birds of many-colored plumage flying and singing around her. Sometimes she has maintained sufficient presence of mind to scribble from dictation the words striking her ear; but the wretched handwriting proves that her attention, all absorbed by the apparition, could not follow the pencil, and that the hand directed it badly. At other times the reverse is the fact. It appears in the course of the vision as though some one took hold of her arm and guided it in spite of herself; the result is splendid calligraphies, wholly different from her own handwriting, executed without her knowledge, and during the execution of which her mind was wholly absent, if we can judge from the surprise she shows on awaking when she finds before her these strange writings, and from analogous scenes which transpire at the seances.

The preceding is applicable especially to the more frequent cases—that is, to the morning or evening visions which happen to her at home, in that intermediate condition between sleep and waking, always so favorable, as we know, to the development of unconscious cerebration. But there are innumerable shades and gradations between this middle type, so to speak, and its opposite extremes; on the one hand is the fortunately very exceptional case where she is seized with ecstasy while at her place of business; and, on the other hand, that in which the automatism limits itself to inscribing some unknown characters or words in another hand than her own in her correspondence and writings—peculiar *lapsus calami*, which she is not slow to perceive on coming to herself.

The following is an example of a case of ecstasy:

Having ascended one day to an upper story, to look for something in a dark store-room, she had an apparition of a man in a turban and large white cloak, whom she had the impression of recognizing, [1] and whose presence filled her with a delightful calm and profound happiness. She could not recall the conversation which passed between them, which, though in an unknown language, she nevertheless had the feeling of having perfectly comprehended. On the departure of the mysterious visitor she was astonished to find herself brought back to sombre reality, and stupefied on noting by her watch that the interview had lasted much longer than it had seemed to do. She preserved all that day a delicious feeling of wellbeing as the effect of the strange apparition.

The phenomenon of mingling strange writing with her own is of relatively frequent occurrence, and we shall see divers specimens of it in the following chapters, apropos of the romances to which it especially belongs. I will give here only one complex example, which will serve at the same time as an illustration of a special kind of automatism, very harmless, to which Hélène is also subject, and which consists in making verses, not without knowing, but at least without intending to do so, and in connection with the most trifling matters.

There are times when, in spite of herself, she feels compelled to speak in distinct rhymes of eight feet, which she does not prepare, and does not

---

[1] Vision relating to the Oriental cycle; the man was the Arab sheik, the father of Simandini.

perceive until the moment she has finished uttering them.[1] In this particular case it is by a quatrain (a very unusual occurrence) that she replies to some one who had consulted her in regard to some blue ribbon. But this quatrain, by its style, by the vision of the blond head of a child which accompanies it, and by the manner also in which she writes it, causes us to hazard the conjecture that it is an inspiration depending on the underlying Royal cycle; while in the following letter, in which she narrates the affair to M. Lemaître, her pen inscribes, all unknown to her, strange characters evidently due to the cropping out of the Martian cycle, of which she speaks in the letter (see Fig. 1, a passage of that letter making a Martian M and V in the words *vers* and *rimait*):

Hier matin dans la matinée j'ai de nouveau parlé en vers sans m'en douter ce n'est qu'en finissant ma phrase que j'ai senti qu'elle rimait

Fig. 1. Fragment of a letter (normal handwriting) of Mlle. Smith, containing two Martian letters. (Collection of M. Lemaître.)

"I have heard some Martian words this afternoon, but have not been able to retain them in my mind. I send you those heard a few days ago, when I had the vision of which I am about to make you the design (Martian lamp). Yesterday morning I for the first time spoke in verse, without being aware of it; it was only on finishing the sentence that I perceived that it rhymed, and I reconstructed it to assure myself of the fact. A little later, on

---

[1] The following are some of these impromptu rhymes, surely up to the level of the circumstances which inspired them, but by which we ought not to judge the *conscious* poetic faculties of Mlle. Smith:
To a little girl proud of her new shoes:
  "Marcelle est là, venez la voir,
  Elle a ses petits souliers noirs."
In a "culinary" discussion:
  "Vous détestez les omelettes,
  Autant que moi les côtelettes."
To a person slightly vain:
  "Vos richesses, ma chère amie,
  Ne me font point du tout envie!"

examining some ribbons, I began anew to speak in verse, and I send those also: they will amuse you. It is a curious thing that I had at that same moment the vision of the blond curly head of a child bound with a blue ribbon. The vision lasted more than a minute. What is still more curious, I do not at all recollect having worn ribbons of that shade as a child: I remember some rose-colored, some red, but I have no recollection whatever of any blue ribbons. I really do not know why I spoke these words; it is the more amusing. I was obliged to speak them, I assure you, in spite of myself. I was eager to put them on paper, and I noticed in writing them down that, for a moment, the handwriting was not regular, that is, it was slightly different from mine."

Here is the quatrain, the pencil impression of which is too faint to enable a fac-simile to be reproduced here, and in it I have indicated by italics the words and syllables the calligraphy or orthography of which differs from that of Hélène and becomes the style of automatic handwriting called that of Marie Antoinette:

> "Les nuances de ces rubans
> *Me* rappelent *mes* jeunes ans;
> Ce bleu *ver*di, je m'en sou*vien*,
> Sans mes cheveux *alloit* si bien!"

The head of curly blond hair, ornamented with blue ribbons, also figures in the visions of the Royal cycle, and appears to belong, as is here the case, sometimes to Marie Antoinette herself, sometimes to one or other of her children, especially the Dauphin.

While it is generally easy to connect these eruptions of the subliminal volcano with the various dreams from which they emanate, such is not always the case, and there are visions the origin of which is doubtful and ambiguous. We must not forget that, alongside of the grand cycles of Hélène which are better known, there also float in her latent imagination innumerable small accessory systems, more or less independent, which supply a large part of the seances, such as revelations of former events connected with the families of the sitters, etc.; it is not always possible to identify the fragments coining from these isolated dreams.

3. *Teleological automatisms.*—The spontaneous phenomena of this category, possessing as a common characteristic a practical utility for

Hélène more or less marked, can be subdivided into two classes, according to their direct attachment to the personality of Leopold, or their not belonging to any distinct personality, and which only express in a vivid manner the result of the normal working, although more or less unconscious, of the faculties of memory and of reason. I confine myself now to citing one case of each of these classes, of which we shall see other examples in the chapters relating to Leopold and to supernormal appearances.

One day Mlle. Smith, wishing to take down a large and heavy object from a high shelf, was prevented from so doing by the fact that her uplifted arms seemed as though petrified and incapable of being moved for some seconds; she saw in this a warning and gave up her intention. In a later seance Leopold said that it was he himself who had caused Hélène's arms to become rigid, in order to prevent her from attempting to lift the object which was too heavy for her and would have caused some accident to befall her.

On another occasion a clerk who sought vainly for a certain pattern asked Hélène if she knew what had become of it. Hélène replied mechanically and without reflection, "Yes, it was sent to Mr. J." (a customer of the firm); at the same time there appeared before her in large black figures about eight or ten inches in height the number 18, and she added, instinctively, "It was eighteen days ago." This statement caused the clerk to smile, because of its improbability, the rule of the house being that customers to whom patterns were lent for examination must return them inside of three days or a messenger would be sent for them. Hélène, struck by this objection, and having no conscious recollection of the affair, replied, "Really, perhaps I am wrong." Meanwhile, an investigation of the date indicated in the records of the house showed that she was perfectly correct. It was through various negligences, with which she had nothing at all to do, that the pattern had not been sent for or recovered. Leopold, on being asked, has no recollection of this circumstance, and does not appear to have been the author of this automatism of cryptomnesia, nor of many other analogous phenomena through which Hélène's subconscious memory renders her signal services and has gained for her a well-merited and highly valued reputation.

Thus we see that if the spontaneous automatisms of Mlle. Smith are often the vexatious result of her moments of suggestibility, or the tempestuous irruption of her subliminal reveries, they also often assume the form of useful messages. Such compensation is not to be despised.

IV. THE SEANCES

Mlle. Smith has never been hypnotized. In her instinctive aversion, which she shares with the majority of mediums, to anything that seems like an attempt to experiment upon her, she has always refused to allow herself to be put to sleep. She does not realize that in avoiding the idea she has actually accepted the reality, since her spiritistic experiences in reality constitute for her an auto-hypnotization, which inevitably degenerates into a hetero-hypnotization, as she is brought under the influence of one or other of the persons present at the seance.

All her seances have somewhat of the same psychologic form, the same method of development running through their immense diversity of content. She places herself at the table with the idea and the intention of bringing into play her mediumistic faculties. After an interval, varying from a few seconds to a quarter of an hour, generally in a shorter time if the room is well darkened and the sitters are perfectly silent, she begins to have visions, preceded and accompanied by very varied sensory and motor disturbances, after which she passes into a complete trance. In that state, it rarely happens, and then only for a few moments, that she is entirely unconscious of the persons present, and, as it were, shut up within her personal dream and plunged into profound lethargy (hypnotic syncope) . Ordinarily she remains in communication, more or less close, with one of the sitters, who thus finds himself in the same relation towards her as a hypnotizer towards his subject, and able to take advantage of that *rapport*, by giving her any immediate or future suggestions that he may desire. When the seance consists only of waking visions, it lasts generally only a short time—an hour to an hour and a half—and is ended quickly by three sharp raps upon the table, after which Mlle. Smith returns to her normal state, which she scarcely seems to have left. If the somnambulism has been complete, the seance is prolonged to double that length of time, and often longer, and the return to the normal state comes slowly through phases of deep sleep, alternating with relapses into somnambulistic gestures and attitudes, moments of catalepsy, etc. The final awakening is always preceded by several brief awakenings, followed by relapses into sleep.

Each of these preliminary awakenings, as well as the final one, is accompanied by the same characteristic movements of the features. The eyes, which have been for a long time closed, open wide, stupidly staring into vacancy, or fix themselves slowly on the objects and the sitters within their range of vision, the dilated pupils do not react, the face is an impassive and rigid mask, devoid of expression. Hélène seems altogether absent. All at once, with a slight heaving of the breast and raising of the head, and a quick breath, a gleam of intelligence illumines her countenance, the mouth is gracefully opened, the eyes become brilliant, the entire countenance lights up with a pleasant smile and gives evidence of her recognition of the world and of her return to herself. But with the same suddenness with which it appeared, that appearance of life lasts but a second or two, the physiognomy resumes its lifeless mask, the eyes becoming haggard and fixed close again, and the head falls on the back of the chair. This return of sleep will be followed by another sudden awaking, then perhaps by several more, until the final awaking, always distinguished, after the smile at the beginning, by the stereotyped question, "What time is it?" and by a movement of surprise on learning that it is so late. There is no memory of what has transpired during the seance.

A complete description of the psychological and physiological phenomena which present themselves, or which might be obtained in the course of the seances, would detain me too long, since there is absolutely nothing constant either in the nature or in the succession of the phenomena, and no two seances are evolved exactly in the same manner. I must confine myself to some striking characteristics.

Three principal symptoms, almost contemporaneous generally, announce that Mlle. Smith is beginning to enter into her trance.

There are on the one side emotional or cœnæsthetic modifications, the cause of which is revealed a little later in the subsequent messages. Hélène is, for instance, seized by an invincible desire to laugh, which she cannot or will not explain; or she complains of sadness, fear, of different unpleasant sensations, of heat or of cold, of nausea, etc., according to the nature of the communications which are approaching and of which these emotional states are the forerunners.

There are, on the other hand, phenomena of systematic anæsthesia (negative hallucinations), limited to those sitters whom the coming messages concern. Hélène ceases to see them, while continuing to hear their voices and feel their touch; or, on the contrary, she is astonished to no longer hear them, though she sees their lips moving, etc.; or, finally, she does not perceive them in any manner, and demands to know why they are leaving when the seance is hardly begun. In its details this systematic anæsthesia varies infinitely, and extends sometimes to but one part of the person concerned, to his hand, to a portion of his face, etc., without it always being possible to explain these capricious details by the content of the following visions; it would seem that the incoherence of the dream presides over this preliminary work of disintegration, and that the normal perceptions are absorbed by the subconscious personality eager for material for the building up of the hallucinations which it is preparing.

Systematic anæsthesia is often complicated with positive hallucinations, and Hélène will manifest her surprise at seeing, for example, a strange costume or an unusual coiffure. This, in reality, is the vision which is already being installed.

The third symptom, which does not manifest itself clearly in her, but the presence of which can be often established before all the others by investigation, is a complete allochiria, [1] ordinarily accompanied by various other sensory and motor disturbances. If, at the beginning of the seance, Hélène is asked, for example, to raise her right hand, to move the left index-finger, or to close one eye, she begins straightway to carry into effect these different acts; then all at once, without knowing why and without hesitation, she deceives herself in regard to the side, and raises her left hand, moves her right index-finger, closes the other eye, etc. This indicates that she is no longer in her normal state, though still appearing to retain her ordinary consciousness, and with the liveliness of a normal person discusses the question of her having mistaken her right hand or eye for her left, and vice versa. It is to be noted that Leopold, on such occasions of pronounced allochiria, does not share this error in regard to the side. I have assisted at some curious discussions between him and Hélène, she insisting that such a hand was her right, or that the Isle Rousseau is on the left as one passes the bridge of Mont Blanc or coming from the railway station,

---

[1] The confusion of sensations in the two sides of the body, as when a person locates in the right leg a touch upon the left leg.

and Leopold all the while, by means of raps upon the table, giving her clearly to understand she was wrong. [1]

A little after the allochiria, and sometimes simultaneously with it, are to be found various other phenomena, extremely variable, of which I here cite only a few One of her arms is contractured as it rests upon the table, and resists the efforts of the sitters to lift it up, as though it were a bar of iron; the fingers of the hand also participate in this rigidity. Sometimes this contracture does not exist before, but establishes itself at the same instant that some one touches the forearm, and increases in proportion to the efforts which are made to overcome it. There is no regularity in the distribution of the anæsthesia (changing from one instant to another), the contractures, or convulsions which the hands and arms of Hélène exhibit. It all seems due to pure caprice, or to depend only on underlying dreams, of which little is known.

Certain analogous and likewise capricious phenomena of anæsthesia, paralysis, sensations of all sorts, of which Hélène complains, often appear in her face, her eyes, her mouth, etc. In the midst of all these disturbances the visions announce themselves, and the somnambulism is introduced with modifications, equally variable, of other functions, evidenced by tears, sobbings, sighs, repeated hiccoughs, various changing of the rhythm of respiration, etc.

If Hélène is experimented upon and questioned too long, the development of the original visions is obstructed, and she easily reaches a degree of sensibility where she falls into the standard class of public representations of hypnotism—a charmed and fascinated state in which she remains riveted before some brilliant object, as, for example, the ring, trinkets, or cuff-button of one of the sitters; then precipitates herself in a frenzy upon the object, and tries to secure it; or assumes emotional attitudes and poses under the influence of joyous airs upon the piano; experiences suggested hallucinations of all kinds, sees terrible serpents, which she pursues with a pair of pincers; beautiful flowers, which she smells with deep respirations and distributes to the sitters; or, again, bleeding wounds which have been made on her hand, and which cause her to shed tears. The common-place character of these phenomena causes their long continuance to be

---

[1] See, on allochiria, P. Janet, *Stigmates mentaux des hysteriques*, pp. 66-71; and *Nevroses et ideés fixes*, vol. i. p. 234.

deprecated, and the ingenuity of all is exercised in endeavoring by different means, none of which is very efficacious or very rapid, to plunge her into profound and tranquil sleep, from which she is not long in passing of her own accord into complete somnambulism and in taking up the thread of her personal imaginations.

If all these disturbing investigations have been successfully avoided, the spontaneous development of the automatisms is effected with greater rapidity and fulness. It is possible then to behold, in the same seance, a very varied spectacle, and to listen, besides, to certain special communications made in a semi-waking state to one or other of the sitters; then, in complete somnambulism, a Hindoo vision is presented, followed by a Martian dream, with an incarnation of Leopold in the middle, and a scene of Marie Antoinette to wind up with. Ordinarily two of these last creations will suffice to fill up a seance. One such representation is not performed without the loss of considerable strength by the medium, which shows itself by the final sleep being prolonged sometimes for an hour, interrupted, as I have said, by repetitions of the preceding somnambulistic scenes, easily recognizable by certain gestures or the murmuring of characteristic words. Passing through these diverse oscillations and the ephemeral awaking, of which I have spoken above, Hélène finishes by returning to her normal state; but the seances which have been too long continued or too full of movement leave her very much fatigued for the rest of the day. It has also sometimes happened to her to re-enter the somnambulism (from which she had probably not completely emerged) during the course of the evening or on returning home, and only to succeed in recovering her perfectly normal state through the assistance of a night's sleep.

As to the real nature of Hélène's slumbers at the end of the seances, and her states of consciousness when she awakes, it is difficult for me to pronounce, having only been able to observe them under unfavorable conditions—that is, in the presence of sitters more or less numerous and restless. The greater part certainly consist of somnambulisms, in which she hears all that passes around her, since although she seems profoundly asleep and absent, the suggestions then given her to be carried out after awaking are registered and performed wonderfully—at least when Leopold, who is almost always on hand and answers by movements of one finger or another to questions put to him, does not make any opposition or declare that the suggestion shall not be carried out ! There are also brief moments when Hélène seems to be in a profound state of coma and kind of syncope without trace of psychic life; her pulse and respiration continue to be regular, but she does not react to any excitation, her arms, if raised, fall heavily, no sign of Leopold can be obtained, and suggestions made at that instant will not be acted upon.

These lethargic phases, during which all consciousness seems to be abolished, are generally followed by cataleptic phases in which the hands and arms preserve every position in which they may be placed, and continue the movements of rotation or of oscillation which may be forced upon them, but never for more than one or two minutes.

In default of more complete experiments, I submit the following comparison of Hélène's muscular force and of her sensibility to pain before and after a seance lasting nearly three hours, the second half being in full somnambulism. At 4.50 o'clock, on sitting down at the table three dynamometric tests with her right hand gave kilos. 27.5, 27, 25—average, 26.5. The sensibility to pain measured on the back of the median phalanx of the index-finger with the algesiometer of Griesbach, gave for the right, grs. 35, 40, 20, 20—average, 29; for the left, 35, 20, 20, 15—average, 22.5 grs. (Sensibility slightly more delicate than that of another lady present at the seance, not a medium and in perfect health.)

At 7.45 o'clock, some minutes after the final awaking: dynamometer, right hand, 8, 4.5, 4.5—average, 5.7; algesiometer, complete analgesia both as to right and left, on the whole of the back of the index as well as the rest of the hand and wrist, the maximum of the instrument (100 grs.) was attained and passed without arousing any painful sensation but only an impression of contact.

One hour later, after dinner: dynamometer 22, 22, 19—average, 21; algesiometer, 20, 18 for the right: 15, 20 for the left. It is possible, then, to say that her muscular force and sensibility to pain, both normal immediately before her entrance upon the seance, are still abolished in the first fifteen minutes after awaking, but are found to be restored in about an hour. Perception of colors, on the contrary, appeared to be as perfect immediately after awaking as before the seance. The tremor of the index-finger; normal before the seance, is very much exaggerated in its amplitude for a certain time after awaking and reflects sometimes the respiratory movements, as can be seen by the curves of Fig. 2. This denotes a great diminution of kinesthetic sensibility and of voluntary control over the immobility of the hand.

The state in which Mlle. Smith carries out the post-hypnotic suggestions made to her in the course of her somnambulisms, when they do not come into collision with either the pronounced opposition of Leopold or the states of lethargy of which I have spoken, is interesting on account of its varied character, which seems to depend upon the greater or less ease with which the hallucination or the act suggested can be reconciled with Hélène's normal personality. Their execution in the full waking state seems to be confined to suggestions of simple acts, free from absurdity, the idea of which would be easily accepted and carried out by the normal self when the desired moment arrived. If, on the contrary, it is a question of more complicated and difficult things, compatible, however, with the rational points of view of the normal waking state, Hélène falls momentarily into somnambulism for the execution of the order given, unless she has permanently remained in that state, in spite of her apparent awaking, in order not to re-enter definitely and completely upon her ordinary state until after the execution of the order, of which there then remains to her no recollection whatever.

From the foregoing facts we may conclude that little or nothing of that which goes on around her escapes her subconscious intelligence, and it is from this source that her somnambulistic romances are nourished afresh.

A word more as to the preparation for the seances. I do not refer to a conscious preparation, but to a subliminal incubation or elaboration, unknown by her, showing itself on the level of her ordinary personality in the form of fugitive gleams and fragmentary images during her sleep at night or the moments of awaking in the morning. Mlle. Smith, in reality, has no hold, possesses no influence, upon the nature of her visions and somnambulisms. She is able, undoubtedly, up to a certain point, to aid their appearance in a general way, by cultivating tranquillity of mind, securing darkness and silence in the room, and by abandoning herself to a passive attitude of mind; or to hinder it, on the other hand, by movement, or distraction of attention; but with the fixed and concrete content itself of her automatisms she has nothing to do and no share in the responsibility for it. So far as her great cycles or her detached messages are concerned, they are fabricated in her in spite of herself, and without her having a word to say about their production, any more than one has in the formation of his dreams. When it is recollected, on the other hand, that the phenomena of incubation, of subliminal preparation, or unconscious cerebration, are universal facts, playing their rôle in the psychology of every human being, we can rely upon finding them also among the mediums, and upon their holding a place with them much more important than with others, owing to the fact that their subconscious life is so much more fully developed.

Fig. 2. Tremor of right index-finger. A, B, C, fragments of curves taken in the normal state before the seance (A and C with closed eyes; B, with open eyes looking at the index-finger); D, E, F, fragments of curves received in succession a quarter of an hour after the seance. The curve F reflects the respiratory oscillations. The curves go from right to left, and the interval between the two vertical lines is ten seconds.

With each one of us the expectation or the simple perspective of any event—a departure, a visit, an errand, or undertaking to do anything, a letter to write, in short, all the more insignificant incidents of daily existence, when they are not absolutely unforeseen—promote a psychological adaptation more or less extended and profound.

Alongside of and underneath the conscious expectancy, certain physical or mental attitudes, voluntarily assumed in view of the event, always effect an underlying preparation of an inward kind, a change which we may regard, according to the side from which we consider the individual, as a peculiar psychical orientation or cerebral adjustment, a modification in the association of ideas or in the dynamics of the cortical nerves. But everything points to the fact that in persons gifted with mediumship this underlying preparation is capable of assuming on occasion a greater importance than is the case with ordinary mortals, a much more complete independence of the ordinary consciousness

To return to Mlle. Smith, when she knows some time in advance who will be present at her next seance, and what people she will almost surely meet there, it would be altogether natural that such previous knowledge of the environment and of the sitters would influence her subliminal thoughts and in some degree direct the course of the latent incubation. It may well be asked, therefore, whether the varied spectacle which the seances furnish is really always impromptu and has its birth on the spur of the moment like ordinary dreams, or whether it has been subconsciously thought out, the seance being only the performance of an arrested programme, the representation *coram populo* of scenes already ripened in the deep subliminal strata of the medium.

Neither of these two hypotheses, held to exclude the other, answers to the facts, but there is some truth in both of them.
The *menu* of the seances—if the expression is permissible—is always composed of one or two *plats de résistance*, carefully prepared in advance in the subliminal laboratories, and of various *hors d'oeuvres* left to the inspiration of the moment. To speak more exactly, the general plot, the chief lines and more striking points of the scenes which unfold themselves are fixed according to a previous arrangement, but the details of execution and accessory embellishments are entirely dependent upon chance circumstances. The proof of this is found, on the one hand, in the suppleness, the perfect ease, the appropriateness with which Hélène's automatisms—if we can still apply the word automatism to those cases in which spontaneity, self-possession, free use of all the faculties constitute the dominant characteristics—often adapt themselves to unexpected situations in the environment or capricious interruptions on the part of the sitters; on the other hand, in the fact that Leopold, interrogated at the beginning of the seance, ordinarily knows very well and announces the

principal vision or incarnations which are about to make their appearance, provided, at least, the spectators do not hinder their unfolding by their tempestuous clamor for something else.

The animated conversations, sometimes full of spirited repartee, between Leopold or Marie Antoinette and the sitters, could not have been prepared in advance, and are altogether opposed to the stereotyped repetition which is generally expected of automatic phenomena. But, on the other hand, such repetition, almost entirely mechanical and devoid of sense, presents itself on frequent occasions. I have, for instance, seen somnambulistic scenes presented which were entirely misplaced, and constituted at the time veritable anachronisms, which would have perfectly fitted the situation eight days previously in another environment, and for which the aforesaid scenes had been evidently intended; but, having been withheld until the last moment by unforeseen circumstances, the following seance gets the benefit of these postponed messages.

Here is proof that Hélène's subliminal imagination prepares up to a certain point her principal productions, in view of the conditions and surroundings under which the seance will probably take place, and also that these products, once elaborated, must be eliminated and poured forth with a sort of blind necessity, at the right or the wrong time, whenever the entrance of Hélène into a favorable hypnoid state furnishes them an opportunity so to do. It follows also that her normal personality has nothing whatever to do with the preparation of the seances, since she can neither suppress nor change scenes badly adapted to the actual environment, the appearance of which sometimes greatly annoys Mlle. Smith when they are recounted to her after the seance; nor can she provoke the messages, the production of which she desires and vainly hopes for—as, for example, a medical consultation with Leopold, the incarnation of a deceased parent, or a scene from one cycle rather than from the others, for the benefit of a sitter who particularly desires it, and whom she is very desirous to please.

Much more could be said concerning the psychological side of the seances of Mlle. Smith, but I must limit myself. It will be possible to gain a more complete idea of this subject by studying the illustrations in the following chapters on the chief cycles of her brilliant subliminal fantasy.

THE PERSONALITY OF LEOPOLD

IS Leopold really Joseph Balsamo, as he pretends? Or, since he has nothing in common with the famous thaumaturgist of the last century, save a certain superficial resemblance, is he, at any rate, a real being, separate from, and independent of, Mlle. Smith? Or, finally, is he only a pseudo-reality, a kind of allotropic modification of Hélène herself, a product of her subliminal imagination, just like our dream creations and the rôles suggested to a hypnotic subject?

Of these three suppositions it is the last which to my mind is undoubtedly the true one, while in Mlle. Smith's eyes it is as certainly the false view. It would be hard to imagine a more profound difference of opinion than that which exists between Mlle. Smith and myself on this subject. It is I, always, who get the worst of a discussion with her concerning it. I yield for two reasons. First, out of politeness; and, secondly, because I understand Hélène perfectly, and, putting myself in her place, realize that I should think exactly as she does about the matter.

Given her surroundings and personal experiences, it is impossible for her to do otherwise than believe in the objective distinct existence of that mysterious being who constantly enters into her life in a sensible and quasi-material way, leaving her no room to doubt. He presents himself before her endowed with corporeality like that of other people, and hides objects which are behind him exactly as an ordinary individual of flesh and bone would do He talks into her ears, generally into the left, in a characteristic voice, which appears to come from a variable distance, sometimes about six feet off, sometimes much farther. He jars the table on which she has placed her immobile arms, takes hold of her wrist and writes with her hand, holding the pen in a manner unlike her, and with a handwriting wholly different from hers. He puts her to sleep without her knowledge, and she is astonished to learn upon awaking that he has gesticulated with her arms and spoken through her mouth in the deep bass voice of a man, with an Italian accent, which has nothing in common with the clear and beautiful quality of her feminine voice.

Moreover, he is not always on hand. He by no means answers Hélène's appeals on all occasions; is not at her mercy; far from it. His conduct, his manifestations, his comings and goings cannot be predicted with any certainty, and testify to an autonomous being, endowed with free-will, often otherwise occupied or absent on his own affairs, which do not permit of his holding himself constantly at the disposal of Mlle. Smith. Sometimes he remains for weeks without revealing himself, in spite of her wishing for him and calling upon him. Then, all at once, he makes his appearance when she least expects him. He speaks for her in a way she would have no idea of doing, he dictates to her poems of which she would be incapable. He replies to her oral or mental questions, converses with her, and discusses various questions. Like a wise friend, a rational mentor, and as one seeing things from a higher plane, he gives her advice, counsel, orders even sometimes directly opposite to her wishes and against which she rebels. He consoles her, exhorts her, soothes, encourages, and reprimands her; he undertakes against her the defence of persons she does not like, and pleads the cause of those who are antipathetic to her. In a word, it would be impossible to imagine a being more independent or more different from Mlle. Smith herself, having a more personal character, an individuality more marked, or a more certain actual existence.

Hélène is also fortified in this conviction by the belief not only of members of her own family, but by that of other cultivated people who, having attended many of her seances, have no doubt whatever of Leopold's objective and separate existence. There are those who believe so firmly in the reality of this superior being, invisible to them, that they are in the habit of calling upon him during the absence of Mlle. Smith. Naturally they obtain responses, through the table or otherwise, and that causes unforeseen complications sometimes when she comes to learn of it. For while she admits theoretically—and Leopold himself has often declared the same thing—that he extends his surveillance and protection from afar over other spiritistic groups, and especially over all Hélène's friends and acquaintances, in practice and in fact, however, it happens that neither he nor she will willingly admit the authenticity of those pretended communications from Leopold obtained in the absence of the medium of his predilection. It is generally some deceiving spirit who has manifested in his place on these occasions. These denials, however, do not prevent those who have become believers from continuing to believe in the omnipresence of this good genius, or from teaching their children to revere him, to make vows and address prayers to him. It must not be forgotten that spiritism is a religion. This also explains the great respect shown to mediums, which is like that accorded to priests.

It follows that, without in the least refraining from speaking ill of them whenever they think they have a grievance against them, on the other hand they bestow on them the same marks of respect as are only accorded to the most sublime product of the human race.

I have known a *salon* where, on the centre table, in full view and in the place of honor, were two photographs in beautiful frames: on the one side the head of Christ, on the other the portrait of—Mlle. Hélène Smith. Among other believers, with less ideal but more practical aspirations, no business matter of importance is closed, no serious decision made, until Leopold has been consulted through Hélène as an intermediary, and the cases are too numerous to mention in which he has furnished important information, prevented a heavy precuniary loss, given an efficacious medical prescription, etc.

It is easily seen how all the successes obtained by Leopold, and the mystical veneration which many very estimable persons accord him, must contribute to strengthen the faith of Hélène in her all-powerful protector. It is in vain that, against this absolute assurance, one seeks to avail one's self of the arguments of contemporary psychology. The example of the fictions of the dream, the analogies taken from hypnotism and from psychopathology, considerations of mental disintegration, the division of the consciousness and the formation of second personalities, all these refined subtleties of our modern scientists break in pieces like glass against immovable rock. I shall not undertake to combat a proposition which, for her, has incontestably so much evidence in its favor, and which resolves all difficulties in the most felicitous manner and in conformity to good common-sense.

Nevertheless, since each individual has a right to his own opinion in the world, I beg leave to assume, for the time being, that Leopold does not exist outside of Mlle. Smith, and to try to discover his possible genesis in the mental life of the latter—solely by hypothesis and by means of psychological experiment. Therefore, readers who have little taste for this kind of academic composition had better skip this chapter.

I. PSYCHOGENESIS OF LEOPOLD

A description of the development of Leopold is not easy, since he has a double origin, apparent and real, like the cranial nerves which give so much trouble to the students of anatomy.

His apparent origin, or, I should say, the moment when he is outwardly separated from the personality of Hélène, and manifests as an independent "spirit," is relatively clear and well marked; but his actual origin, profoundly enfolded in the most inward strata of Hélène's personality and inextricably mixed up with them, presents great obscurities and can only be determined in a very conjectural manner. Let us begin with the apparent origin, or the first appearance of Leopold at the seances.

It is easy to understand that, once initiated into spiritism and plunged into a current of ideas where the comforting doctrine of spirit-guides and protectors holds an important place, Mlle. Smith did not delay in coming into possession of, like all good mediums, a disincarnate spirit specially attached to her person. She even had two in succession, Victor Hugo and Cagliostro. It is not a question of a simple change of name of the guide of Hélène, who presented himself first under the aspect and the name of the great poet and then afterwards adopted that of the renowned thaumaturgist, but there were, at least at the beginning, two different personalities, apparently hostile to each other, one of whom by degrees supplanted the other, after a struggle, a trace of which is found in the very incomplete reports of the seances of that period. Three phases can also be distinguished in the psychogenesis of Mlle. Smith's guide: an initial phase of five months, during which Victor Hugo reigns alone; a phase of transition of about a year, when the protection of Victor Hugo is seen to be powerless to protect Hélène and her spiritistic group against the invasion of an intruder called Leopold, who claims and manifests an increasing authority over the medium by virtue of mysterious relations in the course of a previous existence; finally, the present period, which has lasted for six years past, in which Victor Hugo no longer figures, and which may be dated approximately from the moment when it was revealed that Leopold is only an assumed name, under which he hides in reality the great personality of Joseph Balsamo.

I do not find any fact worthy of mention in the first phase, in which Victor Hugo, who seems to have appeared as the guide of Mlle. Smith about the 1st of April, 1892 (see above, p. 38), played a rôle of no importance. In the second phase, however, it is necessary to cite some extracts from the reports of the seances of the N. group, in order to throw light upon the singular character which Leopold manifested there from the beginning.

August 26, 1892.—"A spirit announces himself under the name of Leopold. He comes for Mlle. Smith, and seems to wish to have a great authority over her. She sees him for some moments, he appears to be about thirty-five years of age, and is clothed altogether in black. The expression of his countenance is rather pleasing, and through answers to some questions which we put to him we are given to understand that he knew her in another existence, and that he does not wish her to give her heart to any one here below. . . Mlle. Smith recognizes her guide, Victor Hugo. She is made happy by his arrival, and asks his protection against the obsession of this new spirit. He answers that she has nothing to fear, that he will always be present. She is joyful at being guarded and protected by him, and feels that she has nothing to fear."

September 2.—. . . "Leopold comes also, but Mlle. Smith fears nothing, since her guide (Victor Hugo) is there to protect her."

September 23.—. . . "An unpleasant evening. A spirit announces himself. It is Leopold. He speaks to us at once: 'I am here. I wish to be master of this sitting.' We are very much disappointed, and do not expect any good of him. He tries, as he had already done once before, to put Mlle. Smith to sleep, who has great difficulty in struggling against this sleep. She rises from the table, hoping by this means to rid herself of him, and that he will give up his place to others. She returns in about ten minutes, but he is still there, and apparently has no intention of abandoning his place. We summon our friends (spiritual) to our aid. . . . They take Leopold's place momentarily, but very soon Leopold returns; we struggle with him, we desire him to go away, but neither soft nor hard words have any effect; before that dogged determination we realize that all our efforts will be useless, and we decide to close the seance."

October 3.—"[Manifestation by the favorite spirits of the group, who declare] that they have not been able to come, as they would have liked to do; that they were prevented by the spirit of Leopold, who is trying to introduce himself to us; that we should repulse him as much as possible, persuaded that he does not come for any good end. I do not know whether we shall be able to rid ourselves of him, but we greatly fear that he will injure us and retard our advancement."

October 7.—. . . "Leopold announces himself. We try to reason with him; we do not wish to forbid his coming, but we ask of him that he shall come as a friend to all, and not in the rôle of master. He is not satisfied; appears to bear much malice. We trust he will come to have better feelings. He shows himself, walks around the table, bows to us, and salutes each one with his hand, and retires again, leaving his place to others."

October 14.—"[After a quarter of an hour of motionless and silent waiting in darkness around the table Mlle. Smith is questioned, and she is shaken in vain.] She is asleep. By the advice of persons present we allow her to remain asleep, when, at the end of five minutes, the table raises itself, a spirit announces himself. It is Victor Hugo; we ask if he has anything to say; he answers yes, and spells out: *Wake her; do not allow her ever to sleep.* We try to do so. We are nervous about that sleep; we have great difficulty in awakening her."

January 6, 1893.—"After twenty minutes of waiting, Leopold arrives, and, as is his habit, puts the medium to sleep for some minutes; he torments us, and prevents our friends (disincarnate) from coming to the table. He vexes us in every way, and goes contrary to all our wishes. In presence of that rancor the sitters regret the indications of ill-humor they have shown towards him, and deplore having to pay so dear for them. It is with difficulty that the medium can be awakened."

February, 1893.—"In one of the seances of this month a remarkable thing happened: the spirit of Leopold, who was very much irritated on that day, twice in succession took away her chair from our medium and carried it to the farther end of the room, while Mlle. Smith fell heavily to the floor. Not expecting this wretched farce, Mlle. Smith struck her knee so hard that for several days she suffered pain in walking. We were obliged to terminate the seance; we were not comfortable. Why this animosity?"

This word *animosity* describes very well the conduct and the feelings that Leopold seemed to have towards the N. group and against his placid rival, Victor Hugo. The personal recollections of the sitters whom I have been able to interrogate confirm the substantial physiognomy of the two figures. That of Hugo is, in effect, effaced and altogether eclipsed by the totally opposite character of the arrogant Leopold, who takes a peculiar pleasure in the rôle of vindictive and jealous mischief-maker, obstructing the appearance of the "spirits" desired by the group, putting the medium to sleep, or causing her to fall on the floor, forbidding her to give her heart to another, and breaking up the seances as far as he is able. It seems to have finally resulted in the meetings of the N. group coming to an end at the beginning of the summer; then comes a break of six months, after which I find Mlle. Smith on the 12th of December inaugurating a new series of seances, with an entirely different spiritistic group organized by Prof. Cuendet. Here Victor Hugo very rarely appears, and never in the rôle of guide, which rôle is freely accorded, without objection, to Leopold, whose real identity (Cagliostro) was no secret to any one in the new environment. It was, therefore, in the course of the year 1893, at a period which cannot be precisely determined from the records, that the rivalry of these two personalities was terminated by the complete triumph of the second.

It follows from the preceding recital that the appearance of Leopold in seances of the N. group was a phenomenon of manifest contrast, of hostility, and of antagonism towards that group.

It is a difficult and delicate task to pronounce upon the complex spirit of an environment of which one was not a part, and in regard to which one possesses only a few and not very concordant incidents. The following, however, seem to be the facts:

The N. group, much more numerous than is convenient in seances of that kind, was composed of very varied elements. Alongside of serious believers were ordinarily some students who boarded with one of the ladies of the group, and who do not appear to have felt the seriousness of spiritistic reunions.

That age has no mercy, and the profound signification of the seances often escaped their superficial and frivolous intelligence. Under such conditions Mlle. Smith was inevitably compelled to experience two contrary impressions. On the one hand, she perceived herself admired, made much of, fêted, as the unrivalled medium, which she really was, and upon whom the group depended for its existence; on the other hand, her secret instincts and high personal dignity could not but be offended by the familiarities to which she was exposed in this mixed environment.

I regard the two rival and successive guides of Hélène as the expression of this double sentiment. If she had been brought up like an American woman, or if her nature had been a degree less fine, the frivolity of the seances would undoubtedly have only given more warmth and brilliancy to Victor Hugo; instead of which, the victorious colors of Leopold are raised over a nature of great native pride, extremely sensitive on the point of feminine dignity, and whose severe and rigid education had already exalted her sense of self-respect. After a struggle of a year between these two personifications of opposite emotional tendencies, the second, as we have seen, finally triumphs; and Mlle. Smith withdraws from the N. group, which at the same time breaks up.

The idea I have formed of Leopold is now apparent. He represents, to my mind, in Mlle. Smith, the synthesis, the quintessence—and the expansion, too—of the most hidden springs of the psychological organism. He gushes forth from that deep and mysterious sphere into which the deepest roots of our individual existence are plunged, which bind us to the species itself, and perhaps to the Absolute, and whence confusedly spring our instincts of physical and moral self-preservation, our sexual feelings. When Hélène found herself in an environment not exactly dangerous, but where she simply ran the risk, as in the N. group, of yielding to some inclination contrary to her fundamental aspirations, it is then that Leopold suddenly springs up, speaking as the master, taking possession of the medium for himself, and indicating his unwillingness that she should attach herself to any one here below. We here recognize the same principle of self-protection and self-preservation which was already active in her as a young girl in the teleological automatisms arising on the occasion of certain emotional shocks, of which I have spoken on p. 25.

But, by these considerations, we have travelled very far from the original appearance of Leopold in the seance of the 26th of August, 1892, towards his actual, more ancient origin. This seems to date from a great fright which Hélène had in the course of her tenth year. As she was walking along the street, on her way home from school, she was attacked by a big dog. The terror of the poor child can well be imagined, and from which she was happily delivered by a personage clothed in a long brown robe with flowing sleeves and with a white cross on the breast, who, appearing to her suddenly and as by a miracle, chased the dog away, and disappeared before she had time to thank him. But, according to Leopold, this personage was no other than himself, who on this occasion for the first time appeared to Hélène, and saved her by driving away the dog.

This explanation was given by Leopold on the 6th of October, 1895, in a seance in which Hélène experienced, in a somnambulistic state, a repetition of that scene of fright, with heart-rending cries, gestures of struggle and defence, attempts at flight, etc. In the waking state she very well recalls this episode of her childhood, but cannot accept Leopold as the person who came to her rescue, but believes it to have been a priest or member of some religious order who rushed to her assistance and drove the animal away. Her parents also recollected the incident, which she told them one day on returning from school in a very excited state, and after which she could not for a long time encounter a dog in the street without hiding herself in the folds of her mother's dress. She has since always preserved an instinctive aversion towards dogs.

We have seen (p. 31) that after this first incident, matters remained *in statu quo* for four years, up to the time when the age of puberty began to favor the development of the Oriental visions. Here, Leopold, to whom we owe this information, does not altogether agree with himself, for at one time he says that it was he himself who furnished Mlle. Smith with her visions of India, at another time he says that they are reminiscences of one of her former existences.

Alongside of these varied visions, Leopold has clearly appeared under the form of the protector in the dark robe in a number of cases. I will only cite two examples, one very remote, the, other quite recent.

One day Hélène went to consult her family physician for some trifling ailment, who, having known her for a long time and being an old friend of her family, presumed to give her an innocent kiss. He was quite unprepared for the explosion of wrath which this familiarity provoked, and hastened to make his apologies: but what is of interest to us in this connection is the fact that under the shock of this emotion her defender of the brown robe appeared before her in the corner of the room, and did not leave her side until she had reached home.

A short time ago this same protector, always in the same costume, accompanied her several days in succession while she was traversing a little-frequented part of the route towards her place of business. One evening, also, he appeared to her at the entrance to the street leading to the locality in question, in the attitude of baring the way, and obliged her to make a detour to regain her house.

Mlle. Smith has the impression—and several indications go to show that she is not deceived—that it is with the purpose of sparing her some unpleasant sight or a dangerous encounter that Leopold, in the brown robe, appears to her under perfectly well-known conditions. He rises before her always at a distance of about ten yards, walks, or rather glides, along in silence, at the same rate as she advances towards him, attracting and fascinating her gaze in such a manner as to prevent her turning her eyes away from him either to the right or the left, until she has passed the place of danger. It is to be noted that whereas Leopold, under other circumstances—for instance, at the seances—shows himself to her in the most varied costumes and speaks on all subjects, it is always under his hieratic aspect, silent, and clothed in his long dark robe, that he appears to her on those occasions of real life in which she is exposed to feelings of fright peculiar to her sex, as he appeared to her on that first occasion in her tenth year.

The hints I have given sufficiently justify, I think, my opinion that the real and primordial origin of Leopold is to be found in that deep and delicate sphere in which we so often encounter the roots of hypnoid phenomena, and to which the most illustrious visionaries, such as Swedenborg,[1] seem to owe a great part not only of the intellectual content but. of the imaginative form, the hallucinatory wrapping, of their genius. There is a double problem to be solved in Mlle. Smith's case. Why have these instinctive feelings and emotional tendencies which are common to the entire human race succeeded in developing in her a product so complex and highly organized is is the personality of Leopold? and why, in the second place, does that personality believe itself to be Joseph Balsamo?

I instantly reply that these two results are, to my mind, entirely the effect of autosuggestion. To explain the first, the simple fact of her being occupied with spiritism and engaged in mediumistic experiments, is sufficient. Take any individual having in her subconsciousness memories, scruples, emotional tendencies, put into her head spiritistic leanings, then seat her at a table, or put a pencil in her hand: even though she may not be of a very impressionable or suggestible temperament, or inclined to the mental disintegration which the general public calls the mediumistic faculty, nevertheless, it will not be long before her subliminal elements group themselves and arrange themselves according to the "personal"

---

[1] See Lehmann's *Auberglaube and Zauberei*, p. 217 *et seq.* Stuttgart, 1898.

form to which all consciousness tends,[1] and which discloses itself outwardly by communications which have the appearance of coming directly from disincarnate spirits.

In the case of Mlle. Smith, Leopold did not exist under the title of a distinct secondary personality before Hélène began to be occupied with spiritism. It was at the seances of the N. group, by an emotional reaction against certain influences, as we have seen, that he began, little by little, to take shape, aided by memories of the same general tone, until he finally grew into an apparently independent being, revealing himself through the table, manifesting a will and a mind of his own, recalling analogous former incidents of Hélène's life, and claiming for himself the merit of having intervened in it in the rôle of her protector.

Once established, this secondary self could not do otherwise than to grow, and to develop and strengthen itself in all directions, assimilating to itself a host of new data favoring the state of suggestibility which accompanies the exercise of mediumship. Without the spiritism and the autohypnotization of the seances, Leopold could never have been truly developed into a personality, but would have continued to remain in the nebulous, incoherent state of vague subliminal reveries and of occasional automatic phenomena.

The second problem, that of explaining why this secondary personality, once established, believes itself to be Cagliostro rather than any other celebrated personage, or of remaining simply the anonymous guardian angel of Mlle. Smith, would demand a very complete knowledge of the thousand outside influences which have surrounded Hélène since the beginning of her mediumship, and which may have involuntarily influenced her.

But on this point I have only succeeded in collecting a very few incidents, which leave much still to be desired, and are of such a character that it is entirely permissible for any one to claim that the purely psychological origin of that personality is not clearly established, and to prefer, if he chooses, the actual intervention of the disincarnate Joseph Balsamo to my hypothesis of autosuggestion.

---

[1] W. James, "Thought Tends to Personal Form." *Principles of Psychology*, vol. i. p. 225 *et seq*. New York, 1890.

The following, however, are the facts advanced by me in support of the latter:

The authoritative and jealous spirit, the evident enemy of the N. group, who manifested himself on the 26th of August, 1892, under the name of Leopold, did not reveal his identity as that of Cagliostro until some time afterwards, under the following circumstances:

One of the most regular attendants at the reunions of the N. group was a Mme. B., who had long been an adherent of spiritism, and who had previously attended numerous seances at the house of M. and Mme. Badel, a thoroughly convinced couple of amateurs, now deceased, whose salon and round table have held a very honorable place in the history of Genevese occultism. But I learned from Mme. B. that one of the disincarnate spirits who manifested himself oftenest at the seances of M. and Mme. Badel was this very Joseph Balsamo. There is, indeed, no figure in history which accords better with the idea of a posthumous return to the mysteries of the round table than that of the enigmatic Sicilian, especially since Alexandre Dumas, *père*, has surrounded him with an additional halo of romance.

Not content with the public reunions of the N. group, Mme. B. often invited Hélène to her house for private seances, of which no record was made. At one of these, Hélène having had a vision of Leopold, who pointed out to her with a wand a decanter, Mme. B. suddenly thought of a celebrated episode in the life of Cagliostro, and after the seance she proceeded to take from a drawer and show to Hélène an engraving taken from an illustrated edition of Dumas, representing the famous scene of the decanter between Balsamo and the Dauphin at the château of Taverney. At the same time she gave utterance to the idea that the spirit who manifested himself at the table by means of Hélène's hands was certainly Joseph Balsamo; and she expressed her astonishment that Hélène had given him the name of Leopold, to which Helene replied that it was he himself who had given that name. Mme. B., continuing her deductions, told Mlle. Smith that perhaps she had formerly been the medium of the great magician, and consequently had been Lorenza Feliciani in a former life. Hélène at once accepted the idea, and for several weeks considered herself to be the reincarnation of Lorenza, until one day a lady of her acquaintance remarked that it was impossible, Lorenza Feliciani having never existed save in the imagination and the romances of Alexandre Dumas, *père*. [1]

Thus dispossessed of her supposed former existence, Hélène was not long in declaring through the table that she was Marie Antoinette. As to Leopold, a short time after Mme. B. had hypothetically identified him with Cagliostro, he himself confirmed that hypothesis at a seance of the N. group, dictating to the table that his real name was Joseph Balsamo.

The origin of the name of Leopold is very obscure, and many hypotheses have been advanced to account for it without our being able to establish any of them with certainty.

One fact, however, is certain, namely, that save for the vague affirmation that he had known Hélène in a previous existence, Leopold had never pretended to be Cagliostro, or given any reason for being thought so, before the reunion where Mme. B., who had been for some time accustomed to manifestations of that personage, announced the supposition and showed Mlle. Smith immediately after the seance (at a moment when she was probably still in a very suggestible state) an engraving from Dumas' works representing Balsamo and the Dauphin. From that day Leopold, on his part, never failed to claim that personality, and progressively to realize the character of the rôle in a very remarkable manner, as we shall see.

II. PERSONIFICATION OF BALSAMO BY LEOPOLD

There is no need, I think, to remind the reader of the well-known fact—so often described under the names of objectivity of types, personification, change of personality, etc.—that a hypnotized subject can be transformed by a word into such other living being as may be desired, according to the measure in which his suggestibility on the one hand and the vividness of his imagination and the fulness of his stored-up knowledge or- memories on the other, enables him to fulfil the rôle which is imposed upon him. Without investigating here to what extent mediums may be likened to hypnotized subjects, it is undeniable that an analogous phenomenon takes place in them; but the process is more gradual, and may extend itself over several years. In place of the immediate metamorphosis which modifies at one stroke and instantly, conformably to a prescribed type, the attitude,

---

[1] Alexandre Dumas, *père*, *Memoirs of a Physician*, chap. xv.

the physiognomy, the gestures, the words, the intonations of voice, the style, the handwriting, and other functions besides, we are, in the case of the medium, in the presence of a development formed by successive stages arranged according to grades, with intervals of different lengths, which finally succeed in creating a complete personality, all the more astonishing, at first sight, because the involuntary suggestions have not been noticed, the accumulations of which have little by little caused its birth. This process of development is present in a high degree in the case of Mlle. Smith, in the elaboration of her secondary personality, Leopold-Cagliostro.

In the beginning, in 1892 and 1893, this "spirit" only manifested himself by the brief periods of sleep which he induced in Hélène at certain seances, by raps struck upon the table, by visions in which he showed himself clothed in black and of youthful appearance, and, more rarely, by auditive hallucinations. His character and the content of his messages were summed up in imperious, authoritative, domineering manners, with the pretension of claiming Mlle. Smith all for himself, of defending her against the influences of the N. group, and, finally, of detaching her from that environment.

There was nothing, however, in this general character of monopoly and of protection which specially recalled the Balsamo of history or of romance. The personification of complete objectivity of this established type really began only in 1894, when Leopold had no longer to struggle with an environment foreign to his nature. The subconscious psychological task of realization of the proposed model could then be followed by him more freely; in spiritistic terms, Joseph Balsamo was able to manifest himself and make himself known in a manner more complete through Hélène as an intermediary, while continuing to follow and protect her as the reincarnation of the royal object of his passion.

At the seances held with M. Cuendet, Leopold frequently showed himself to Hélène clothed after the fashion of the last century and with a face like that of Louis XVI., under the different phases of his multiplex genius. He also showed himself to her in his laboratory, surrounded by utensils and instruments appropriate to the sorcerer and alchemist that he was; or, again, as the physician and possessor of secret elixirs, the knowledge of which is productive of consultations or remedies for the use of sitters who need them; or, again, as the illumined theosophist, the verbose prophet of the brotherhood of man, who diffuses limping Alexandrine verses—which seem to have been inherited from his predecessor, Victor Hugo—containing exhortations a little weak at times, but always stamped with a pure moral tone, elevated and noble sentiments, and a very touching religious spirit—in short, a fine example of that "ethico-deific verbiage" (if I may be allowed the expression, which is an Americanism), which, both in prose and in verse, is one of the most frequent and estimable products of mediumship.

But it was not until 1895 that Leopold, benefiting by the progress made by the automatic phenomena in Hélène, multiplied and perfected his processes of communication. The first step consisted in substituting, in his dictations by spelling, the movements of the hand or of a single finger for those of the whole table. This was the immediate result of a suggestion of mine.

Quand même tu serois satisfait
Aurois-tu pour cela plus de joie
Et crois-tu que là-haut, dans
L'esprit s'agite et vit sans ch

Home
Je veux tenir ma promesse
mais tu comprendras sans nul
te, qu'aujourd'hui à cet instant
je suis force d'être d'une grande
et dois m'abstenir de beaucoup

Fig. 3. Handwriting of Leopold. Fragments of two letters, one in Alexandrine verse, the other in prose, entirely in the hand of Leopold, automatically written by Mlle. Smith in spontaneous hemisomnambulism.

The second step in advance was the handwriting, which shows two stages. In the first, Leopold gave Hélène the impression of a phrase (verbo-visual hallucination), which she copied in pencil on a sheet of paper, in her own handwriting. The second, which was only accomplished five months later, and which consisted in writing directly with Hélène's hand, permitted the immediate establishment of three curious facts. One is, that Leopold holds his pen in the usual manner, the handle resting between the thumb and the index-finger, while Hélène, in writing, always holds her pen-handle or pencil between the index and middle fingers, a very rare habit with us. The next is that Leopold has an entirely different handwriting from that of Hélène, a calligraphy more regular, larger, more painstaking, and with marked differences in the formation of the letters (see Figs. 3 and 4). The third is that he uses the style of handwriting of the last century, and puts an *o* instead of an *a* in the tenses of the verbs, *j'amois*, for *j'amais*, etc. These three characteristics he has never departed from during all the four years that I have been accumulating specimens of his handwriting.

Fig. 4. Normal handwriting of Mlle. Smith.

The following is a résumé of the seances at which these two innovations took place.

April 21, 1895.—As I had just asked Leopold a question which he did not like, Hélène, being in a state of hemisomnambulism, with a pencil and some sheets of paper placed before her, in the hope of obtaining some communication (not from Leopold), seemed about to plunge into a very interesting perusal of one of the blank sheets; then, at my request, which she with difficulty comprehended, she commenced to write rapidly and nervously on another sheet, in her usual handwriting, a copy of the imaginary text which Leopold was showing her ("in fluid letters," as he said afterwards at the seance) as follows: "*My thoughts are not thy thoughts, and thy wishes are not mine, friend Flournoy—Leopold.*" At the final awakening Hélène recognized perfectly her own handwriting in his phrase, but had no recollection of the occurrence.

September 22, 1895.—After different visions and some stanzas of Victor Hugo, dictated by the table, Hélène appeared to suffer considerably in her right arm, which she was holding at the wrist with her left hand, when the table at which she was seated gave out the following, dictated by Leopold: "I shall hold her hand," meaning that it was he, Leopold, who was causing Mlle. Smith to suffer pain by seizing her right hand. As she seemed to feel very badly and began to weep, Leopold was asked to desist; but he refused, and, still speaking through the table, said, "Give her some paper," then, "More light." Writing material was furnished her and the lamp brought in, which Hélène gazed at fixedly, while Leopold continued to dictate (this time with the little finger of her left hand), "Let her gaze on the lamp until she forgets the pain in her arm." She then seemed, in fact, to forget her pain, and to find satisfaction in looking at the lamp; then she fastened her eyes on the paper, and seemed to read something there which she endeavored to copy in pencil. But here the right hand began a curious alternation of contrary motions, expressing in a very clear manner a contest with Leopold, who was trying to compel her to hold the pencil in a certain way, which Hélène refused to do, with a great pretence of anger. She persisted in holding it between the index and middle fingers, as was her wont, while Leopold wanted her to hold it in the usual way, between the thumb and the index-finger, and said: "I do not wish her to . . . she is holding the pencil very badly." The right index-finger then went through a very comical gymnastic performance, being seized with a tremor, which caused her to place it on one side or the other of the pencil, according to whether it was Leopold or Hélène who was victorious; during this time she frequently raised her eyes, with a look sometimes reproachful, sometimes supplicating, as if to gaze at Leopold standing by her side endeavoring to force her to hold the pencil in the manner he preferred. After a contest of nearly twenty minutes, Hélène, vanquished and completely subdued by Leopold, seemed to be absent, while her hand, holding the pencil in the manner she did not like, wrote slowly the two following lines, followed by a rapid and feverish signature of Leopold:

> "Mes vers sont si mauvais que pour toi j'aurois dû
> Laisser à tout jamais le poète têtu.—LEOPOLD."

An allusion, which was of no importance, to a remark made by me at the commencement of the seance on the verses of Victor Hugo and those of Leopold frequently dictated by the table. The seance lasted some time longer; on awakening, Hélène vaguely remembered having seen Leopold, but knew nothing more concerning the handwriting scene.

It is a fact that while her other incarnations are always accomplished passively and without any struggle, that of Leopold has the peculiarity of regularly provoking more or less resistance on the part of Hélène. " I do not make of her all that I wish . . . she is headstrong. . . . I do not know whether I shall succeed. . . . I do not believe I can master her to-day . . . " replies he often when asked to incarnate himself or write with her hand, and, indeed, his efforts often fail. There exists between Hélène and her guide a curious phenomenon of contrast and opposition, which only breaks out in the higher and more recent forms of motor automatism, the handwriting, the speech, or the complete incarnation, but from which the sensory messages and simple raps on the table or of the finger are free. It is very possible that the idea, very antipathetic to Hélène, of the hypnotizer mastering his subjects in spite of themselves—of the disincarnated Cagliostro using his medium as a simple tool—has been subconsciously the origin of this constant note of revolt against the total domination of Leopold, and of the intense suffering which accompanied his first incarnations, and which has slowly diminished through her becoming accustomed to the process, though it has never been completely banished.

After the handwriting, in its turn came speech, which also was attained by means of two stages. In a first attempt Leopold only succeeded in giving Hélène his intonation and pronunciation after a seance in which she suffered acutely in her mouth and in her neck, as though her vocal organs were being manipulated or removed; she began to talk in a natural tone, and was apparently wide awake and feeling well, but spoke with a deep bass voice, and a strong, easily recognizable Italian accent. It was not until a year later that Leopold was finally able to speak himself by the mouth of Mlle. Smith, while she was completely entranced, and who did not retain on awakening any memory of this strange occurrence. Since then the complete control of the medium by her guide is a frequent occurrence at the seances, and affords a tableau very characteristic and always impressive.

Leopold succeeds in incarnating himself only by slow degrees and progressive stages. Hélène then feels as though her arms had been seized, or as if they were absent altogether; then she complains of disagreeable sensations, which were formerly painful, in her throat, the nape of her neck, and in her head; her eyelids droop; her expression changes; her throat swells into a sort of double chin, which gives her a likeness of some sort to the well-known figure of Cagliostro. All at once she rises, then, turning slowly towards the sitter whom Leopold is about to address, draws herself up proudly, turns her back quickly, sometimes with her arms crossed on her breast with a magisterial air, sometimes with one of them hanging down while the other is pointed solemnly towards heaven, and with her fingers makes a sort of masonic sign, which never varies. Soon after a series of hiccoughs, sighs, and various noises indicate the difficulty Leopold is experiencing in taking hold of the vocal apparatus; the words come forth slowly but strong; the deep bass voice of a man, slightly confused, with a pronunciation and accent markedly foreign, certainly more like Italian than anything else. Leopold is not always easily understood, especially when his voice swells and thunders out a reply to some indiscreet question or to the disrespectful remarks of some skeptical sitter. He speaks thickly, pronounces *g* like *j*, and all his *u's* like *ou*, accents the final syllables, embellishes his vocabulary with obsolete words, or words which do not fit the circumstances, such as *fiole* for *bouteille*, *omnibus* for *tramways*, etc. He is pompous, grandiloquent, unctuous, sometimes severe and terrible, sometimes also sentimental. He says "thee" and "thou" to everybody, and appears to believe that he is still grand-master of the secret societies, from the emphatic and sonorous manner in which he pronounces the words "Brother" or "And thou, my sister," by which he addresses the sitters. Although he generally addresses himself to one of them in particular, and holds very little collective discourse, he is in touch with every one, listens to everything that is said, and each one may have his turn in conversation with him. Ordinarily he keeps his eyelids closed: he has, nevertheless, been persuaded to open his eyes in order to permit the taking of a photograph by a flash light. I regret that Mlle. Smith would not consent to the publication of her photographs, either in her normal state or in that of Leopold, in connection with the reproduction of a portrait of Cagliostro.[1] The reader

---

[1] The one which is found, for example, at the beginning of the Vie de Joseph Balsamo, etc., translated from the Italian (3d edition, Paris, 1791), and which has been several times reproduced. Mlle. Smith has hanging over her fireplace a fine copy of this portrait.

may assure himself that when she incarnates her guide she really assumes a certain resemblance of features to him, and there is something in her attitude which is sometimes somewhat theatrical, but sometimes really majestic, which corresponds well to the generally received idea of this personage, whether he is regarded as a clever impostor or as a wonderful genius.

Speech is the apogee of the incarnations of Leopold; often interrupted by fits of hiccoughs and spasms, it seems to be injurious to Hélène's organism, and there are some seances at which attempts to produce it fail to succeed. Leopold, on these occasions, indicates his impotence and the fatigue of the medium by his gestures, and is then reduced to the necessity of expressing himself by digital dictations or handwriting, or else to giving Hélène verbo-auditive hallucinations, the content of which she repeats in her natural voice.

From the point of view of ease and mobility of the entire organism, there is a notable difference between Leopold and the other incarnations of Hélène: these last seem to be effected with much more facility than in the case of that of her guide par excellence. In the case of the Hindoo princess and that of Marie Antoinette, the perfection of the play, the suppleness and freedom of movement, are always admirable. It is true there is no question here, according to the spiritistic doctrine and the subconscious ideas of Mlle. Smith, of incarnations properly so called, since it is she herself who simply returns to that which she formerly was, by a sort of reversion or prenatal ecmnesia; she does not undergo, in consequence, any foreign possession, and can in these rôles preserve her natural identity and the entire disposition of her faculties. But still the occasional incarnation of different personalities, such as those of deceased parents or friends of the spectators, are often more easily and quickly effected than that of Leopold. Hélène moves in these cases with more vivacity and changes of attitude. In the rôle of Cagliostro, on the other hand, with the exception of the grandiose and not very frequent movements of the arms, once standing, she remains motionless, or only with difficulty advancing a little way towards the person to whom she addresses her discourse.

The content of the oral conversations of Leopold, as well as of his other messages by the various sensory and motor processes, is too varied for me to describe here: the numerous examples scattered through this work only can give an idea of it.

III. LEOPOLD AND THE TRUE JOSEPH BALSAMO

It would naturally be supposed that Leopold would have given us, by means of the psychological perfection of his partial or total incarnations and by the content of his messages; such a living likeness of Cagliostro that there would have been occasion to ask whether it is not really the latter who actually "returns," in the same way that Dr. Hodgson and his colleagues ask themselves whether it is not actually George Pelham who manifests himself through Mrs. Piper. Let us suppose, for example, that Leopold possessed a handwriting, an orthography, a style identical with that which is found here and there in the manuscripts of Joseph Balsamo; that he spoke French, Italian, or German, as that cosmopolitan adventurer did, and with all the same peculiarities; that his conversations and messages were full of precise allusions to actual events in his life, and also of unpublished but verifiable facts, etc. In that case the difficult and delicate task of proving that Mlle. Smith had no knowledge through normal methods of these thousand exact features would still remain, and we should not be forced to ask whether this soi-disant authentic revenant is simply a very well-gotten-up simulacrum, an admirable reconstruction, a marvellous imitation, such as the subliminal faculties are only too glad to produce for the diversion of psychologists and the mystification of the simple.

This problem is not given to us. I regret it, but it is true, nevertheless—to my mind, at least, for in these matters it is prudent to speak only for one's self—that there is no reason to suspect the real presence of Joseph Balsamo behind the automatisms of Mlle. Smith.

That there are very curious analogies between what is known to us of Cagliostro and certain characteristic traits of Leopold, I do not deny, but they are precisely such as accord very well with the supposition of the subliminal medley.

Fragment of a letter to his wife, reproduced in *L'Isographie des Hommes célèbres*.

Let us consider first the handwriting. To facilitate the comparison, I have reproduced here (see pp. 109 and 111) some fragments of letters of Cagliostro and of Leopold and of Hélène. Let us suppose—which is, perhaps, open to discussion—that the handwriting of Leopold, by its regularity, its firmness, resembles that of Balsamo more than that of Mlle. Smith; the degree of resemblance does not, I think, go beyond that which might be expected considering the notorious fact that handwriting reflects the psychological temperament and modifies itself in accordance with the state of the personality. [1]

It is well known how the calligraphy of a hyptonized subject varies according to the suggestion that he shall personate Napoleon, Harpagon, a little girl, or an old man; there is nothing surprising in the fact that the hypnoid secondary personality of Hélène, which imagines itself to be the powerful and manly Count of Cagliostro, should be accompanied by muscular tensions communicating to the handwriting itself a little of that solidity and breadth which are found in the autograph of Balsamo. To this, however, the analogy is limited. The dissimilarities in the detail and the

---

[1] See, *e.g.*, Ferrari, Hericourt, and Richet, "Personality and Handwriting," *Revue philosophique*, vol. xxi. p. 414.

formation of the letters are such that the only conclusion which they warrant is that Mlle. Smith, or her subconsciousness, has never laid eyes on the manuscripts of Cagliostro. They are, indeed, rare, but the facilities she might have had, of which she has riot thought of taking

Fig. 6. Normal handwriting of Mlle. Smith.

Fig. 7. Handwriting of Leopold. Fragment and signature of one of his letters, written by Mlle. Smith, in spontaneous hemisomnambulism.

Fragment and signature of one of his letters, written by Mlle. Smith, in spontaneous hemisomnambulism.

advantage, for consulting in the Geneva public library the same volume from which I took Fig. 5, would prove, at least, her good faith and her honesty, if it were in the least necessary. The extravagant signature of

Leopold with which all his messages are subscribed (see Fig. 7) recalls in no wise that of Alessandro di Cagliostro at the bottom of Fig. 5.

The archaic forms of orthography, *j'aurois* for *j'aurais*, etc., which appear above the first autograph of Leopold (see p. 99), and which occur again in the messages of Marie Antoinette, constitute a very pretty hit, of which the ordinary self would probably never dream by way of voluntary imitation, but by which the subconscious imagination has seen fit to profit. It is undoubtedly a matter for wonderment that Mlle. Smith, who has not gone very deep into literary studies, should, nevertheless, have retained these orthographic peculiarities of the eighteenth century; but we must not overlook the fineness of choice, the refined sensibility, the consummate, albeit instinctive, art which presides over the sorting and storing away of the subconscious memories. By some natural affinity, the idea of a personage of a certain epoch attracts and gathers into its net everything that the subject can possibly learn or hear spoken concerning the fashion of writing, of speaking, or acting, peculiar to that epoch. I do not know whether Balsamo ever used the French language and the orthography that Leopold employs. Even if he did, it would not weaken the hypothesis of the subliminal imitation, but if, on the other hand, it should be ascertained that he did not, the hypothesis would be greatly strengthened thereby.

As for the speech, I am ignorant as to how, with what accent and what peculiarities of pronunciation, Balsamo spoke the French tongue, and to what degree, in consequence, his reconstruction by Hélène's subliminal fantasy correctly hits it. If this point could be cleared up, it would probably be found to be just like that of the handwriting. Nothing could be more natural than to ascribe to the *chevalier d'industrie* of Palermo a very masculine, deep-bass voice, and, it goes without saying, as Italian as possible. It must be noted, too, that Mlle. Smith often heard her father speak that language, which he knew very well, with several of his friends; but that, on the other hand, she does not speak it, and has never learned it. Leopold, however, does not know Italian, and turns a deaf ear when any one addresses him in that language. The intonation, the attitude, the whole physiognomy, in short, accord with these remarks. As to the extremely varied content of the conversations and messages of Leopold, we are not obliged to consider Balsamo as their necessary author. When everything relating to Mlle. Smith and the sitters, but which has nothing to do with the last century, has been swept aside, together with the spiritistic dissertations in regard to the "fluid" manner in which Leopold exists, perceives, and moves, the three subjects or categories of communications still remain, which merit a rapid examination.

In the first place, there. are the answers of Leopold to the questions put to him concerning his terrestrial life. These answers are remarkably evasive or vague. Not a name, not a date, not a precise fact does he furnish. We only learn that he has travelled extensively, suffered greatly, studied deeply, done much good, and healed a great many sick folk; but now he sees things too lofty to think any more about historic details of the past, and it is with unconcealed disgust or direct words of reproach for the idle curiosity of his carnal questioners that he hastens to turn the conversation, like Socrates, to moral subjects and those of a lofty philosophy, where he feels evidently more at ease. When he is further pressed he becomes angry sometimes, and sometimes ingenuously avows his ignorance, enveloping it meanwhile in an air of profound mystery. " They are asking the secret of my life, of my acts, of my thoughts. I cannot answer." This does not facilitate investigation of the question of identity.

In the second place come the consultations and medical prescriptions. Leopold affects a lofty disdain for modern medicine and phenic acid. He is as archaic in his therapeutics as in his orthography, and treats all maladies after the ancient mode. Baths of pressed grape-skins for rheumatism, an infusion of coltsfoot and juniper-berry in white wine for inflammations of the chest, the bark of the horse-chestnut in red wine and douches of salt water as tonics, tisanes of hops and other flowers, camomile, oil of lavender, the leaves of the ash, etc.; all these do not accord badly with what Balsamo might have prescribed a century or more ago. The misfortune, from the evidential point of view, is that Mlle. Smith's mother is extremely well versed in all the resources of popular medicine where old recipes are perpetuated. She has had occasion to nurse many sick people in her life, knows the virtues of different medicinal plants, and constantly employs, with a sagacity which I have often admired, a number of those remedies spoken of as "old-women's," which make the young doctors fresh from the clinic smile, but to which they will more than once resort in secret after a few years of medical experience.

Finally, there still remain the sentiments of Leopold for Hélène, which he claims are only the continuation of those of Cagliostro for Marie Antoinette. My ignorance of history does not permit me to pronounce categorically on this point. That the Queen of France did have some secret interviews with the famous "gold-maker," due to simple curiosity or to questions of material interest, there is no doubt, I believe; but that his feelings for his sovereign were a curious combination of the despairing passion of Cardinal Rohan for the queen, with the absolute respect which Alexandre Dumas, *père*, ascribes to Joseph Balsamo towards Lorenza Feliciani, appears to me less evident.

In short, if the revelations of Leopold have truly unveiled to us shades of feeling of Count Cagliostro hitherto unsuspected, and of which later documentary researches shall confirm the historic correctness—why, so much the better, for that will finally establish a trace of the supernormal in the mediumship of Hélène!

IV. LEOPOLD AND MLLE. SMITH

The connection between these two personalities is too complex for a precise description. There is neither a mutual exclusion, as between Mrs. Piper and Phinuit, who appear reciprocally to be ignorant of each other and to be separated by the tightest of partitions; nor a simple jointing, as in the case of Felida X., whose secondary state envelops and overflows the whole primary state. This is more of a crossing of lines, but of which the limits are vague and with difficulty assignable. Leopold knows, foresees, and recalls very many things of which the normal personality of Mlle. Smith knows absolutely nothing, not only of those which she may simply have forgotten, but of those of which she never had any consciousness. On the other hand, he is far from possessing all the memories of Hélène; he is ignorant of a very great part of her daily life; even some very notable incidents escape him entirely, which explains his way of saying that, to his great regret, he cannot remain constantly by her, being obliged to occupy himself with other missions (concerning which he has never enlightened us) which oblige him often to leave her for a time.

These two personalities are, therefore, not co-extensive; each one passes beyond the other at certain points, without its being possible for us to say which is, on the whole, the more extended. As to their common domain, if it cannot be defined by one word with entire certainty, it appears, nevertheless, to be chiefly constituted by its connection with the innermost ranges of the being, both physiological and psychological, as might be suspected from what I remarked above concerning the real origin of Leopold. Physician of the soul and of the body, director of conscience, and at the same time hygienic counsellor, he does not always manifest himself immediately, but he is always present when Hélène's vital interests are involved. This will be made clearer by two or three concrete examples, which will at the same time illustrate some of the psychological processes by which Leopold manifests himself to Hélène.

It must be admitted that there is a disagreement and opposition as complete as possible (but how far does this "possible" go?) when Hélène, in at least an apparently waking state, converses with her guide, manifestly by a partial sensory or motor automatism; for example, in the case cited on page 64, where Leopold, not sharing the allochiria of Hélène, declared by the table that she was wrong, so emphatically that she protested and became angry; also, when in verbo-auditive hallucinations, or by automatic handwriting, he enters into discussion with her, and she holds her own with him; or, again, when the organism seems to be divided up between two different persons, Leopold speaking by Hélène's mouth, with his accent, and uttering his own ideas to her, and she complaining, in writing, of pains in her head and throat, without understanding their cause. Nevertheless, in these cases of division of the consciousness, which appear to amount to its cutting in two, it is doubtful whether this plurality is more than apparent. I am not positive of having ever established with Hélène a veritable simultaneity of different consciousnesses. At the very moment at which Leopold writes by her hand, speaks by her mouth, dictates to the table, upon observing her attentively I have always found her absorbed, preoccupied, as though absent; but she instantaneously recovers her presence of mind and the use of her waking faculties at the end of the motor automatism. In short, that which from the outside is taken for the coexistence of distinct simultaneous personalities seems to me to be only an alternation, a rapid succession between the state of Hélène-consciousness and the state of Leopold-consciousness; and, in the case where the body seems to be jointly occupied by two independent beings—the right side, for instance, being occupied by Leopold, and the left by Hélène, or the Hindoo princess—the psychical division has never seemed to me to be radical, but many indications have combined to make me of the opinion that behind all was an individuality perfectly self-conscious, and enjoying thoroughly, along with the spectators, the comedy of the plural existences.

A single fundamental personality, putting the questions and giving the answers, quarrelling with itself in its own interior—in a word, enacting all the various rôles of Mlle. Smith—is a fitting interpretation, which accords very well with the facts as I have observed them in Hélène, and very much better than the theory of a plurality of separate consciousnesses, of a psychological polyzoism, so to speak. This last theory is doubtless more convenient for a clear and superficial description of the facts, but I am not at all convinced that it conforms to the actual condition of affairs.

It is a state of consciousness sui generis, which it is impossible adequately to describe, and which can only be represented by the analogy of those curious states, exceptional in the normal waking life, but less rare in dreams, when one seems to change his identity and become some one else.

Hélène has more than once told me of having had the impression of *becoming* or *being* momentarily Leopold. This happens most frequently at night, or upon awakening in the morning. She has first a fugitive vision of her protector; then it seems that little by little he is submerged in her; she feels him overcoming and penetrating her entire organism, as if he really became her or she him. These mixed states are extremely interesting to the psychologist; unhappily, because they generally take place in a condition of consecutive amnesia, or because the mediums do not know how, or do not wish, to give a complete account of them, it is very rare that detailed descriptions are obtained.

Between the two extremes of complete duality and complete unity numerous intermediate states are to be observed; or, at least, since the consciousness of another cannot be directly penetrated, these mixed states may be inferred from the consequences which spring from them.

It has happened, for example, that, believing they were dealing with Leopold alone, thoroughly incarnated and duly substituted for the personality of Mlle. Smith, the sitters have allowed to escape them on that account some ill-timed pleasantry, some indiscreet question or too free criticisms, all innocent enough and without evil intention, but still of a nature to wound Hélène if she had heard them, and from which the authors would certainly have abstained in her presence in a waking state.

Leopold has not stood upon ceremony in putting down these imprudent babblers, and the incident, generally, has had no further consequences. But sometimes the words and bearing of Mlle. Smith for days or weeks afterwards show that she was aware of the imprudent remarks, which proves that the consciousness of Leopold and her own are not separated by an impenetrable barrier, but that osmotic changes are effected from the one to the other. It is ordinarily pointed and irritating remarks which cause the trouble, which goes to prove that it is the feelings of self-love or personal susceptibility that form in each one of us the inmost fortifications of the social self, and are the last to be destroyed by somnambulism, or that they constitute the fundamental substratum, the common base by which Leopold and Mlle. Smith form a whole and mingle themselves in the same individuality.

The psychological process of this transmission is varied from another cause. Sometimes it appears that the consecutive amnesia of the trance has been broken as to the most piquant details, and that Hélène clearly remembers that which has been said, in the presence of Leopold, disagreeable to herself. Some times it is Leopold himself who repeats to her the unpleasant expressions which have been used, with commentaries calculated to lessen their effect and to excuse the culprits: for it is an interesting trait of his character that he undertakes with Hélène the defence of those same persons whom he reprimands and blames, a contradiction not at all surprising when it is psychologically interpreted, considering the habitual conflict of emotional motives or tendencies, the warfare which opposite points of view is incessantly carrying on in our inmost being. Sometimes, again, it is in a dream that the junction is effected between the somnambulistic consciousness of Leopold and the normal consciousness of Hélène.

Apropos of the last case, here is an example containing nothing disagreeable, in which Hélène remembered in her waking state a nocturnal dream, which was itself a repetition or echo, in natural sleep, of a somnambulistic scene of the previous evening.

In a seance at which I assisted, shortly after my recovery from an attack of congestion of the lungs, Hélène, completely entranced, has a vision of Leopold-Cagliostro, who, in the rôle of sympathetic physician, comes to hold a consultation with me. After some preliminaries she kneels down by my chair, and, looking alternately at my chest and at the fictitious doctor standing between us, she holds a long conversation with him, in which she explains the condition of my lungs, which she sees in imagination, and the treatment which Leopold prescribes, somewhat as follows: ". . . It is the lungs . . . it is darker . . . it is one side which has been affected . . . You say that it is a severe inflammation—and can that be healed? . . . Tell me, what must be done . . . Oh, where have I seen any of these plants? . . . I don't know what they are called . . . those . . . I don't understand very well . . . those synantherous? . . . Oh, what a queer name . . . Where are they to be found? . . . You say it belongs to the family of . . . then it has another name? Tell me what it is . . . some *tissulages* [sic] . . . Then you think this plant is good for him? . . . Ah! but explain this to me . . . the fresh leaves or the dried flowers? Three times a day, a large handful in a pint . . . and then honey and milk. . . . I will tell him that he must drink three cups a day . . ." etc. Then followed very detailed directions as to treatment, various infusions, blisters, etc. The whole scene lasted more than an hour, followed by complete amnesia, and nothing was said to Hélène about it, as it was half-past six in the evening, and she was in haste to return home. The next day she wrote me a seven-page letter in which she described a very striking dream she had had during the night. ". . . I fell asleep about two o'clock in the morning and awaked at about five. Was it a vision? Was it a dream I had? I don't really know what to consider it and dare not say; but this I do know, I saw my dear friend Leopold, who spoke to me a long time about you, and I think I saw you also. I asked him what he thought of your state of health. . . . He replied that in his opinion it was far from re-established, That the pain you feel in the right side came from an inflammation of the lung which has been seriously affected . . . You will doubtless laugh when I tell you that he also described the remedies you ought to take. . . . One of them is a simple plant, which is called, as nearly as I can remember, Tissulage or Tussilache, but has also another name, which I cannot recollect, but the first name will doubtless suffice, since he says you are familiar with the plant . . ." etc.

What I have said concerning Leopold is also applicable to the other personifications of Mlle. Smith. The normal consciousness of Hélène mingles and fuses itself in every way with the somnambulistic consciousness of Simandini, of Marie Antoinette, or some other incarnation, as we shall soon see. I pass now to the examination of some detailed examples, destined to throw light upon the rôle which Leopold plays in Hélène's existence.

Let us begin by listening to Leopold himself. Among his numerous messages, the following letter, written in his fine handwriting by the hand of Mlle. Smith—in response to a note in which I had begged him (as a spiritual being and distinct from her) to aid me in my " psychic researches"—contains information for which I had not asked, but which was none the less interesting. It must not be forgotten that it is the disincarnate adorer of Marie Antoinette who is writing:

"FRIEND,—I am pleased and touched by the mark of confidence you have deigned to accord me. The spiritual guide of Mademoiselle [Smith], whom the Supreme Being in his infinite goodness has permitted me to find again with ease, I do all I can to appear to her on every occasion when I deem it necessary; but my body, or, if you prefer, the matter of little solidity of which I am composed, does not always afford me the facility of showing myself to her in a positive human manner. [He, in fact, appeared to her often under the form of elementary visual hallucinations, a luminous trail, whitish column, vaporous streamer, etc.]

"That which I seek above all to inculcate in her is a consoling and true philosophy, which is necessary to her by reason of the profound, unhappy impressions, which even now still remain to her, of the whole drama of her past life. I have often sown bitterness in her heart [when she was Marie Antoinette], desiring only her welfare. Also, laying aside everything superfluous, I penetrate into the most hidden recesses of her soul, and with an extreme care and incessant activity I seek to implant there those truths which I trust will aid her in attaining the lofty summit of the ladder of perfection.

"Abandoned by my parents front my cradle, I have, indeed, known sorrow early in life. Like all, I have had many weaknesses, which I have expiated, and God knows that I bow to His will!

"Moral suffering has been my principal lot. I have been full of bitterness, of envy, of hatred, of jealousy. Jealousy, my brother! what a poison, what a corruption of the soul!

"Nevertheless, one ray has shone brightly into my life, and that ray so pure, so full of everything that might pour balm on my wounded soul, has given, me a glimpse of heaven!

"Herald of eternal felicity! ray without spot! God deemed best to take it before me! But to-clay it is given back to me! May His holy name be blessed!

"Friend, in what manner shall I reply to you? I am ignorant myself, not knowing what it will please God to reveal to you, but through her whom you call Mademoiselle [Smith], God willing, perhaps we shall be able to satisfy you.

"Thy friend,

"LEOPOLD."

We can see, under the flowing details of the spiritistic ideas and his rôle as the repentant Cagliostro, that the dominant characteristic of Leopold is his deep platonic attachment for Mlle. Smith, and an ardent moral solicitude for her and her advance towards perfection. This corresponds perfectly with the character of the numerous messages which he addresses to her in the course of her daily existence, as may he seen from the following specimen. He is referring to a case where, after having warned her on two occasions during the day by auditive hallucinations that he would manifest himself in the evening, he gives her, in fact, by automatic writing in his own hand, the encouragement she was actually in need of under the circumstances in which she found herself.

One morning, at her desk, Hélène heard an unknown voice, stronger and nearer to her than is usual with Leopold, say to her: "Until this evening"; a little later the same voice, which she now recognized as that of Leopold, but of a quality rougher and nearer to her than was his habit, said to her: "You understand me well, until this evening." In the evening, having returned home, she was excited at supper, left the table in haste towards the end of the meal, and shut herself up in her room with the idea that she would learn something; but, presently, the instinctive agitation of her hand indicated to her that she should take her pencil, and having done so, she obtained in the beautiful calligraphy of Leopold the following epistle. (She says that she remained wide awake and self-conscious while writing it, and it is the only occasion of a similar character when she had knowledge of the content.)

"MY BELOVED FRIEND,—Why do you vex yourself, torment yourself so? Why are you indignant, because, as you advance in life, you are obliged to acknowledge that all things are not as you had wished and hoped they might be? Is not the route we follow on this earth always and for all of us strewn with rocks? is it not an endless chain of deceptions, of miseries? Do me the kindness, my dear sister, I beg of you, to tell me that from this time forth you will cease from endeavoring to probe too deeply the human heart. In what will such discoveries aid you? What remains to you of these things, except tears and regrets? And then this God of love, of justice, and of life—is not He the one to read our hearts? It is for Him, not for thee, to see into them.

"Would you change the hearts? Would you give them that which they have not, a live, ardent soul, never departing from what is right, just, and true? Be calm, then, in the face of all these little troubles. Be worthy, and, above all, always good! In thee I have found again that heart and that soul, both of which will always be for me all my life, all my joy, and my only dream here below.

"Believe me: be calm: reflect: that is my wish."

"Thy friend,

"LEOPOLD."

I have chosen this example for the sake of its brevity. Hélène has received a number of communications of the same kind, sometimes in verse, in which the moral and religious note is often still more accentuated. In the greater part we meet with, as in the next to the last phrase of the foregoing letter, an allusion to the presumed affection of Cagliostro for Marie Antoinette. It is to be noticed that there is nothing in these excellent admonitions that a high and serious soul like that of Mlle. Smith could not have drawn from its own depths in a moment of contemplation and meditation.

Is it a benefit or an injury to the moral and truly religious life to formulate itself thus clearly in verbal hallucinations rather than to remain in the confused but more personal state of experienced aspirations and strongly expressed emotions? Do these inspirations gain or lose in inward authority and subjective power by assuming this exterior garb and this aspect of objectivity? This is a delicate question, probably not susceptible of a uniform solution.

In the following incident, which I relate as an example among many other similar ones, it is no longer, properly speaking, the moral and religious sentiments personified in Leopold, but rather the instinct of reserve and of defence peculiar to the weaker sex, the sense of the proprieties, the self-respect, tinctured with a shade of exaggeration almost amounting to prudery.

In a visit to Mlle. Smith, during which I inquired whether she had received any recent communications from Leopold, she told me she had only seen him two or three times in the last few days, and had been struck by his "restless and unhappy" air, instead of the air "so pleasant, so sweet, so admirable," which he generally has. As she did not know to what to attribute this change of countenance, I advised her to take her pencil and to wrap herself in meditation, with the hope of obtaining some automatic message.

In about a minute her expression indicated that she was being taken possession of; her eyes were fixed on the paper, upon which her left hand rested, the thumb and little finger being agitated and continually tapping (about once a second), the right hand having tried to take the pencil between the index and middle finger (the manner of Hélène), ended by seizing it between the thumb and the index finger, and traced slowly in the handwriting of Leopold:

"Yes, I am restless | pained, even in anguish. | Believest thou, friend, that it is with satisfaction | that I see you every day accepting the attentions, the flatteries; | I do not, call them insincere, but of little worth, and little praiseworthy | on the part of those from whom they come." |

This text was written at six separate times (marked by the vertical bars), separated by brief moments of full wakefulness, when the tappings of the left hand ceased, and when Hélène, repeating in a loud voice what she was about to write, is very much astonished, does not know to what Leopold alludes, then at my request takes her pencil to obtain an explanation, and falls asleep again during the following fragment. At the end of this bit, as she persists in saying that she is ignorant of what he refers to, I proceed to question Leopold, who replies that for several days Hélène has permitted herself to be courted by a M. V. (perfectly honorably), who often found himself on the same street-car with her, had made a place for her beside him the last few mornings, and had paid her some compliments on her appearance.

These revelations excited the laughter and protestations of Hélène, who commenced to deny that it could have come from Leopold, and accused me of having suggested it to her little finger; but the right hand took the pencil and traced these words in the handwriting and with the signature of Leopold: "I only say what I think, and I desire that you refuse henceforth all the flowers that he may offer you.—Leopold." This time Hélène remembered the incident, and recollected that yesterday morning he had offered her a rose which he was wearing as a boutonnière.

Eight days later I paid another visit to Hélène, and after an effort to secure some handwriting, which was not successful, but resulted in a Martian vision (see Martian text No. 14), she had a visual hallucination of Leopold, and losing consciousness of the actual environment and of my presence also, as well as that of her mother, she flung herself into a running conversation with him in regard to the incident of eight days previously: "Leopold . . . Leopold . . . don't come near me [repulsing him]. You are too severe, Leopold! . . . Will you come on Sunday? I am going to be at M. Flournoy's next Sunday. You will be there . . . but take good care that you do not . . . No, it is not kind of you always to disclose secrets. . . . What must he have thought? . . . You seem to make a mountain out of a molehill. . . . And who would think of refusing a flower? You don't understand at all. . . . Why, then? It was a very simple thing to accept it, a matter of no importance whatever . . . to refuse it would have been impolite. . . . You pretend to read the heart. . . . Why give importance to a thing that amounts to nothing? . . . It is only a simple act of friendship, a little token of sympathy . . . to make me write such things on paper before everybody! not nice of you!" In this somnambulistic dialogue, in which we can divine Leopold's replies, Hélène took for the moment the accent of Marie Antoinette (see below, in the "Royal cycle"). To awaken her, Leopold, who had possession of Hélène's arms, made some passes over her forehead, then pressed the frontal and suborbital nerves of the left side, and made me a sign to do the same with those of the right. The seance of the next day but one, at my house, passed without any allusion by Leopold to the incident of the street-car, evidently on account of the presence of certain sitters to whom he did not wish to reveal Hélène's secrets. But, three days after, in a new visit, during which she told me of having had a waking discussion concerning the future life (without telling me with whom), she again wrote, in the hand of Leopold: "It is not in such society as this that you ought so seriously to discuss the immortality of the soul." She then confessed that it was again on the street-car, and with M. V., that she had held that conversation while a funeral procession was passing. There was never anything that might have been of a compromising character in the exchange of courtesies and the occasional conversations of Mlle. Smith with her neighbor of the street-car. The trouble that it caused poor Leopold was very characteristic of him, and well indicated the severe and jealous censor who formerly had worried the N. group; there can be heard again the echo of that voice, "which has absolutely nothing to do with the conscience" (see pp. 27 and 82), and which has hitherto prevented Hélène from accepting any of the suitors whom she has encountered in the course of her journey through life. This austere and rigorous mentor, always wide awake, and taking offence at the least freedom which Mlle. Smith allows herself in the exchange of trifling courtesies, represents, in fact, a very common psychological attribute; it is not every well-bred feminine soul that carries stored in one of its recesses, where it manifests its presence by scruples more or less vaguely felt, certain hesitations or apprehensions, inhibiting feelings or tendencies of a shade of intensity varying according to the age and the temperament.

It is not my part to describe this delicate phenomenon. It suffices me to remark that here, as in the ethico-religious messages, the personality of Leopold has in no way aided the essential content of those inward experiences of which Mlle. Smith is perfectly capable by herself; the form only of their manifestation has gained in picturesque and dramatic expression in the *mise-en-scène* of the automatic handwritings and of the somnambulistic dialogue. It seems as though the suggestive approach of my presence and my questions had been necessary to excite these phenomena; it is, however, very probable, to judge from other examples, that my influence only hastened the explosion of Leopold in formulated reproaches, and that his latent discontent, hitherto noticed in the "restless and suffering air" of his fugitive visual apparitions, would have terminated, after a period of incubation more or less prolonged, in breaking out into spontaneous admonitions, auditive or written.

It can be divined that in this rôle of vigilant guardian, of an almost excessive zealousness for the honor or the dignity of Mlle. Smith, Leopold is again, to my mind, only a product of psychological duplication. He represents a certain grouping of inward desires and secret instincts, which the hypnoid predisposition, encouraged by spiritism, has brought into a peculiar prominence and given an aspect of foreign personality; in the same way, in the phantasmagoria of the dream, certain after-thoughts, almost unperceived while awake, rise to the first plane and become transformed into contradictory fictitious personages, whose cutting reproaches astonish us sometimes on awakening by their disturbing truthfulness.

A final example will show us Leopold, in his rôle of watcher over the health of Mlle. Smith and adviser of precautions which she ought to take. He is not troubled about her general health; when she had *la grippe*, for instance, or when she is simply worn out with fatigue, he scarcely shows himself. His attention is concentrated upon certain special physiological functions, of the normal exercise of which he takes care to be assured. He does not otherwise seem to exercise a positive action upon them, and cannot modify them in any way; his office seems to be confined to knowing beforehand their exact course, and to see that Hélène is not guilty of any imprudence which may impede them.

Leopold here shows a knowledge and prevision of the most intimate phenomena of the organism which has been observed in the case of secondary personalities, and which confers upon them, in that respect at least, an unquestionable advantage over the ordinary personality. In the case of Mlle. Smith, the indications of her guide are always of a prohibitive nature, calculated to prevent her from taking part in spiritistic reunions at a time at which she believes herself able to do so with impunity, but which he, endowed with a more refined cœnæsthetic sensibility, thinks she ought not to undertake. He has for several years formally laid his ban upon every kind of mediumistic exercises at certain very regular periods.

He has also on numerous occasions compelled her by various messages, categorical auditive hallucinations, diverse impulses, contractures of the arms, forcing her to write, etc., to modify her plans and to abandon seances already arranged. This is a very clear form of teleological automatism.

As a specimen of this spontaneous and hygienic intervention of Leopold in the life of Hélène, I have selected the letter given below, because it combines several interesting traits. It well depicts the energy with which Mlle. Smith is compelled to obey her guide.

The passage from the auditive to the graphic form of automatism is also to be noticed in it. Apropos of this, in the page of this letter reproduced in Fig. 8 (see p. 137), it is made clear that the transition of the hand of Hélène to that of Leopold is accomplished brusquely and in a decided manner. The handwriting is not metamorphosed gradually, slowly, but continues to be that of Mlle. Smith, becoming more and more agitated, it is true, and rendered almost illegible by the shocks to the arm of which Leopold takes hold up to the moment when, suddenly and by a bound, it becomes the well-formed calligraphy of Cagliostro.

"*January* 29, 6.15 A.M.

"MONSIEUR,—I awoke about ten minutes ago, and heard the voice of Leopold telling me in a very imperious manner, 'Get up out of your bed, and quickly, very quickly, write to your dear friend, M. Flournoy, that you will not hold a seance to-morrow, and that you will not be able to go to his house for two weeks, and that you will not hold any seance within that period.' I have executed his order, having felt myself forced, compelled in spite of myself, to obey. I was so comfortable in bed and so vexed at being obliged to write you such a message; but I feel myself forced to do what he bids me.
"At this moment I am looking at my watch; it is 6.25 o'clock. I feel a very strong shock in my right arm—I might better speak of it as an electric disturbance—and which I perceive has made me . write crooked. I hear also at this instant the voice of Leopold. I have much difficulty in writing what he tells me: '6.42½ . Say to him this: *I am, sir, always your very devoted servant, in body and mind, healthy and not unbalanced.*'

"I stopped for some moments after writing these words, which I saw very well, after having written them, were in the handwriting of Leopold. Immediately afterwards, a second disturbance, similar to the first, gave me a fresh shock, this time from my feet to my head. It all passed so quickly that I am disturbed and confused by it. It is true that I am not yet quite well. Is this the reason why Leopold prevents my going to Florissant tomorrow? I do not know, but, nevertheless, am anxious to follow his advice. . . ."

Mlle. Smith always submits obediently to the commands of her guide, since, whenever she has transgressed them, through forgetfulness or neglect, she has had cause to repent it.

It is clear that in this rôle of special physician of Mlle. Smith, always au courant of her state of health, Leopold could easily be interpreted as personifying those vague impressions which spring forth continually from the depths of our physical being, informing us as to what is passing there.

A neuralgic toothache is felt in a dream hours before it makes itself felt in our waking consciousness, while some maladies are often thus foreshadowed several days before they actually declare themselves. All literature is full of anecdotes of this kind; and the psychiatrists have observed that in the form of circular alienation, where phases of melancholic depression and maniacal excitation alternately succeed one another more or less regularly with intervals of normal equilibrium, it is frequently in sleep that the first symptoms of the change of humor can be detected which has already begun in the depths of the individuality, but will only break forth on the outside a little later. But all the hypnoid states are connected, and it is not at all surprising that, in the case of a subject inclined to automatism, these confused presentiments should arise with the appearance of a foreign personality which is only a degree higher than the process of dramatization already so brilliantly at work in our ordinary dreams.

It will be useless to lengthen or further multiply examples of the intervention of Leopold in the life of Mlle. Smith. Those which I have given show him under his essential aspects, and suffice to justify Hélène's confidence in a guide who has never deceived her, who has always given her the best counsel, delivered discourses of the highest ethical tone, and manifested the most touching solicitude for her physical and moral health. It is easy to understand that nothing can shake her faith in the real, objective existence of this precious counsellor.

It is really vexatious that the phenomena of dreams should be so little observed or so badly understood (I do not say by psychologists, but by the general public, which prides itself on its psychology), since the dream is the prototype of spiritistic messages, and holds the key to the explanation of mediumistic phenomena. If it is regrettable to see such noble, sympathetic, pure, and in all respects remarkable personalities as Leopold reduced to the rank of a dream creation, it must be remembered, however, that dreams are not always, as idle folk think, things to be despised or of no value in themselves: the majority are insignificant and deserve only the oblivion to which they are promptly consigned. A very large number are bad and sometimes even worse than reality; but there are others of a better sort, and "dream" is often a synonym for "ideal."

> chose ainsi. mais qu'y faire on me
> force je le sens très bien.
> Dans ce moment je regarde ma montre,
> il est 6h. 25 minutes je sens une secousse
> très forte dans mon bras droit, je di-
> rai mieux en disant une commotion
> électrique et qui je m'aperçois me
> fait écrire tout de travers.
> J'entends dans ce moment même la
> voix de Léopold, j'ai beaucoup de
> peine à écrire qui me dit———:
> 6h.4½.
> Dis lui donc ceci !
> Je suis toujours monsieur votre bien
> dévouée, d'esprit et de corps sain
> non déséquilibrée

Fig. 6. A page from a letter of Mlle. Smith, showing the spontaneous irruption of the personality and the handwriting of Leopold during the waking state of Hélène.

To sum up, Leopold certainly expresses in his central nucleus a very honorable and attractive side of the character of Mlle. Smith, and in taking him as her "guide" she only follows inspirations which are probably among the best of her nature.

THE MARTIAN CYCLE

THE title of this book would naturally commit me to a review of the Hindoo romance before investigating the Martian cycle. Considerations of method have caused me to reverse this order. It is better to advance from the simple to the complex, and while we certainly know less concerning the planet Mars than of India, the romance which it has inspired in the subliminal genius of Mlle. Smith is relatively less difficult to explain than the Oriental cycle. In fact, the former seems to spring from pure imagination, while in the latter we meet with certain actual historical elements, and whence Hélène's memory and intelligence have gained a knowledge of them is an extremely difficult problem for us to solve. There is, then, only one faculty at work in the Martian romance, as a professional psychologist would say, while the Oriental cycle calls several into play, making it necessary to treat of it later, on account of its greater psychological complexity.

While the unknown language which forms the vehicle of many of the Martian messages cannot naturally be dissociated from the rest of the cycle, it merits, nevertheless, a special consideration, and the following chapter will be entirely devoted to it. It does not figure in the present chapter, in which I shall treat of the origin and the content only of the Martian romance.

I. ORIGIN AND BIRTH OF THE MARTIAN CYCLE

"We dare to hope," says M. Camille Flammarion, at the beginning of his excellent work on the planet Mars, "that the day will come when scientific methods yet unknown to us will give us direct evidences of the existence of the inhabitants of other worlds, and at the same time, also, will put us in communication with our brothers in space."[1] And on the last page of his book he recurs to the same idea, and says: "What marvels does not the science of the future reserve for our successors, and who would dare to say that Martian humanity and terrestrial humanity will not some day enter into communication with each other?"

---

[1] C. Flammarion, *La Planète Mars et ses conditions d'habitabilité*, p. 3. Paris, 1892.

This splendid prospect seems still far off, along with that of wireless telegraphy, and almost an Utopian dream, so long as one holds strictly to the current conceptions of our positive sciences. But break these narrow limits; fly, for example, towards the illimitable horizon which spiritism opens up to its happy followers, and as soon as this vague hope takes shape, nothing seems to prevent its immediate realization; and the only cause for wonder is found in the fact that no privileged medium has yet arisen to have the glory, unique in the world, of being the first intermediary between ourselves and the human inhabitants of other planets; for spiritism takes no more account of the barrier of space than of time. The "gates of distance" are wide open before it. With it the question of means is a secondary matter; one has only the embarrassment of making a choice. It matters not whether it be by intuition, by clairvoyance, by telepathy, or by double personality that the soul is permitted to leave momentarily its terrestrial prison and make the voyage between this world and others in an instant of time, or whether the feat is accomplished by means of the astral body, by the reincarnation of disincarnate omnisciences, by "fluid beings," or, in a word, by any other process whatever. The essential point is, according to spiritism, that no serious objection would be offered to the possibility of such communication. The only difficulty would be to find a mediumistic subject possessing sufficient psychical faculties. It is a simple question of fact; if such a one has not yet been found, it is apparently only because the time is not yet ripe. But now that astronomers themselves appeal to those "unknown methods of actual science" to put us en rapport with other worlds, no doubt spiritism—which is the science of to-morrow, as definite as absolute religion—will soon respond to these legitimate aspirations. We may, therefore, expect at any moment the revelation so impatiently looked for, and every good medium has the right to ask herself whether she is not the being predestined to accomplish this unrivalled mission.

These are the considerations which, to my mind, in their essential content inspired in the subliminal part of Mlle. Smith the first idea of her Martian romance. I would not assert that the passages from M. Flammarion which I have quoted came directly to the notice of Hélène, but they express and recapitulate wonderfully well one of the elements of the atmosphere in which she found herself at the beginning of her mediumship. For if there are no certain indications of her ever having read any work on the "heavenly worlds" and their inhabitants, either that of M. Flammarion or of any other author, she has, nevertheless, heard such subjects discussed. She is perfectly familiar with the name of the celebrated astronomical writer Juvisy, and knows something of his philosophical ideas, which, by-the-way, is not at all surprising when we consider the popularity he enjoys among spiritists, who find in him a very strong scientific support for their doctrine of reincarnation on other planets.

I also have evidence that in the circle of Mme. N., of which Hélène was a member in 1892, the conversation more than once turned in the direction of the habitability of Mars, to which the discovery of the famous "canals" has for some years specially directed the attention of the general public. This circumstance appears to me to explain sufficiently the fact that Hélène's subliminal astronomy should be concerned with this planet. It is, moreover, quite possible that the first germs of the Martian romance date still further back than the beginning of Hélène's mediumship. The Oriental rôle shows indications of concerning itself with that planet, and the very clear impression which she has of having in her childhood and youth experienced many visions of a similar kind "without her noticing them particularly," gives rise to the supposition that the ingredients of which this cycle is composed date from many years back. Possibly they may have one and the same primitive source in the exotic memories, descriptions, or pictures of tropical countries which later branched out under the vigorous impulsion of spiritistic ideas in two distinct currents, the Hindoo romance on the one side and the Martian on the other, whose waters are mingled on more than one occasion afterwards.

While, on the whole, therefore, it is probable that its roots extend back as far as the childhood of Mlle. Smith, it is nevertheless with the Martian romance, as well as with the others, not a mere question of the simple cryptomnesiac return of facts of a remote past, or of an exhumation of fossil residua brought to light again by the aid of somnambulism. It is a very active process, and one in full course of evolution, nourished, undoubtedly, by elements belonging to the past, but which have been recombined and moulded in a very original fashion, until it amounts finally, among other things, to the creation of an unknown language. It will be interesting to follow step by step the phases of this elaboration: but since it always, unfortunately, hides itself in the obscurity of the subconsciousness, we are only cognizant of it by its occasional appearances, and all the rest of that subterranean work must be inferred, in a manner somewhat hypothetical, from those supraliminal eruptions and the scanty data which we have concerning the outward influences which have exerted a stimulating influence upon the subliminal part of Hélène. It was in 1892, then, that the conversations took place which were to prepare the soil for this work of lofty subliminal fantasy, and planted in Hélène's mind the double idea, of enormous scientific interest, that she could enter into direct relation with the inhabitants of Mars, and of the possibility, unsuspected by scientists, but which spiritism furnishes us, of reaching there by a mediumistic route. I doubt, however, whether that vague suggestion on the part of the environment would have sufficed to engender the Martian dream—since for more than two years no sign of its eruption mainfested itself—without the intervention of some fillip more concrete, capable of giving a start to the whole movement. It is not easy, unfortunately, for want of records of the facts, to assign with precision the circumstances under which and the moment when Hélène's subconscious imagination received that effective impulsion, but an unequivocal trace is discovered, as I am about to show in the contemporaneous report of the proceedings of the first distinctly Martian seance of Mlle. Smith.

In March, 1894, Hélène made the acquaintance of M. Lemaître, who, being exceedingly interested in the phenomena of abnormal psychology, was present with others at some of her seances, and finally begged her to hold some at his house. At the first of these (October 28, 1894), Hélène met a lady, a widow, who was greatly to be pitied. Besides suffering from a very serious affection of the eyes, Mme. Mirbel had been terribly afflicted by the loss of her only son, Alexis, seventeen years old, and a pupil of M. Lemaître. While not yet fully convinced of the truth of spiritism, it is easy to understand that Mme. Mirbel was very anxious to believe in that consolatory doctrine, and ready to accept it, if only some proofs could be furnished her; and what more convincing testimony could she ask or receive than that of a message from her beloved child? Moreover, it was probably not without a secret hope of procuring a communication of this nature that she accepted the invitation which M. Lemaître had sent her with the idea of procuring some moments of distraction for the unhappy mother As happens frequently in Hélène's case, this first seance fully satisfied the desires of the sitters and surpassed their expectations. Speaking only of that which concerns Mme. Mirbel, Hélène had the vision, first, of a young man, in the very detailed description of whom there was no difficulty in recognizing the deceased Alexis Mirbel; then of an old man whom the table called Raspail, brought by the young man that he might treat his mother's eyes, who thus had the double privilege of receiving through. the table words of tenderness from her son, and from Raspail directions for the treatment of the affection of her eyes. Nothing in that seance recalled in any way the planet Mars, and it could not be foreseen from anything that occurred there that Alexis Mirbel, disincarnated, would return later under the name of Esenale as official interpreter of the Martian language.

It was altogether different a month later (November 25), at the second reunion at M. Lemaître's, at which Mme. Mirbel was again present. On this occasion the astronomical dream appeared at once and dominated the entire seance.

From the beginning, says the report of the seance, Mlle. Smith perceived, in the distance and at a great height, a bright light. Then she felt a tremor which almost caused her heart to cease beating, after which it seemed to her as though her head were empty and as if she were no longer in the body. She found herself in a dense fog, which changed successively from blue to a vivid rose color, to gray, and then to black: she is floating, she says; and the table, supporting itself on one leg, seemed to express a very curious floating movement. Then she sees a star, growing larger, always larger. and becomes, finally, "as large as our house." Hélène feels that she is ascending; then the table gives, by raps: "Lemaître, that which you have so long desired!" Mlle. Smith, who had been ill at ease, finds herself feeling better; she distinguishes three enormous globes, one of them very beautiful. "On what am I walking?" she asks. And the table replies: "On a world—Mars." Hélène then began a description of all the strange things which presented themselves to her view, and caused her as much surprise as amusement. Carriages without horses or wheels, emitting sparks as they glided by; houses with fountains on the roof; a cradle having for curtains an angel made of iron with outstretched wings, etc. What seemed less strange, were people exactly like the inhabitants of our earth, save that both sexes wore the same costume, formed of trousers very ample, and a long blouse, drawn tight about the waist and decorated with various designs. The child in the cradle was exactly like our children, according to the sketch which Hélène made from memory after the seance.

Finally, she saw upon Mars a sort of vast assembly hall, in which was Professor Raspail, having in the first row of his hearers the young Alexis Mirbel, who, by a typtological dictation, reproached his mother for not having followed the medical prescription which he gave her a month previously: "Dear mamma, have you, then, so little confidence in us? You have no idea how much pain you have caused me!" Then followed a conversation of a private nature between Mme. Mirbel and her son, the latter replying by means of the table; then everything becomes quiet, the vision of Mars effaces itself little by little; the table takes the same rotary movement on one foot which it had at the commencement of the seance; Mlle. Smith finds herself again in the fogs and goes through the same process as before in an inverse order. Then she exclaims: "Ah! here I am back again!" and several loud raps on the table mark the end of the seance.

I have related in its principal elements this first Martian seance, for the sake of its importance in different respects.

The initial series of cœnæsthetic hallucinations, corresponding to a voyage from the earth to Mars, reflects well the childish character of an imagination which scientific problems or the exigencies of logic trouble very little. Without doubt spiritism can explain how the material difficulties of an interplanetary journey may be avoided in a purely mediumistic, fluid connection; but why, then, this persistence of physical sensations, trouble with the heart, tremor, floating sensation, etc.? However it may be, this series of sensations is from this time on the customary prelude, and, as it were, the premonitory aura of the Martian dream, with certain modifications, throughout all the seances; sometimes it is complicated with auditive hallucinations (rumbling, noise of rushing water, etc.), or sometimes olfactory (disagreeable odors of burning, of sulphur, of a coming storm), oftener it tends to shorten and simplify itself, until it is either reduced to a brief feeling of malaise, or to the initial visual hallucination of the light, generally very brilliant and red, in which the Martian visions usually appear.

But the point to which I wish to call special attention is that singular speech of the table, on the instant at which Mlle. Smith arrives on the distant star, and before it is known what star is concerned: "Lemaître, that which you have so much wished for!" This declaration, which may be considered as a dedication, so to speak, inscribed on the frontispiece of the Martian romance, authorizes us, in my opinion, in considering it and interpreting it in its origin, as a direct answer to a wish of M. Lemaître, a desire which came at a recent period to Hélène's knowledge, and which has enacted with her the initiatory rôle of her astronomical dream.

It is true that M. Lemaître himself did not understand at the moment to what this preliminary warning referred, but the note which he inserted at the end of his report of that seance is instructive in this regard: "I do not know how to explain the first words dictated by the table: 'Lemaître, that which you have so much wished for!' M. S. reminds me that in a conversation which I had with him last summer I said to him: 'It would be very interesting to know what is happening upon other planets.' If this is an answer to the wish of last year, very well."

It must be added that M. S., who had been sufficiently struck by this wish of M. Lemaître to remember it for several months, was, during all of the time referred to, one of the most regular attendants upon the seances of Mlle. Smith; and, to one who knows by experience all that happens at the spiritistic reunions, before, after, and during the seance itself, there could hardly be any doubt but that it was through M. S., as intermediary, that Mlle. Smith had heard mentioned M. Lemaître's regret at our relative ignorance of the inhabitants of other planets. This idea, probably caught on the wing during the state of suggestibility which accompanies the seances, returned with renewed force when Hélène was invited to hold a seance at the house of M. Lemaître, and made more vivid also by the desire, which is always latent in her, of making the visions as interesting as possible to the persons among whom she finds herself. Such is, in my opinion, the seed which, falling into the ground and fertilized by former conversations concerning the inhabitants of Mars and the possibility of spiritistic relations with them, has served as the germ of the romance, the further development of which it remains for me to trace.

One point which still remains to be cleared up in the seance, as I come to sum up, is the singularly artificial character and the slight connection between the Martian vision, properly so called, and the reappearance of Raspail and Alexis Mirbel. We do not altogether understand what these personages have to do with it. What need is there of their being to-day found on the planet Mars simply for the purpose of continuing their interview with Mme. Mirbel, begun at a previous seance, without the intervention of any planet? The assembly-hall at which they are found, while it is located on Mars, is a bond of union all the more artificial between them and that planet in that there is nothing specifically Martian in its description and appears to have been borrowed from our globe. This incident is at bottom a matter out of the regular course, full of interest undoubtedly for Mme. Mirbel, whom it directly concerns, but without intimate connection with the Martian world. It was evidently the astronomical revelation, intended for M. Lemaître, and ripened by a period of incubation, which should have furnished the material for this seance; but the presence of Mme. Mirbel awoke anew the memory of her son and of Raspail, which had occupied the preceding seance, and these memories, interfering with the Martian vision, become, for good or ill, incorporated as a strange episode in it without having any direct connection with it. The work of unification, of dramatization, by which these two unequal chains of ideas are harmonized and fused the one with the other through the intermediation of an assembly-hall, is no more or no less extraordinary than that which displays itself in all our nocturnal phantasmagoria, where certain absolutely heterogeneous memories often ally themselves after an unexpected fashion, and afford opportunity for confusions of the most bizarre character.

But mediumistic communications differ from ordinary dreams in this—namely, the incoherence of the latter does not cause them to have any consequences. We are astonished and diverted for a moment as we reflect upon a dream. Sometimes a dream holds a little longer the attention of the psychologist, who endeavors to unravel the intricate plot of his dreams and to discover, amid the caprices of association or the events of the waking state, the origin of their tangled threads. But, on the whole, this incoherence has no influence on the ultimate course of our thoughts, because we see in our dreams only the results of chance, without value in themselves and without objective signification.

It is otherwise with spiritistic communications, by reason of the importance and the credit accorded them.

The medium who partially recollects her automatisms, or to whom the sitters have detailed them after the close of the seance, adding also their comments, becomes preoccupied with these mysterious revelations; like the paranoiac, who perceives hidden meanings or a profound significance in the most trifling coincidences, she seeks to fathom the content of her strange visions, reflects on them, examines them in the light of spiritistic notions; if she encounters difficulties in them, or contradictions, her conscious or unconscious thought (the two are not always in accord) will undertake the task of removing them, and solving as well as possible the problems which these dream-creations, considered as realities, impose upon her, and the later somnambulisms will bear the imprint of this labor of interpretation or correction.

It is to this point we have come at the commencement of the astronomical romance of Mlle. Smith. The purely accidental and fortuitous conjunction of the planet Mars and Alexis Mirbel in the seance of the 25th of November determined their definitive welding together. Association by fortuitous contiguity is transformed into a logical connection.

II. LATER DEVELOPMENT OF THE MARTIAN CYCLE

This development was not effected in a regular manner; but for the most part by leaps and bounds, separating stoppages more or less prolonged. After its inauguration in the seance of November 25, 1894, it suffered a first eclipse of nearly fifteen months, attributable to new preoccupations which had installed themselves on the highest plane of Mlle. Smith's subconsciousness and held that position throughout the whole of the year 1895.

Compared with the seance of November, 1894, that of February, 1896 (of which a résumé follows), shows interesting innovations. Raspail does not figure in it and henceforth does not appear again, which was probably due to the fact that Mme. Mirbel had failed to make use of the method of treatment which he had prescribed for her eyes. Young Mirbel, on the contrary, sole object of the desires and longings of his poor mother, occupies the highest plane, and is the central figure of the vision. He now speaks Martian and no longer understands French, which complicates the conversation somewhat. Further, not possessing the power of moving tables upon our globe, it is through the intervention of the medium, by incarnating himself momentarily in Mlle. Smith, that he henceforth communicates with his mother. These two latter points in their turn cause certain difficulties to arise, which, acting as a ferment or a suggestion, will later usher in a new step in the progress of the romance: Alexis Mirbel cannot return to incarnate himself in a terrestrial medium if he is imprisoned in his Martian existence; he must first terminate that and return to the condition in which he again floats in interplanetary space; which "fluid" or wandering state permits him at the same time to give us the French translation of the Martian tongue; since, according to spiritism, a complete memory of previous existences, and consequently of the various languages pertaining to them, is temporarily recovered during the phases of disincarnation.

These anticipatory hints will assist the reader in following more easily the thread of the somnambulistic romance in the résumé of its principal stages.

February 2, 1896.—I sum up, by enumerating them, the principal somnambulistic phases of this seance, which lasted more than two hours and a half, and at which Mme. Mirbel assisted.

I. Increasing hemisomnambulism, with gradual loss of consciousness of the real environment—at the beginning the table bows several times to Mme. Mirbel, announcing that the coming scene is intended for her. After a series of elementary visual hallucinations (rainbow colors, etc.), meaning for Mme. Mirbel that she would finally become blind, Hélène arose, left the table, and held a long conversation with an imaginary woman who wished her to enter a curious little car without wheels or horses. She became impatient towards this woman, who, after having at first spoken to her in French, now persisted in speaking in an unintelligible tongue, like Chinese. Leopold revealed to us by the little finger that it was the language of the planet Mars, that this woman is the mother of Alexis Mirbel, reincarnated on that planet, and that Hélène herself will speak Martian. Presently Hélène begins to recite with increasing volubility an incomprehensible jargon, the beginning of which is as follows (according to notes taken by M. Lemaître at the time, as accurately as possible): "**Mitchma mitchmon mimini tchouainem mimatchineg masichinof mézavi patelki abrésinad navette naven navette mitchichénid naken chinoutoufiche**" . . . From this point the rapidity prevented the recognition of anything else, except such scraps as "**téké. . . katéchivist. . . méguetch,**" . . . or "**méketch . . . kété . . . chiméké.**" After a few minutes, Hélène interrupts herself, crying out, "Oh, I have had enough of it; you say such words to me I will never be able to repeat them." Then, with some reluctance, she consents to follow her interlocutrix into the car which was to carry her to Mars.

2. The trance is now complete. Hélène thereupon mimics the voyage to Mars in three phases, the meaning of which is indicated by Leopold: a regular rocking motion of the upper part of the body (passing through the terrestrial atmosphere), absolute immobility and rigidity (interplanetary space), again oscillations of the shoulders and the bust (atmosphere of Mars). Arrived upon Mars, she descends from the car, and performs a complicated pantomime expressing the manners of Martian politeness: uncouth gestures with the hands and fingers, slapping of the hands, taps of the fingers upon the nose, the lips, the chin, etc., twisted courtesies, glidings, and rotation on the floor, etc. It seems that is the way people approach and salute each other up there.

3. This sort of dance having suggested to one of the sitters the idea of performing upon the piano, Hélène suddenly fell upon the floor in an evidently hypnotic state, which had no longer a Martian character. At the cessation of the music she entered into a mixed state, in which the memory of the Martian visions continually mingle themselves with some idea of her terrestrial existence. She talks to herself. "Those dreams are droll, all the same. . . . I must tell that to M. Lemaître. When he [the Martian Alexis Mirbel] said 'Good-day' to me, he tapped himself upon the nose. . . . He spoke to me in a queer language, but I understood it perfectly, all the same," etc. Seated on the ground, leaning against a piece of furniture, she continues, soliloquizing in French, in a low voice, to review the dream, mingling with it some wandering reflections. She finds, for example, that the young Martian (Alexis) was a remarkably big boy for one only five or six years old, as he claimed to be, and that the woman seemed very young to be his mother.

4. After a transitory phase of sighs and hiccoughs, followed by profound sleep with muscular relaxation, she enters into Martian somnambulism and murmurs some confused words: "**Késin ouitidjé**" . . . etc. I command her to speak French to me; she seems to understand, and replies in Martian, with an irritated and imperious tone, I ask her to tell me her name; she replies, "**Vasimini Météche**." With the idea that, perhaps, she "is incarnating" the young Alexis, of whom she has spoken so much in the preceding phase, I urge Mme. Mirbel to approach her, and thereupon begins a scene of incarnation really very affecting; Mme. Mirbel is on her knees, sobbing bitterly, in the presence of her recovered son, who shows her marks of the most profound affection and caresses her hands "exactly as he was accustomed to do during his last illness," all the time carrying on a discourse in Martian (**tin is toutch**), which the poor mother cannot understand, but to which an accent of extreme sweetness and a tender intonation impart an evident meaning of words of consolation and filial tenderness. This pathetic duet lasted about ten minutes, and was brought to an end by a return to lethargic sleep, from which Hélène awakened at the end of a quarter of an hour, pronouncing a short Martian word, after which she instantly recovered the use of her French and her normal waking state.

5. Questioned as to what had passed, Hélène, while drinking tea, narrates the dream which she has had. She has a sufficiently clear memory of her journey and of what she has seen on Mars, with the exception of the young man, of whom she has retained only a recollection of the scene of incarnation.

But suddenly, in the midst of the conversation, she begins to speak in Martian, without appearing to be aware of it, and while continuing to chat with us in the most natural manner; she appeared to understand all our words, and answered in her strange idiom, in the most normal tone, and seemed very much astonished when we told her that we did not understand her language; she evidently believes she is speaking French.[1] By questioning her concerning a visit which she had made a few days before to M. C., and asking her the number and the names of the persons whom she met there, we succeed in identifying the four following Martian words: **Métiche S.**, *Monsieur S.*; **Médache C.**, *Madame C.*; **Métaganiche Smith**, *Mademoiselle Smith;* **kin't'che**, *four*. After which she resumes definitively her French. Interrogated as to the incident which has transpired, she is astounded, has only a hesitating and confused memory of her having spoken at all this evening of her visit to M. C., and does not recognize nor understand the four Martian words given above when they are repeated to her. On several occasions during this seance I had made the suggestion to Hélène that at a given signal, after her awaking, she would recover the memory of the Martian words pronounced by her and of their meaning. But Leopold, who was present, declared that this command would not be obeyed, and that a translation could not be obtained this evening. The signal, though often repeated, was, in fact, without result.

It has seemed to me necessary to describe with some detail this seance, at which the Martian language made its first appearance, in order to place before the reader all the fragments which, we have been able to gather, without, of course, any guarantee of absolute accuracy, since every one knows how difficult it is to note the sounds of unknown words. A curious difference is to be noticed between the words picked up in the course of the seance and the four words several times repeated by Hélène, the meaning and pronunciation of which have been determined with complete accuracy in the posthypnotic return of the somnambulistic dream. Judged

---

[1] Compare the case of Mlle. Anna O. Brener et Frend, *Studien über Hysterie*, p. 19. Vienna, 1895.

by these latter, the Martian language is only a puerile counterfeit of French, of which she preserves in each word a number of syllables and certain conspicuous letters. In the other phrases, on the contrary, also making use of later texts which have been translated, as we shall see hereafter, it cannot be discovered what it is. We are constrained to believe that these first outbreaks of Martian, characterized by a volubility which we have rarely met with since then, was only a pseudo-Martian, a continuation of sounds uttered at random and without any real meaning, analogous to the gibberish which children use sometimes in their games of "pretending" to speak Chinese or Indian, and that the real Martian was only created by an unskilful distortion of French, in a posthypnotic access of hemisomnambulism, in order to respond to the manifest desire of the sitters to obtain the precise significance of some isolated Martian words.

The impossibility, announced by Leopold, of procuring a translation that same evening of the pretended Martian spoken for the first time during that seance, and the fact that it could not again be obtained, give some support to the preceding theory.

The circumstance that Hélène, in remembering her dream in phase No. 3, had the sentiment of having *well understood* this unknown jargon, is not an objection, since the children who amuse themselves by simulating an uncouth idiom—to recur to that example—do not retain the least consciousness of the ideas which their gibberish is assumed to express. It seems, in short, that if this new language was already really established at that time in Hélène's subliminal consciousness to the point of sustaining fluently discourses of several minutes' duration, some phrases at least would not have failed to gush forth, spontaneously sometimes, in the course of ordinary life, and in order to throw light upon visions of Martian people or landscapes. More than seven months had to elapse before that phenomenon, which was so frequent afterwards, began to appear.

May we not see in this half-year a period of incubation, employed in the subliminal fabrication of a language, properly so called—that is to say, formed of precise words and with a definite signification, in imitation of the four terms just referred to—to replace the disordered nonsense of the beginning?

However it may be, and to return to our story, one can imagine the interest which that sudden and unexpected apparition of mysterious speech aroused, and which the authority of Leopold would not allow to be taken for anything other than the language of Mars. The natural curiosity of Hélène herself, as well as that of her friends, to know more about our neighbors of other worlds and their way of expressing themselves should naturally have contributed to the development of the subliminal dream. The following seance, unhappily, did not justify the promise with which it began.

February 16, 1896.—"At the beginning of this seance, Hélène has a vision of Alexis Mirbel, who announces, by means of the table, that he has not forgotten his French, and that he will give a translation of the Martian words another day. But this prediction is not fulfilled. Whether Hélène, for the reason that she is not feeling well to-day, or that the presence of some one antipathetic to her has hindered the production of the phenomena, the Martian somnambulism, which seemed on the point of breaking forth, did not make its appearance. Hélène remains in a crepuscular state, in which the feeling of present reality and the Martian ideas on the level of consciousness interfere with and mutually obscure each other.. She speaks in French with the sitters, but mingling with it here and there a strange word (such as **méche**, **chinit**, **chéque**, which, according to the context, seem to signify *pencil, ring, paper*), and appears far away from her actual surroundings. She is astonished, in particular, at the sight of M. R. occupied in taking notes by the *procès verbal*, and seems to find that manner of writing with a pen or pencil strange and absurd, but without explaining clearly how it was to be otherwise accomplished. The importance of this seance is in the fact that the idea stands out clearly (which was not to be realized until a year and a half later) of a mode of handwriting peculiar to the planet Mars."

This seance, which was almost a failure, was the last of that period. Hélène's health, which became more and more impaired by standing too long on her feet and overwork at her desk, necessitated her taking a complete rest. I have mentioned the fact that during these six months, without any regular seances, she was subject to a superabundance of spontaneous visions and somnambulisms; but these automatisms belonged to the Hindoo or other cycles, and I do not believe that she experienced during that time any phenomena which were clearly related to the Martian romance. On the other hand, as soon as she was re-established in and had returned to her normal mode of life, the latter appeared again with all the more intensity, dating from the following nocturnal vision. (See Fig. 9.)

September 5, 1896.—Hélène narrates that having arisen at a quarter-past three in the morning to take in some flowers that stood upon the window-sill and were threatened by the wind, instead of going back to bed immediately she sat down upon her bed and saw before her a landscape and some peculiar people. She was on the border of a beautiful blue-pink lake, with a bridge the sides of which were transparent and formed of yellow tubes like the pipes of an organ, of which one end seemed to be plunged into the water. The earth was peach-colored; some of the trees had trunks widening as they ascended, while those of others were twisted. Later a crowd approached the bridge, in which one woman was especially prominent. The women wore hats which were flat, like plates. Hélène does not know who these people are, but has the feeling of having conversed with them. On the bridge there was a man of dark complexion (Astané), carrying in his hands an instrument somewhat resembling a carriage-lantern in appearance, which, being pressed, emitted flames, and which seemed to be a flying-machine. By means of this instrument the man left the bridge, touched the surface of the water, and returned again to the bridge. This tableau lasted twenty-five minutes, since Hélène, upon returning to consciousness, observed that her candle was still burning and ascertained that it was then 3.40 o'clock. She is convinced that she did not fall asleep, but was wide awake during all of this vision. (See Figs. 10 and 11.)

From that time the spontaneous Martian visions are repeated and multiplied. Mlle. Smith experiences them usually in the morning, after awaking and before rising from her bed; sometimes in the evening, or occasionally at other times during the day. It is in the course of these visual hallucinations that the Martian language appears again under an auditive form.

September 22, 1896.—During these last days Hélène has seen again on different occasions the Martian man, with or without his flying-machine; for example, he appeared to her while she was taking a bath, at the edge of the bath-tub. She has had several times visions of a strange house the picture of which followed her with so much persistency that she finally painted it (see Fig. 12). At the same time she heard on three different occasions a sentence the meaning of which she does not know, but which she was able to take down with her pencil as follows: "**Dodé né ci haudan té méche métiche Astané ké dé mé véche**." (As was ascertained six weeks after, by the translation given in the seance of the 2d of November, this phrase indicates that the strange house is that of the Martian man, who is called Astané.)

This phrase was undoubtedly Martian, but what was the meaning of it? After having hoped in vain for nearly a month that the meaning would be revealed in some way or other, I decided to try a disguised suggestion. I wrote to Leopold himself a letter, in which I appealed to his omniscience as well as to his kindness to give me some enlightenment in regard to the strange language which piqued our curiosity, and, in particular, as to the meaning of the phrase Hélène had heard. I asked him to answer me in writing, by means of Hélène's hand. We did not have to wait long for a reply. Hélène received my letter the 20th of October, and on the evening of the 22d, seized with a vague desire to write, she took a pencil, which placed itself in the regular position, between the thumb and the index-finger (whereas she always held her pen between the middle and index-finger), and traced rapidly, in the characteristic handwriting of Leopold and with his signature, a beautiful epistle of eighteen Alexandrine lines addressed to me, of which the ten last are as follows, being an answer to my request that the secrets of Martian be revealed to me:

> "Ne crois pas qu'en t'aimant comme un bien tendre frère
> Je te diroi des cieux tout le profond mystère;
> Je t'aideroi beaucoup, je t'ouvriroi la voie,
> Mais à toi de saisir et chercher avec joie;
> Et quand tu la verras d'ici-bas détachée,
> Quand son âme mobile aura pris la volée
> Et planera sur Mars aux superbes couleurs;
> Si tu veux obtenir d'elle quelques lueurs,
> Pose bien doucement, ta main sur son front pâle
> Et prononce bien bas le doux nom d'Esenale!" [1]

---

[1] "Do not think that in loving you as a tender brother
I shall tell you all the profound mysteries of heaven;
I shall help you much, I shall open for you the way,
But it is for you to seize and seek with joy;
And when you shall see her released from here below,
When her mobile soul shall have taken flight
And shall soar over Mars with its brilliant tints;
If you would obtain from her some light,
Place your hand very gently on her pale forehead
And pronounce very softly the sweet name of Esenale!"

I have been very sensible to the pledges of fraternal affection that Leopold has accorded me, but this time I was especially moved, and although the very uncommon name of Esenale meant absolutely nothing to me, I took care not to forget the singular rule which had been furnished me. At the following seance an opportunity for using it presented itself, and Leopold went so far as to direct himself the application of his method by giving us his instructions, sometimes with one finger, sometimes with another, during Hélène's Martian trance.

Monday, November 2, 1896.—After various characteristic symptoms of the departure for Mars (vertigo, affection of the heart, etc.), Hélène went in a deep sleep. I had recourse to the prescribed method, but Leopold, by the fingers of the right hand, indicated that the proper moment had not yet arrived, and said: "When the soul shall again have regained possession of itself thou shalt execute my order; she will then describe to you, while still asleep, that which she shall have seen on Mars." Shortly after he adds, "Make her sit down in an easy-chair" (instead of the uncomfortable one which she had taken, as was her wont); then, as her peaceful sleep still continued, he informs us again that she is en route towards Mars; that once arrived up there she understands the Martian spoken around her, although she has never learned it; that it is not he, Leopold, who will translate the Martian for us—not because he does not wish to do so, but because he cannot; that this translation is the performance of Esenale, who is actually disincarnate in space, but who has recently lived upon Mars, and also upon the earth, which permits him to act as interpreter, etc.

After half an hour of waiting, Hélène's calm sleep gave way to agitation, and she passed into another form of somnambulism, with sighs, rhythmic movements of the head and hands, then grotesque Martian gestures and French words murmured softly to the hearing of Leopold, who seems to accompany her on Mars, and to whom she confides some of her impressions in regard to that which she perceives. In the midst of this soliloquy a 'vertical movement of the arm, peculiar to Leopold, indicates that the moment has arrived for carrying out his directions. I place my hand on Hélène's forehead, and utter the name of Esenale, to which Hélène replies in a soft, feeble, somewhat melancholy voice: "Esenale has gone away . . . he has left me alone . . . but he will return, . . . he will soon return. . . . He has taken me by the hand and made me enter the house [that which she saw in her vision, and of which she made the drawing a month ago—see Fig. 12]. . . . I do not know where Esenale is leading me, but he has said to me, '**Dodé né ci haudan té méche métiche Astané ké dé mé véche**,' but I did not understand; . . . **dodé**, *this;* **né**, *is;* **ci**, *the;* **haudan**, *house;* **te**, *of the;* **méche**, *great;* **métiche**, *man;* **Astané**, *Astané;* **ké**, *whom;* **dé**, *thou;* **mé**, *hast;* **véche**, *seen.* . . . This is the house of the great man Astané, whom thou hast seen. . . . Esenale has told me that. . . . Esenale has gone away. . . . He will return . . . he will soon return . . . he will teach me to speak . . and Astané will teach me to write."

I have abridged this long monologue, constantly interrupted by silences, and the continuation of which I only obtained by having constant recourse to the name of Esenale as the magic word, alone capable of extracting each time a few words from Hélène's confused brain. After the last sentence or phrase, in which one can see a categorical prediction of the Martian writing, her weak, slow voice was finally hushed, and Leopold directs by means of his left middle finger the removal of the hand from the forehead. Then follow the customary alternations of lethargic sleep, sighs, catalepsy, momentary relapses into somnambulism, etc. Then she opens her eyes permanently, very much surprised to find herself in the easy-chair. Her brain is greatly confused. "It seems to me as though I had a great many things on my mind, but I cannot fix upon anything." By degrees she regains a clear consciousness, but of the entire seance, which has lasted an hour and a half, there only remain some fragments of Martian visions and no recollection whatever of the scene with Esenale and that of the translation.

This process of translation, the first application of which is here presented, becomes from this time the standard method.

For more than two years and a half, the imposition of the hand upon Hélène's forehead and the uttering of the name of Esenale at the proper moment during the trance constitute the "open sesame" of the Martian-French dictionary buried in the subliminal strata of Hélène's consciousness. The idea of this ceremonial is evidently to awaken by suggestion—in a certain favorable somnambulistic phase, which Leopold recognizes and himself announces by a gesture of the arm—the secondary personality which has amused itself by composing the phrases of this extraterrestrial language.

In spiritistic terms, it amounts to invoking the disincarnate Esenale, otherwise called Alexis Mir-bel, who, having lived on both planets, can easily devote himself to the functions of an interpreter.

The only difference between this scene of translation and other seances is in the ease and rapidity with which it is performed. Esenale seems sometimes to be thoroughly asleep and difficult to awaken; Hélène persists in replying by the stereotyped refrain, and incessantly repeats, in her soft and melancholy voice, "Esenale has gone away—he will soon return—he has gone away—he will soon return." Then some more energetic passes or friction on the forehead are necessary, instead of the simple pressure of the hand, in order to break up this mechanical repetition, which threatens to go on forever, and in order to obtain, finally, the repetition and translation, word by word, of the Martian texts. Otherwise the voice continues identical with that of the refrain, soft and feeble, and one can never know whether it is Esenale himself who is making use of Hélène's phonetic apparatus without modifying it, or whether it is she herself, repeating in her sleep what Esenale has told her; the categorical distinctness and absence of all hesitation in pronunciation of the Martian are in favor of the former supposition, which is also corroborated by the fact that it was also in this same voice that Alexis Mirbel (Esenale) spoke to his mother in the scenes of incarnation. (See Fig. 13.)

Fig. 13. Martian landscape. Greenish-yellow sky. A man with a yellow complexion, dressed in white, in a boat of brown, yellow, black, and red colors on a blue-green lake: rose-tinted rock, with white and yellow spots; dark green vegetation; buildings of brown, red, and rose-lilac tints, with white window-panes and curtains of bright blue.

It would be wearisome to recount in detail all the further manifestations of the Martian cycle, which occur frequently in numerous seances and also under the form of spontaneous visions in the daily life of Mlle. Smith. The reader can gain an idea of them both from the remarks of the following paragraph, as well as from the explanatory résumés added to the Martian texts, which will be collected in the following chapter. It merely remains for me to say a word here as to the manner in which the pictures of Hélène relative to Mars, and reproduced in autotype in the Figs. 9 to 20, have been made.

None of these pictures has been executed in complete somnambulism, and they have not, consequently, like the drawings of certain mediums, the interest of a graphic product, absolutely automatic, engendered outside of and unknown to the ordinary consciousness. They are nothing more than simple compositions of the normal consciousness of Mlle. Smith. They represent a type of intermediary activity, and correspond to a state of hemisomnambulism. We have seen above (p. 20) that already in her childhood Hélène seems to have executed various pieces of work in a semi-automatic manner. The same performance is often reproduced on the occasion of the Martian visions, which sometimes pursue her so persistently that she decides to execute them with pencil and brush; work which, in anticipation, often frightens her by its difficulty, but which, when the time comes, accomplishes itself, to her great astonishment, with an ease and perfection almost mechanical. Here is an example:

One Tuesday evening, having already retired, Hélène saw on her bed some magnificent flowers, very different from ours, but without perfume, and which she did not touch, for during her visions she has no idea of moving, and remains inert and passive. The afternoon of the following day, at her desk, she found herself enveloped in a red light, and at the same time felt an indefinable but violent affection of the heart (aura of the voyage to Mars). "The red light continues about me, and I find myself surrounded by extraordinary flowers of the kind which I saw on my bed, but they had no perfume. I will bring you some sketches of them on Sunday." She sent them to me, in fact, on Monday, with the following note: "I am very well satisfied with my plants. They are the exact reproduction of those which it afforded me so much pleasure to behold [No. 3, in Fig. 16, which, beforehand, Hélène despaired of being able to render well], which appeared to me on the latter occasion, and I greatly regret that you were not here to see me execute the drawing: the pencil glided so quickly that I did not have time to notice what contours it was making. I can assert without any exaggeration that it was not my hand alone that made the drawing, but that truly an invisible force guided the pencil in spite of me. The various tints appeared to me upon the paper, and my brush was directed in spite of me towards the color which I ought to use. This seems incredible, but it is, notwithstanding, the exact truth. The whole was done so quickly that I marvelled at it."

Fig. 9. Martian landscape. Pink bridge, with yellow railings plunging down into a pale-blue and purple-tinted lake The shores and hills of a red color, no green being visible. All the trees are of a brick-red, purple, or violet tint [From the collection of M Lemaitre]

Fig. 15. Light-brown and yellow trunk and leaves double-lobed flowers of a vivid red, out of which proceed yellow stamens like black threads.

Fig. 16. Large leaves, light yellowish brown; flowers with purple petals with black stamens and black stems covered with little purple leaves like petals.

Fig. 17. Large violet fruit with black spots, surmounted by a yellow and violet plume, The trunk of brown color with black veins, with six branches of the same character ending in a yellow hook. Red-brick soil.

The house of Astané (Fig. 12), and the extensive landscapes of Figs. 13 and 14, are also the products of a quasi-automatic activity, which always gives great satisfaction to Mlle. Smith. It is, in a way, her subliminal self which holds the brush and executes, at its pleasure, its own tableaux, which also have the value of veritable originals. Other drawings, on the contrary (for example, the portrait of Astané, Fig. 11), which have given Hélène much trouble without having satisfied her very well, should be regarded as simple copies from memory, by the ordinary personality, of past visions, the memory of which is graven upon her mind in a manner sufficiently persistent to serve as a model several days afterwards. In both cases, but especially in the first, Hélène's paintings may be considered as faithful reproductions of the tableaux which unfold themselves before her, and consequently give us better than most verbal descriptions an idea of the general character of her Martian visions.

Let us see now what kind of information the messages and somnambulisms of Hélène furnish us in regard to the brilliant planet whose complicated revolutions formerly revealed to a Kepler the fundamental secrets of modern astronomy.

III. THE PERSONAGES OF THE MARTIAN ROMANCE

In using the word "romance" to designate the Martian communications, taken as a whole, I wish to state that they are, to my mind, a work of pure imagination, but not that there are to be found in them characteristics of unity and of internal co-ordination, of sustained action, of increasing interest to the final dénouement. The Martian romance is only a succession of detached scenes and tableaux, without order or intimate connection, and showing no other common traits beyond the unknown language spoken in it, the quite frequent presence of the same personages, and a certain fashion of originality, a color or quality badly defined as "exotic" or "bizarre" in the landscapes, the edifices, the costumes, etc.

Of a consecutive plot or intrigue, properly so called, there is no trace. I naturally speak only of that which we have learned from the seances of Mlle. Smith, or from the spontaneous visions which she recollects sufficiently to narrate afterwards. But this fails to shadow forth the hidden source whence they all spring.

Without determining the question, I am inclined, nevertheless, to accord to the Martian romance, in some profound stratum of Hélène's being, a much greater continuity and extent than would appear from judging it solely by the fragments known to us. We have only, in my opinion, a few pages, taken at hazard from different chapters; the bulk of the volume is wanting, and the little we possess does not enable us to reconstruct it in a satisfactory manner. We must, therefore, be content with sorting this *débris* of unequal importance, according to their content, independently of their chronological order, and grouping them around the principal personages which figure in them.

The anonymous and mixed crowd which forms the base of some of the Martian visions only differs from that of our own country by the large robe common to both sexes, the flat hats, and the sandals bound to the feet by straps. The interest is confined to a small number of more distinct personages having each his own name, always terminating in an *e* with the men and in an *i* with the women, except only in the case of Esenale, who occupies, however, a place by himself in his quality of disincarnated Martian, fulfilling the function of interpreter. Let us begin by saying a few words about him.

ESENALE

We have seen (p. 164) that this name was hinted at by Leopold on the 22d of October, 1896, without any other explanation as a means of obtaining the signification of the Martian words. Then at the first recurrence to this talisman (November 2d, see p. 166) we learn only that he was a deceased inhabitant of Mars, whose acquaintance Leopold had recently made in interplanetary space. It was only at the following seance (November 8th), where we find Mme. Mirbel, that, after an incarnation of her son Alexis, followed by the scene of translation (see text 3) and in response to questions of the sitters—which answered very well the purpose of suggestion—Leopold affirmed by the left index-finger that Esenale was Alexis Mirbel. It cannot be determined whether that identification constituted a primitive fact which it pleased Leopold to keep secret, only revealing it at the end of a seance at which Mme. Mirbel was present, or whether, as I am inclined to regard it, it was only established at that same seance, under the domination of the circumstances of the moment. As a translator of Martian, Esenale did not show great talent. He had to be entreated, and it was necessary often to repeat his name while pressing or rubbing Hélène's forehead, in order to obtain the exact meaning of the last texts which had been given. He possessed, it is true, an excellent memory, and faithfully reproduced, before giving it word by word, the French for the Martian phrases which Hélène had heard several weeks before and only seen again five or six months afterwards (text 24), and of which there had been no previous opportunity to obtain a translation. But it was to these latter texts, not yet interpreted, that he confined his willingness; on two occasions only did he add, of his own accord, some words of no importance (texts 15 and 36. Text No. 19, for instance, has always remained untranslated, and my later efforts (June 4, 1899) to obtain the meaning of the unknown words **milé piri** have been in vain; moreover, Esenale has not been able to fill up the gaps in text No. 24.

Alexis Mirbel, after the two first Martian seances, reported on pp. 146 and 154, called Esenale, often accorded his mother, in scenes of incarnation, somewhat pathetic, touching messages of filial tenderness and consolation (texts 3, 4, 11, 15, and 18). It is to be noted that, although opportunities for continuing this rôle were not wanting, he appears to have completely abandoned it for the last two years: His last message of this kind (October 10, 1897, text 18) followed a month after a curious seance in which Leopold sought to explain to us spontaneously—no one had mentioned the subject—certain flagrant contradictions in the first manifestations of Alexis-Esenale. Here is a résumé of that scene, with the text of Leopold's communication:

September 12, 1897.—After sundry waking visions, Mlle. Smith hears Leopold speaking; her eyes are closed, and, appearing to be asleep, she repeats, mechanically and in a slow and feeble voice, the following words, which her guide addresses to her: "Thou art going to pay close attention. Tell them now [the sitters] to keep as quiet as possible, that is what often mars the phenomena, the comings and goings, and the idle chatter of which you are never weary. You recollect there was, several months ago, a young man, that young man Alexis Mirbel, who came to give counsel to his mother at a reunion you held with M. (I do not understand the name he gave) . . . at Carouge [1] . . . Well, at that moment he happened—that is to say, two days before—to die on . . . (I could not understand the name) . . . where he had been . . . or he had regained life. [2] This is why I have come to tell you to-day he was in that phase of separation of the material part from the soul which permitted him to recollect his previous existence—that is to say, his life here below in this state; he not only recollects his first mother, but can speak once more the -language he used to speak with her. Some time after, when the soul was finally at rest, he no longer recollected that first language; he returns, he hovers about (his mother), sees her with joy, but is incapable of speaking to her in your language. [3] Whether it will return to him I do not know and cannot say, but I believe that it will. And now listen." Here Mlle. Smith seems to awake, opens her eyes, and has a long Martian vision, which she describes in detail. She now sees a little girl in a yellow robe, whose name she hears as **Anini Nikaïné**, occupied with various childish games—*e.g.*, with a small wand she makes a number of grotesque little figures dance in a white tub, large and shallow, full of sky-blue water. Then come other persons, and, finally, Astané, who has a pen in his fingers, and, little by little, takes hold of Hélène's arm and throws her into a deep trance for the purpose of causing her to write text No. 17.

These spontaneous explanations of Leopold are interesting in that they betray clearly the subliminal desire to introduce some order and logic into the incoherences of the mediumistic reveries. It is a form of the process of justification and retrospective interpretation intended to make the incidents of the past accord with the dominant ideas of the present (see p. 95). In appearance, the theory upon which Leopold rested, after having doubtless meditated long, is quite awkward; but perhaps it was difficult for him to do better, since no one can accomplish the impossible.

ASTANÉ

"The great man Astané" is the reincarnation on Mars of the Hindoo fakir Kanga, who was a devoted companion and friend of Simandini. He has preserved in his new existence the special character of savant or of sorcerer, which he formerly possessed in India, and he has equally retained all his affection for his princess of old, who has been restored to him in

---

[1] Allusion to the seance of November 25, 1894, at M. Lemaître's. See p. 146.
[2] That is to say, he died on Mars, where he had been reincarnated.
[3] Allusion to seance of February 2, 1896. See p. 154.

Mlle. Smith; he frequently utilizes his magic powers to evoke her—that is to say, to re-enter into spiritual communication with her, notwithstanding the distances between their actual places of habitation. The ways and means of that evocation remain, however, enveloped in mystery. We cannot say whether it was Hélène that rejoined Astané on Mars during her somnambulism, or whether it was he who descended "fluidly" towards her and brought to her the odors of the far-distant planet.

When Astané says to Hélène, during a seance: "Come to me an instant. Come and admire these flowers," etc. (text 8), or shows her the curiosities of his Martian abode, it seems as though he had really called her to him through space; but when he appears to her, while awake, at the edge of her bathtub, and expresses his chagrin at finding her still on this miserable earth (text 7), it must be admitted that it is he who has descended to her and inspires her with these visions of an upper world. It is of no importance, on the whole. It is here to be noted that, in these evocations, Astané only manifests himself in visual and auditive hallucinations, never in tactile impressions or those of general sensibility; in the sphere of emotion his presence is accompanied by a great calm on the part of Hélène, a profound bliss, and an ecstatic disposition, which is the correlative and pendant of the happiness experienced by Astané himself (texts 10, 17, etc.) at finding himself in the presence of his idol of the past. The social state of Astané—I should rather say his name, his quality of sorcerer, and his previous terrestrial existence in the body of Kanga—was not immediately revealed.

Nevertheless, at his first apparition (September 5, 1896, see p. 162), he rises superior to the crowd, inasmuch as he alone possesses a flying-machine incomprehensible to us. In the following weeks Mlle. Smith hears his name, and sees him again on many occasions, as well as his house (Fig. 12), but it is only at the end of two months and a half that his identity and his "evocative" powers become known, at a seance at which I was not present, and during which Hélène did not, contrary to her usual custom, fall completely asleep. The following is a résumé of the notes, which I owe to the kindness of M. Cuendet:

November 19, 1896.—Contrary to the experience of the preceding seances, Mlle. Smith remained constantly awake, her arms free on the table, conversing and even laughing all the while with the sitters. The messages were obtained by means of visions and typtological dictations. Hélène having asked Leopold how it happens that she had been able to communicate with a being living on Mars, she has a vision in which Astané appears to her in a costume more Oriental than Martian. " Where have I seen that costume?" asks she; and the table replies, "*In India*," which indicates that Astané is an ex-Hindoo reincarnated on Mars. At the same time Hélène has a vision of an Oriental landscape which she believes she has already seen before, but without knowing where. She sees Astané there, carrying under his arm rolls of paper of a dirty white color, and bowing in Oriental fashion before a woman, also clothed in Oriental garments, whom she also believes she has seen before. These personages appear to her to be "inanimate, like statues." The sitters ask whether the vision was not a simple tableau (of the past) presented by Leopold; the table replies in the affirmative, then inclines itself significantly towards Mlle. Smith, when some one asked who that Oriental woman might be, and the idea is put forth that possibly she represents Simandini. Finally, to further questions of the sitters, the table (Leopold) dictates again that Astané in his Hindoo existence was called *Kanga*, who was a "*sorcerer of the period*"; then that "*Astané on the planet Mars possesses the same faculty of evocation which he had possessed in India*." Leopold is then asked if the power of Astané is greater than his. "*A different power, of equal strength*," replies the table. Finally, Hélène desiring to know whether Astané when he evokes her sees her in her real character or that of her Hindoo incarnation, the table affirms that he sees her in her Hindoo character, and adds: "*and, in consequence, under those characteristics which she [Hélène] possesses to-day and which are in such striking harmony with those of Sima*N*dini*," insisting on the *N* in the middle of the name.

It is to be remarked that at this sitting it was Leopold who gave all the information in regard to the past of Astané, and that he recognizes in him a power over Hélène almost equal to his own. It is strange that the accredited guide of Mlle. Smith, ordinarily so jealous of his rights over her and ready to take offence at all rival pretensions, so freely accords such prerogatives to Astané. This unexpected mildness is still more surprising when the singular similarity of position of these two personages in regard to Hélène is considered. Kanga, the Hindoo fakir, holds in the life of Simandini exactly the same place as Cagliostro in the life of Marie Antoinette, the place of a sorcerer giving beneficial counsel, and at the same time of a platonic adorer, and both of them in their actual rôles of Astané and of Leopold preserve for Mlle. Smith the respectful attachment which they had for her illustrious former existences. How is it these two extraterrestrial pretenders do not hate each other the more cordially since their rival claims upon Hélène have identical foundations? But, far from in the least disputing her possession, they assist each other in the most touching fashion. When Astané writes in Martian by Mlle. Smith's right hand that the noise of the sitters threatens to make him insane (see text 20) it is Leopold who comes to his rescue in making them keep silent by his gestures with the left arm. When Leopold indicates to me that the moment for pressing Hélène's forehead has arrived, it is Astané who lends him his pencil in order that the message may be written (see below, seance of September 12, 1897, and Fig. 23), and the exchange of powers takes place between them without the medium experiencing the least shock, and without its betraying itself outwardly otherwise than by the difference of their handwriting. It is true that Leopold's apparitions to Hélène are infinitely more frequent and his incarnations much more complete than those of Astané, who shows himself to her at increasing intervals, and has never attained to speaking by her mouth. It makes no difference: these two personages resemble each other too much for mutual toleration—if they are really two.

My conclusion presses. Astané is, at bottom, only a copy, a double, a transposition in the Hindoo-Martian manner of Leopold. They are two variations of one primitive theme. In regarding these two beings, as I do, in the absence of proof to the contrary, not as real and objective individualities, but as pseudo-personalities, dream fictions, fantastic subdivisions of the hypnoid consciousness of Mlle. Smith, it may be said that it is the same fundamental emotion which has inspired these twin rôles, the details of which have been adapted by the subliminal imagination to correspond to the diversity of the circumstances. The contradiction painfully felt between the proud aspirations of the *grande dame* and the vexing ironies of reality has caused the two tragic previous existences to gush forth—intrinsically identical, in spite of the differences of place and epoch—of the noble girl of Arabia, having become Hindoo princess, burned alive on the tomb of her despot of a husband, and of her Austrian highness, having become Queen of France and sharing the martyrdom of her spouse.

On parallel lines, in these two dreams issuing from the same emotional source, it is the universal and constant taste of the human imagination for the marvellous, allied to the very feminine need of a respectful and slightly idolatrous protector, which on the one side has created out of whole cloth the personage of Kanga-Astané, and on the other hand has absorbed, without being careful in modifying authentic history, that of Cagliostro-

Leopold. Both are idealistic sorcerers, of profound sagacity, tender-hearted, who have placed their great wisdom at the service of the unfortunate sovereign and made for her, of their devotion, amounting almost to adoration, a tower of strength, a supreme consolation in the midst of all the bitternesses of real life. And as Leopold acts as guide for Hélène Smith in the general course of her actual earthly existence, so Astané seemingly plays the sane rôle in the moments of that life in which Hélène leaves our sublunar world to fly away to the orb of Mars.

If, then, Astané is only a reflection, a projection of Leopold in the Martian sphere, he has there assumed a special coloring, and has outwardly harmonized himself with this new situation.

Fig. 12. House of Astané. Blue sky; soil, mountains, and walls of a red color. The two plants, with twisted trunks, have purple leaves; the others have long green lower leaves and small purple higher leaves. The frame-work of the doors, windows, and decorations are in the shape of trumpets, and are of a brownish-red color. White glass (?) and curtains or shades of a turquoise-blue. The railings of the roof are yellow, with blue tips.

He is clothed in a voluminous, embroidered robe; he has long hair, no beard, a yellow complexion, and carries in his hand a white roll, on which he writes with a point fastened to the end of the index-finger.

His house (Fig. 12) is quadrangular, with gates and windows, and reminds one by its exterior aspect of some Oriental structure, with a flat roof embellished with plants.

Fig. 14. Martian landscape. Sky of yellow; green lake; gray shores bordered by a brown fence; bell-towers on the shore, in yellow-brown tones, with corners and pinnacles ornamented with pink and blue balls; hill of red rocks, with vegetation of a rather dark green interspersed with rose, purple, and white spots (flowers); buildings at the base constructed of brick-red lattice-work; edges and corners terminating in brown-red trumpets; immense white window-panes, with turquoise-blue curtains; roofs furnished with yellow-brown bell-turrets, brick-red battlements, or with green and red plants (like those of Astané's house, Fig. 12). Persons with large white head-dresses and red or brown robes.

The inside is also appropriate. The furniture recalls ours by force of contrast. We have few details; with the exception of a musical instrument with vertical cylinders, closely related to our organs, upon which Hélène sometimes sees and hears Astané playing, seated on a stool with one foot, resembling a milking-stool.

When we pass to the garden the same amalgam of analogies and unlikenesses to our flora are discovered. We have seen that Hélène has been often haunted in the waking state by visions of Martian plants and flowers, which she finally draws or paints with a facility approaching automatism; these specimens, as also the trees scattered over the landscapes, show that Martian vegetation does not differ essentially from ours. Of the animals we do not know much. Astané has often with him an ugly beast, which caused Hélène much fright on account of its grotesque form—about two feet long, with a flat tail; it has the "head of a cabbage," with a big green eye in the middle (like the eye of a peacock feather), and five or six pairs of paws, or ears all about (see Fig. 18). This animal unites the intelligence of the dog with the stupidity of the parrot, since on the one hand it obeys Astané and fetches objects at his command (we do not know how), while, on the other hand, it knows how to write, but in a manner purely mechanical. (We have never had a specimen of this handwriting). (See Fig. 18.)

In fact, as to other animals, beyond the little black bird cited, without description (text 20), and a species of female deer for the purpose of nursing infants (text 36), Hélène saw only horrid aquatic beasts like big snails, which Astané caught by means of iron nets stretched over the surface of the water.

Astané's property is enclosed by large red stones, on the border of the water, where Hélène loves to retire with her guide to converse in peace and to recall to mind with him the ancient and melancholy memories of their Hindoo existence; the general tone of these conversations is entirely the same as that of her conversations with Leopold.

There is a mountain also of red rocks, where Astané possesses some excavated dwelling-places, a kind of grotto appropriate to the sorcerer-savant which he is.

The corpse of Esenale, admirably preserved, is also to be seen there, among other things, about which the disincarnate Esenale sometimes floats in "fluid" form, and which Hélène still finds soft to the touch, when, after much hesitation, and not without fright, she gained courage to touch it with the end of her finger, at the invitation of Astané. It is also in this house, excavated in the rock, that Astané has his observatory, a pit traversing the mountain, by means of which he contemplates the heavens (text 9), our earth included, by means of a telescope, which the beast with the head of a cabbage brings him.

Fig. 18. Astané's ugly beast. The body and tail are rose-colored; the eye is green with a black centre; the head is blackish; the lateral appendices are brownish-yellow, covered, like the whole body, with pink hair.

Fig. 19. Martian lamp, standing against a rose and blue-colored tapestry.

To these qualities of savant Astané joins those of wise counsellor and of patriarchal governor. We also see a young girl named Matêmi coming to consult him frequently (texts 22 and 28), perhaps on matrimonial affairs, since Matêmi reappears on several occasions with her lover or her *fiancé*, Siké, and, among others, at a great family *fête*, presided over by Astané. (See Fig. 19.)

The following are some details concerning that vision, which occupied the greater part of a seance (November 28, 1897). Hélène sees, in a vast, red, initial light, a Martian street appear, lighted neither by lamps nor electricity, but by lights shining through small windows in the walls of the houses. The interior of one of these houses becomes visible to her: a superb, square hall, lighted at each angle by a kind of lamp, formed of four superposed globes,—two blue and two white—not of glass (Fig. 19); under each lamp a small basin, over which was a kind of cornucopia pouring forth water. There were many ornamental plants. In the middle of the hall, a grove, around which are placed a number of small tables with a polished surface like nickel. There are young people in Martian robes; young girls with long hair hanging down their backs, and wearing at the back of the head a head-dress of roses; colored blue or green butterflies attached to the neck.

There were at least thirty speaking Martian (but Hélène did not hear them distinctly). Astané appeared "in a very ugly robe to-day," and showed himself full of friendly gallantry towards the young girls. He seats himself alone at one of the tables while the young people take their places at others, two couples at each. These tables are adorned with flowers different from ours: some blue, with leaves in the shape of almonds; others starry, and as white as milk, scented like musk; others, again, the most beautiful, have the form of trumpets, either blue or fire colored, with large rounded leaves, with black figures. (See Fig. 20.)

Hélène hears Astané pronounce the name "Pouzé." Then come two men in long white trousers with a black sash; one wears a coat of rose color, the other a white one. They carry ornamented trays, and, passing in front of each table, they place square plates upon them, with forks without handles, formed of three teeth an inch in length: for glasses they had goblets like tea-cups, bordered with a silver thread. Then they brought in a kind of basin a cooked animal resembling a cat, which is placed before Astané, who twists it and cuts it rapidly with his fingers, tipped with sharp silver tips; square pieces are distributed, among the guests, on square plates with furrows around the edges for the juice. Every one is filled with a wild gayety. Astané sits at each table in succession, and the girls pass their hands through his hair. New basins melt, and are eaten like the flowers. Then the guests wash their hands at little fountains in the corners of the room.

Now one of the walls is raised, like the curtain of a theatre, and Hélène sees a magnificent hall adorned with luminous globes, flowers, and plants, with the ceiling painted in pink clouds on a pink sky, with couches and pillows suspended along the walls. Then an orchestra of ten musicians arrive, carrying a kind of gilded funnel about five feet in height, with a round cover to the large opening, and at the neck a kind of rake, on which they placed their fingers. Hélène hears music like that made by flutes and sees every one moving; they arrange themselves by fours, make passes and gestures, then reunite in groups of eight. They glide about gently, for it could not be called dancing. They do not clasp each other's waists, but place their hands on each other's shoulders, standing some distance apart. It is terribly warm. It is "boiling hot." They stop, walk, talk, and it is then that Hélène hears a tall young brunette (Matêmi) and a short young man (Siké) exchange the first words of text No. 20. Then they depart in the direction of a large bush with red flowers (*tamiche*) and are soon followed by Ramié and his companion

Fig. 10 Flying-machine held by Astané, emitting yellow and red flames. [From the collection of M. Lemaître.]

At this moment the vision, which has lasted an hour and a quarter, passes away. Hélène, who had remained standing during the whole description, now enters into complete somnambulism, and Astané causes her to write Martian phrases which she had heard and repeated a short time before.

During the entire vision Leopold occupied her left hand, which was hanging anæsthetically down her body, and replied by his index-finger to the questions which I asked in a low voice. I thus learned that this Martian scene was not a wedding, or any special ceremony, but a simple family *fête;* that it was no recollection or product of Hélène's imagination but a reality actually passing on Mars: that it was not Leopold but Astané who furnished this vision and caused her to hear the music: that Leopold himself neither saw nor heard anything of it all, yet knows all that Mlle. Smith sees and hears, etc.

Fig. 20. Plant of Martian design. Fire-red flowers; violet-gray leaves.

This résumé of a family *fête*, presided over by Astané, gives the measure of the originality of the people of Mars. The visions relating to other incidents are of the same order: read the description of the Martian nursery (text 36), of the voyage in a *miza* a sort of automobile, the mechanism of which is entirely unknown to us (text 23), of the operation of chirurgery (text 29), of the games of the little Anini (p. 176, etc.). We see always the same general mixture of imitation of things which transpire among us, and of infantile modifications of them in the minute details.

POUZÉ RAMIÉ—VARIOUS PERSONAGES

Of the other personages who traverse the Martian visions we know too little to waste much time upon them. The name of the one who appears most frequently is Pouzé. He is present at the banquet, and we meet him also in the company of a poor little withered old man with a trembling voice, in connection with whom he occupies himself with gardening or botany, in an evening promenade by the shore of the lake (text 14). He also figures again by the side of an unknown person named Paniné, and he has a son, Saïne, who had met with some accident to his head and had been cured of it, to the great joy of his parents (texts 23 and 24).

Finally, we must devote a few words to Ramié, who manifests himself for the first time in October, 1898, as the revealer of the ultra-Martian world, of which we shall soon take cognizance. Ramié seems to be a relative of Astané, an astronomer, not so brilliant as Astané, but possessing the 'same privilege, which the ordinary Martians do not seem to enjoy, of being able to take hold of Hélène's arm, and of writing with her hand. There is, to my mind, no fundamental difference between Leopold, Astané, and Ramié, in their relation to Hélène; they are only a reproduction in triplicate of one identical emotional relation, and I do not think I am mistaken in regarding these three figures as three very transparent disguises of the same fundamental personality, which is only a hypnoid subdivision of the real being of Mlle. Smith.

It is much wiser to leave to the future—if the Martian and ultra-Martian romances continue to develop—the task of enlightening ourselves more completely as to the true character of Ramié. Possibly some day we shall also know more concerning the couple called Matêmi and Siké, as well as many others, such as Sazéni, Paniné, the little Bullié, Romé, Fédié, etc., of whom we now know scarcely more than their names, and understand nothing in regard to their possible relationships to the central figures of Astané and Esenale.

IV. CONCERNING THE AUTHOR OF THE MARTIAN ROMANCE

The general ideas which the Martian cycle suggests will most assuredly differ, according to whether it is considered as an authentic revelation of affairs on the planet Mars, or only as a simple fantasy of the imagination of the medium; and meanwhile, holding, myself, to the second supposition, I demand from the Martian romance information in regard to its author rather than its subject-matter.

There are two or three points concerning this unknown author which strike me forcibly:

First: He shows a singular indifference—possibly it may be due to ignorance—in regard to all those questions which are most prominent at the present time, I will not say among astronomers, but among people of the world somewhat fond of popular science and curious concerning the mysteries of our universe. The canals of Mars, in the first place—those famous canals with reduplication—temporarily more enigmatical than those of the Ego of the mediums; then the strips of supposed cultivation along their borders, the mass of snow around the poles, the nature of the soil, and the conditions of life on those worlds, in turn inundated and burning, the thousand and one questions of hydrography, of geology, of biology, which the amateur naturalist inevitably asks himself on the subject of the planet nearest to us—of all this the author of the Martian romance knows nothing and cares nothing. Questions of sociology do not trouble him to a much greater extent, since the people occupying the most prominent place in the Martian visions, and making the conversation, in no wise enlighten us as to the civil and political organization of their globe, as to the fine arts and religion, commerce and industry, etc. Have the barriers of the nations fallen, and is there no longer a standing army up there, except that of the laborer occupied in the construction and maintenance of that gigantic net-work of canals for communication or irrigation? Esenale and Astané have not deigned to inform us. It seems probable from certain episodes that the family is, as with us, at the foundation of Martian civilization; nevertheless, we have no direct or detailed information in regard to this subject. It is useless to speculate. It Is evident that the author of this romance did not care much for science, and that, in spite of her desire to comply with the wishes of M. Lemaître (see p. 149), she had not the least conception of the questions which arise in our day, in every cultivated mind, as to the planet Mars and its probable inhabitants.

Secondly: If, instead of quarrelling with the Martian romance about that which it fails to furnish us, we endeavor to appreciate the full value of what it does give us, we are struck by two points, which I have already touched upon more than once in passing—viz., the complete identity of the Martian world, taken in its chief points, with the world n which we live, and its puerile originality in a host of minor details. Take, for example, the family fête (p. 188). To be sure, the venerable Astané is there saluted by a caress of the hair instead of a hand-shake; the young couples while dancing grasp each other not by the waist but by the shoulder; the ornamental plants do not belong to any species known to us: but, save for these insignificant divergences from our costumes and habits, as a whole, and in general tone, it is exactly as with us.

The imagination which forged these scenes, with all their decoration, is remarkably calm, thoughtful, devoted to the real and the probable. The miza, which runs without a visible motor power, is neither more nor less extraordinary to the uninitiated spectator than many of the vehicles which traverse our roads. The colored globes placed in an aperture of the walls of the houses to light the streets recall strongly our electric lamps. Astané's flying-machine will probably soon be realized in some form or other. The bridges which disappear under the water in order to allow boats to pass (text 25) are, save for a technical person, as natural as ours which accomplish the same result by lifting themselves in the air. With the exception of the "evocative" powers of Astané, which only concern Mlle. Smith personally and do not figure in any Martian scene, there is nothing on Mars which goes beyond what has been attained or might be expected to be accomplished by ingenious inventors here below.

A wise little imagination of ten or twelve years old would have deemed it quite droll and original to make people up there eat on square plates with a furrow for the gravy, of making an ugly beast with a single eye carry the telescope of Astané to him, of making babies to be fed by tubes running directly to the breasts of animals like the female deer, etc. There is nothing of the *Thousand and One Nights*, the *Metamorphoses* of Ovid, fairy stories, or the adventures of Gulliver, no trace of ogres nor of giants nor of veritable sorcerers in this whole cycle. One would say that it was the work of a young scholar to whom had been given the task of trying to invent a world as different as possible from ours, but *real*, and who had conscientiously applied himself to it, loosening the reins of his childish fancy in regard to a multitude of minor points in the limits of what appeared admissible according to his short and narrow experience.

Thirdly: By the side of these arbitrary and useless innovations the Martian romance bears in a multitude of its characteristics a clearly Oriental stamp, upon which I have already often insisted. The yellow complexion and long black hair of Astané; the costume of all the personages—robes embroidered or of brilliant hues, sandals with thongs, flat white hats, etc., the long hair of the women and the ornaments in the form of butterflies for their coiffures; the houses of grotesque shapes, recalling the pagoda, kiosk, and minaret, the warm and glowing colors of the skies, the water, the rocks, and the vegetation (see Figs. 13 and 14), etc.: all this has a sham air of Japanese, Chinese, Hindoo. It is to be noted that this imprint of the extreme East is purely exterior, not in any wise penetrating to the characters or manners of the personages.

All the traits that I discover in the author of the Martian romance can be summed up in a single phrase, its profoundly infantile character. The candor and imperturbable naïveté of childhood, which doubts nothing because ignorant of everything, is necessary in order for one to launch himself seriously upon an enterprise such as the pretended exact and authentic depictions of an unknown world. An adult, in the least cultivated and having some experience of life, would never waste time in elaborating similar nonsense—Mlle. Smith less than any one, intelligent and cultivated as she is in her normal state.

This provisional view of the author of the Martian cycle will find its confirmation and its complement in the following chapters, in which we shall examine the Martian language, from which I have until now refrained.

THE MARTIAN CYCLE (CONTINUED)—THE MARTIAN LANGUAGE

OF the various automatic phenomena, the "speaking in tongues" is one which at all times has most aroused curiosity, while at the same time little accurate knowledge concerning it has been obtainable, on account of the difficulty of collecting correctly the confused and unintelligible words as they gush forth.

The phonograph, which has already been employed in some exceptional cases, like that of Le Baron, will doubtless some day render inestimable service to this kind of study, but it leaves much still to be desired at the present moment, from the point of view of its practical utilization in the case of subjects not in their right mind, who are not easily manageable, and who will not remain quiet long enough while uttering their unusual words to allow the instrument to be adjusted and made ready.

There are different species of glossolalia. Simple, incoherent utterances, in a state of ecstasy, interspersed with emotional exclamations, which are sometimes produced in certain surcharged religious environments, is another matter altogether from the creation of neologisms, which are met with in the dream, in somnambulism, mental alienation, or in children. At the same time this fabrication of arbitrary words raises other problems— as, for example, the occasional use of foreign idioms unknown to the subject (at least, apparently), but which really exist. In each of these cases it is necessary to examine further whether, and in what measure, the individual attributes a fixed meaning to the sounds which he utters, whether he understands (or has, at least, the impression of understanding) his own words, or whether it is only a question of a mechanical and meaningless derangement of the phonetic apparatus, or, again, whether this jargon, unintelligible to the ordinary personality, expresses the ideas of some secondary personality. All these forms, moreover, vary in shades and degrees, and there are, in addition, those mixed cases, possibly the more frequent, where all the forms are mingled and combined. The same individual, and sometimes in the course of the same spasm, also exhibits a series of neologisms, comprehended or uncomprehended, giving way to a simple, incoherent verbiage in common language, or vice versa, etc.

A good description and rational classification of all these categories and varieties of glossolalia would be of very great interest. I cannot think of attempting such a study here, having enough already to fully occupy my attention, by reason of having involved myself with the Martian of Mlle. Smith. This somnambulistic language does not consist, as we have already discovered, either in speaking ecstatically or in religious enthusiasm, nor yet in the use of a foreign language which really exists; it represents rather neologism carried to its highest expression and practised in a systematic fashion, with a very precise signification, by a secondary personality unknown to the normal self. It is a typical case of "glosso-poesy," of complete fabrication of all the parts of a new language by a subconscious activity. I have many times regretted that those who have witnessed analogous phenomena—as, for example, Kerner, with the *Seeress of Prevost*—have not gathered together and published in their entirety all the products of this singular method of performing their functions on the part of the verbal faculties. Undoubtedly each case taken by itself seems a simple anomaly, a pure arbitrary curiosity, and without any bearing; but who knows whether the collection of a large number of these psychological bibelots, as yet few enough in their total, would not end in some unexpected light? Exceptional facts are often the most instructive.

In order to avoid falling into the same errors of negligence, not knowing where to stop, in case I wished to make a choice, I have taken the course of setting forth here in full all the Martian texts which we have been able to gather. I will have them follow a paragraph containing certain remarks which that unknown language has suggested to me; but, very far from flattering myself that I have exhausted the subject, I earnestly hope that it will find readers more competent than myself to correct and complete my observations, since I must acknowledge that as a linguist and philologist I am very much like an ass playing the flute. It is expedient, in beginning, to give some further details regarding the various psychological methods of manifestation of that unknown tongue.

I. VERBAL MARTIAN AUTOMATISMS

I have described in the preceding chapter, and will not now return to it, the birth of the Martian language, indissolubly bound up with that of the romance itself, from the 2d of February, 1896, up to the inauguration of the process of translation by the entrance of Esenale upon the scene on the 2d of November following (see pp. 154-165). During several months thereafter the Martian language is confined to the two psychological forms of apparition in which it seems to have been clothed during the course of that first year.

First: *Verbo-auditive* automatism, hallucinations of hearing accompanying visions in the waking state. In the case of spontaneous visions, Hélène notes in pencil, either during the vision itself or immediately afterwards, the unintelligible sounds which strike her ear; but to her great regret many of them escape her, since she is sometimes only able to gather the first or the last phrase of the sentences which her imaginary personages address to her, or scattered fragments of conversations which she holds with herself; these fragments themselves often contain inaccuracies, which are ultimately rectified at the moment of translation, Esenale having the good habit of articulating very clearly each Martian word before giving its French equivalent. In the case of the visions which she has at the seances, Hélène slowly repeats the words she hears without understanding them, and the sitters make note of them more or less correctly.

Secondly: *Vocal* automatism ("verbo-motor hallucinations of articulation," in the cumbersome official terminology). Here again it is the sitters who gather as much as they can of the strange words pronounced in a state of trance, but that is very little, since Hélène, in her Martian state, often speaks with a tremendous volubility. Moreover, a distinction must be made between the relatively clear and brief phrases which are later translated by Esenale, and the rapid and confused gibberish the signification of which can never be obtained, probably because it really has none, but is only a pseudo-language (see pp. 154-159).

A new process of communication, the handwriting, made its appearance in August, 1897, with a delay of perhaps eighteen months as to the speech (the reverse of Leopold's case, who wrote a long time before speaking). It is produced, also, under two forms, which constitute a pendant to the two cases given above, and also complete the standard quartette of the psychological modalities of language.

Thirdly: *Verbo-visual* automatism—that is, apparitions of exotic characters before Hélène's eyes when awake, who copies them as faithfully as possible in a drawing, without knowing the meaning of the mysterious hieroglyphics.

Fourthly: *Graphic* automatism—*i.e.*, writing traced by the hand of Hélène while completely entranced and incarnating a Martian personage. In this case the characters are generally smaller, more regular, better formed than in the drawings of the preceding case. A certain number of occasions, when the name has been pronounced by Hélène before being written, and especially the articulation of Esenale at the moment of translation, have permitted the relations between her vocal sounds and the graphic signs of the Martian language to be established.

It is to be noted that these four automatic manifestations do not inflict an equal injury upon the normal personality of Mlle. Smith. As a rule, the verbo-auditive and verbo-visual hallucinations only suppress her consciousness of present reality; they leave her a freedom of mind which, if not complete, is at least sufficient to permit her to observe in a reflective manner these sensorial automatisms, to engrave them on her memory, and to describe them or make a copy of them, while she often adds remarks testifying to a certain critical sense. On the contrary, the verbo-motor hallucinations of articulation or of writing seem to be incompatible with her preservation of the waking state, and are followed by amnesia. Hélène is always totally absent or entranced while her hand writes mechanically, and if, as seldom happens, she speaks Martian automatically, outside of the moments of complete incarnation, she is not aware of it, and does not recollect it. This incapacity of the normal personality of Mlle. Smith to observe at the time or remember afterwards her verbo motor automatisms denotes a more profound perturbation than that she experiences during her sensory automatisms.

The Martian handwriting only appeared at the end of a prolonged period of incubation, which betrayed itself in several incidents, and was certainly stimulated by various exterior suggestions during a year and a half at least. The following are the principal dates of this development.

February 16, 1896.—The idea of a special handwriting belonging to the planet Mars occurs for the first time to Hélène's astonishment in a Martian semi-trance (see p. 162).

November 2.—Handwriting is clearly predicted in the phrase, "Astané will teach me to write," uttered by Hélène in a Martian trance, after the scene of the translation by Esenale (see p. 166).

November 8.—After the translation of text No. 3, Leopold, being questioned, replies that Astané will write this text for Mlle. Smith, but the prediction is not fulfilled.

May 23, 1897.—The announcement of Martian handwriting becomes more precise. "Presently," says Astané to Hélène, "thou wilt be able to trace our handwriting, and thou wilt possess in thy hands the characters of our language" (text 12).

June 20.—At the beginning of a seance, a Martian vision, she demands of an imaginary interlocutor "a large ring which comes to a point, and with which one can write." This description applies to M. R., who has with him some small pocket-pens of this kind, capable of being adjusted to the end of the index-finger.

June 23.—I hand Hélène the two small pocket-pens which M. R. has brought for her, but they do not please her. After trying to use one, she throws it away and takes up a pencil, saying that if she must write Martian, the ordinary means will suffice as well as those peculiar pocket-pens. In about a minute she falls asleep, and her hand begins automatically to trace a message in Leopold's handwriting. I then ask that individual whether the pocket-pens of M. R. do not meet the exigencies of Martian, and whether Mlle. Smith will some day write that language, as has already been announced. Hélène's hand thereupon responds in the beautiful calligraphy of Leopold: "I have not yet seen the instrument which the inhabitants of the planet Mars use in writing their language, but I can and do affirm that the thing will happen, as has been announced to you.—LEOPOLD."

June 27.—In the scene of the translation of text 15, Hélène adds to her usual refrain, "Esenale has gone away; he will soon return; he will soon write."

August 3.—Between four and five o'clock in the afternoon Hélène had a vision at her desk, lasting ten or fifteen minutes, of a broad, horizontal bar, flame-colored, then changing to brick-red, and which by degrees became rose-tinted, on which were a multitude of strange characters, which she supposes to be the Martian letters of the alphabet, on account of the color. These characters floated in space before and round about her. Analogous visions occur in the course of the weeks immediately following.

August 22.—Hélène for the first time writes in Martian. After various non-Martian visions Mlle. Smith turns away from the window (it rained hard, and the sky was very gray) and exclaims, "Oh, look, it is all red! Is it already time to go to bed? M. Lemaître, are you there? Do you see how red it is? I see Astané, who is there, in that red; I only see his head and the ends of his fingers; he has no robe; and here is the other (Esenale) with him. They both have some letters at the ends of their fingers on a bit of paper. Quick, give me some paper!" A blank sheet and the pocket-pen are handed to her, which latter she disdainfully throws down. She accepts an ordinary pencil, which she holds in her customary fashion, between her middle and index-finger, then writes from left to right the three first lines of Fig. 21, looking attentively towards the window at her fictitious model before tracing each letter, and adding certain oral notes, according to which there are some words which she sees written in black characters on the three papers—or, more correctly, on three white wands, a sort of narrow cylinder, somewhat flattened out—which Astané, Esenale, and a third personage whose name she does not know but whose description corresponds with that of Pouzé, hold in their right hands. After which she a gain sees another paper or cylinder, which Astané holds above his head, and which bears also some words which she undertakes to copy (the three last lines of Fig. 21, p. 205). " Oh, it is a pity," says she, on coming to the end of the fourth line, "it is all on one line, and I have no more room." She then writes underneath the three letters of line 5, and without saying anything adds line 6. Then she resumes: "How dark it is with you . . . the sun has entirely gone down" (it still rains very hard). "No one more! nothing more!" She remains in contemplation before that which she has written, then sees Astané again near the table, who again shows her a paper, the same, she thinks, as the former one. "But no, it is not altogether the same there is one mistake, it is there [she points to the fourth line towards the end] . . . Ah, I do not see more!" Then, presently she adds: "He showed me something else; there was a mistake, but I was not able to see it. It is very difficult. While I was writing, it was not I myself, I could not feel my arms. It was difficult, because when I raised my head I no longer saw the letters well. It was like a Greek design."

At this moment Hélène recovered from the state of obscuration, from which she emerged with difficulty, which had accompanied the Martian vision and the automatic copy of the verbo-visual text. But a little later in the evening she only vaguely remembered having seen strange letters, and was altogether ignorant of having written anything.

The very natural supposition that the three first words written were the names of the known personages (Astané, Esenale, Pouzé), who bore them on their wands, led to the discovery of the meaning of many of the Martian characters and permitted the divining of the sense of the three last words.

The new alphabet was enriched by certain other signs on the following days, thanks to the echoes of that seance in the ordinary life of Hélène, who happened on several occasions to write not the true Martian as yet, but French in Martian letters, to her great stupefaction when she found herself after a while in the presence of these unknown hieroglyphics.

Fig. 21. Text No. 16; seance of August 22, 1897.—First Martian text written by Mlle Smith (according to a visual hallucination). Natural size. [Collection of M. Lemaitre.]—Herewith its French notation.

astane
esenale
pouze
mene simand
ini.
mira.

[Martian script line]

Fig. 22. Examples of isolated French words (*française, lumière, prairie*) automatically traced in Martian characters by Mlle. Smith in her normal handwriting. See also Fig. 1, p. 56.

The first manifestation of that graphic automatism, being as yet concerned only with the form of the letters and not the vocabulary, dates from the day after the following seance:

August 23.—"Here," wrote Hélène to me at noon, sending me some memoranda from which I have taken the three examples of Fig. 22—"here are some labels which I made it my business to make this morning at ten o'clock, and which I have not been able to finish in a satisfactory manner. I have only just now emerged from the rose-colored fog in which I have been continuously enwrapped for almost two hours."

Three weeks later a complete automatic Martian handwriting was produced in a seance at my house, of which the following is a summary.

[Martian text, several lines]

mets ta main sur son front

Fig. 23. Martian text No. 17; seance of September 12, 1897. Written by Mlle. Smith incarnating Astané (then Leopold for the French words at the end). See the translation, p. 222. Too many *l*'s at the end of the first line immediately produced the scrawls intended to strike them out. (Reproduction one-half natural size.)

September 12, 1897.—At the end of a quite long Martian vision, Mlle. Smith sees Astané, who has something at the end of his finger and who signs to her to write. I offer her a pencil, and after various tergiversations she slowly begins to trace some Martian characters (Fig. 23). Astané has possession of her arm, and she is, during this time, altogether anæsthetic and absent. Leopold, on the contrary, is at hand, and gives various indications of his presence.

At the end of the sixth line she seems to half awaken, and murmurs, "I am not afraid; no, I am not afraid." Then she again falls into a dream in order to write the four last words (which signify "*Then do not fear*," and which are the response of Astané to her exclamation).

Almost immediately Leopold substitutes himself for Astané and traces on the same sheet, in his characteristic handwriting (considerably distorted towards the end): "*Place thy hand on her forehead*," by means of which he indicates to me that the time has arrived to pass on to the scene of translation by Esenale.

We may conclude from these successive stages that the Martian handwriting is the result of a slow

Fig 24. Martian alphabet, summary of the signs obtained. (Never has been given as such by Mlle. Smith.)

autosuggestion, in which the idea of a special writing instrument, and its handling, for a long time played the dominant rôle, then was abandoned, without doubt, as impracticable to realize. The characters themselves then haunted for several weeks Hélène's visual imagination before they appeared to her on the cylinders of the three Martians in a manner sufficiently clear and stable to enable her to copy them and afterwards to be capable of subduing her graphomotor mechanism. Once manifested outwardly, these signs, which I have assembled under the form of an alphabet in Fig. 24, have not varied for two years.

Moreover, some trifling confusion, of which I shall speak a little later, shows well that the personality which employs them is not absolutely separated from that of Hélène, although the latter, in a waking state, might hold the same relation to Martian which she holds to Chinese—that is, she knows its general very characteristic aspect, but is ignorant of the signification of the characters, and would be incapable of reading it.

Hélène's Martian handwriting is not stereotyped, but presents, according to circumstances, some variations in form, especially in the size of the letters.

This may be established by Figs. 21 to 32, in which I have reproduced the greater part of the texts obtained by writing. When the Martian gushes forth in verbo-visual hallucinations, Hélène transcribes it in strokes of large dimensions, lacking firmness, full of repetitions (Figs. 21, 26, 31), and she always remarks that the original, which is before her eyes, is much smaller and clearer than her copy. In the texts which have come automatically from her hand—*i.e.*, supposedly traced by the Martians themselves—the handwriting is really smaller and more precise. Here again are some curious differences. Astané has a calligraphy less voluminous than that of Esenale, and Ramié has a much finer one than Esenale (Figs. 28 and 29).

It would be altogether premature for me to launch myself upon the study of Martian graphology, and, therefore, leaving that line to my successors, I take up the texts which have been collected in their chronological order.

II. THE MARTIAN TEXTS

It is not always easy to represent a language and its pronunciation by means of the typographical characters of another. Happily the Martian, in spite of its strange appearance and the fifty millions of leagues which separate us from the red planet, is in reality so near neighbor to French that there is scarcely any difficulty in this case.

The dozen written texts [1] which we possess, and which Mlle. Smith either copied from a verbo-visual hallucination, or which were traced by her hand in an access of graphomotor automatism, are readily translated into French, since each Martian letter has its exact equivalent in the French alphabet. I have confined myself to placing accents on the vowels (there are none in the Martian writing), conformably to the pronunciation of Esenale at the moment of translation. It is only necessary to read the following texts aloud, articulating them as though they were French, in order to secure the Martian words almost exactly as they proceed from the mouth of M le. Smith; I say almost, because there still remains, naturally, in the speech of Esenale, as in that of every one, a special mannerism of strengthening certain syllables and slurring others—in short, that of delicate shades of accentuation, which cannot be adequately represented, and which the hearers did not attempt to take note of at the seances.

In the auditive or vocal texts, those which have not been obtained by writing, I have adopted the more probable orthography, according to the pronunciation of Esenale, but (with the exception of words known by means of the written texts) I naturally cannot guarantee their absolute correctness.

The manner in which Hélène takes down in pencil the Martian phrases which strike her ear is not of great assistance to us in that respect, because, as I have said above (p. 158), she finds herself at the time of these verbo-auditive hallucinations in the situation of a person who hears some unknown words, and spells them as well as she is able, after a quite arbitrary and often faulty fashion. She writes, for example, "**hezi darri né ciké taisse,**" which, according to the pronunciation of Esenale and other written texts, should be "**êzi darié siké tés**"; or, again, "**misse messe as si lé,**" instead of "**mis mess ass ilé.**" We cannot, therefore, depend upon the orthography of Hélène, but I have naturally followed it in every case in which there seemed to be no good reason to depart from it. In stating that the following texts should be articulated like French, two remarks must be added: First, the final consonant, very rare in Martian, is always aspirated; the word **ten** is pronounced as in the French *gluten;* **essat**, like *fat;* **ames**, like *aloes;* **mis** and **mess**, like *lis* (flower), and mess (of an officer), etc. In the second place, for the different values of the *e* I have adopted the

---

[1] These are texts 16-20, 26, 28, 31, 34, 37-39. They are further distinguished by an asterisk.

following rule: the *e* broad is always indicated by the accent grave *è*; the *e* medium, which is only found at the beginning and in the middle of a word, is marked with the acute accent *é*; the *e* short, by the acute accent at the end of a word (or before a final *e* mute), and by the circumflex at the beginning or in the middle; the *e* mute, or demimute, remains without accent.

The pronunciation, therefore, will be, for example, the *e*'s of the Martian words **mété, bénézee**, like those of the French words *été, répétée;* **êvé**, like *rêvé,* **tès**, as in *Lutèce*, etc.

There will be found in italics, underneath the Martian texts, their French equivalents, word for word, as given by Esenale in the manner described above (see pp. 166-168).[1] I have also indicated the kind of automatism— auditive, visual, vocal, or graphic—by means of which each text was obtained, also the date of its appearance, and (in parentheses) that of the seance, often quite remote, at which it was translated. I have also added such explanations as seemed to me to be necessary.

1.	**métiche C.**	**médache C.**	**métaganiche S.**	**kin't'che**
	Monsieur C.	*Madame C.*	*Mademoiselle S.*	*quatre.*
	Mr. C.	Mrs. C.	Miss C.	Four.

Vocal. February 2, 1896. See above, p. 157.

2.	**dodé**	**né**	**ci**	**haudan**	**té**	**mess**	**métiche**	**astané**	**ké**	**dé**
	Ceci	*est*	*la*	*maison*	*du*	*grand*	*homme*	*Astané*	*que*	*tu*
	mé	**véche.**								
	as	*vu.*								

This is the house of the great man Astané, whom thou hast seen.

Auditive. About September 20, 1896 (translated November 2).—Heard by Hélène at the same time at which she had the vision of Fig. 12 (see p. 166).

3.	**modé**	**iné**	**cé**	**di**	**cévouitche**	**ni**	**êvé**	**ché**	**kiné**	**liné**

---

[1] A literal English translation of each text will be found immediately beneath the French equivalents of the Martian words.

| *Mère* | *adorée,* | *je* | *te* | *reconnais* | | *et* | *suis* | *ton* | *petit* | *Linet.* |

Adored mother, I recognize thee, and am thy little Linet.

Words addressed to Mme. Mirbel by her son Alexis (Esenale) in a scene of incarnation altogether analogous to that described on p. 156.

4.	i	**modé**	**meté**	**modé**	**modé**	**iné**	**palette**	**is**
	O	*mère,*	*tendre*	*mère,*	*mère*	*bien-aimée,*	*calme*	*tout*
	ché	**péliché**	**ché**	**chiré**	**né**	**ci ten**	**ti**	**vi**
	ton	*souci,*	*ton*	*fils*	*est*	*près*	*de*	*toi.*

Oh, mother, tender mother, dearly loved mother, calm all thy care, thy son is near thee.

Vocal. November 29, 1896 (translated same seance).—Spoken by Esenale and addressed to Mine. Mirbel, in a scene of incarnation analogous to the preceding. At the moment of translation., Esenale repeated, very distinctly, the last words, as follows: "**né ci,** *est près* ["is near"], **ten ti vi,** *de toi* ("thee"). This was evidently an error, since it appears from numerous later texts that est près de toi corresponds to **né ten ti vi**; it follows that it would be natural to translate the word **ci** by *là, ici,* or *tout,* if these words had not been differently rendered in other texts. (A confusion of the adverb *là* with the article *la,* translated by **ci** in text 2, might also be suspected.)

5.	i	**kiché**	**ten**	**ti**	**si**	**ké**	**di**	**êvé dé**	**étéche**	**mêné**
	Oh!	*pourquoi*	*près*	*de*	*moi*	*ne*	*te*	*tiens-tu*	*toujours,*	*amie*
	izé	**bénézée**								
	enfin	*retrouvée!*								

Oh! Why dost thou not keep thyself always near me, friend, at last found again?

Auditive. December 4, 1896 (translated December 13). Fragment of a long discourse by Astané to Hélène, during an apparition which she had of him about nine o'clock in the evening, as she was about to go to bed. This sentence, which he uttered twice, is the only one which she has been able to recall with sufficient precision to note down immediately after the vision. She has the feeling of having understood Astané's whole discourse while he was delivering it, and thinks she would have been able to translate it into French, perhaps not word for word, but in its general sense. She expected to transcribe it the following day, but in the morning when she awoke she was unable to recall either the words of Astané or their meaning, not even that of this sentence, written on the previous evening. Heard again, as the second part of the following text, in the seance of the 13th of December.

6 ti	iche	cêné	éspênié	ni	ti	êzi	atèv	astané	êzi		
De	notre	belle	"Espénié"	et	de	mon	être	Astané,	mon		
érié	vizé	é	vi...	i	kiché	ten	ti	si	ké	di	êvé
âme	descend	à	toi...	oh!	pourquoi	près	de	moi	ne	te	tiens
dé	étéche	mêné	izé	bénézée							
tu	toujours,	amie	enfin	retrouvée!							

From our beautiful "Espénié" and from my being Astané, my soul descends to thee—Oh! why dost thou not keep thyself always near to me, friend, at last found again?

Auditive. December 13, 1896 (translated same seance).—Heard in the far-away voice of Astané, Hélène having all the while a painful sensation, as though the skin of her face around her eyes, on the back of her wrists and hands, was being torn off. In the translation the word *Espénié* remains as it is, being a proper name; the left index-finger (Leopold) points heavenward, and says that it might be rendered by *terre, planète, demeure*.

7 cé	êvé	plêva	ti	di	bénèz	éssat	riz	tès	midée		
Je	suis	chagrin	de	te	retrouver	vivant	sur	cette	laide		
durée	cé	ténassé	riz	iche	éspênié	vétéché	ié	ché	atèv	hêné	
terre;	je	voudrais	sur	notre	Espénié	voir	tout	ton	être	s'élever	
ni	pové	ten	ti	si	éni	zée	métiché	oné	gudé	ni	zée	darié
et	rester	près	de	moi;	ici	les	hommes	sont	bons	et	les	cœurs
grêvé												
larges												
.

I am sorry to find you again living on this wretched earth; I would on our Espénié see all thy being raise itself and remain near me; here men are good and hearts large.

Auditive. December 15, 1896 (translated January 17, 1897).—Words spoken by Astané to Hélène in a morning vision. The following fragment of the letter in which she sent me this text merits being cited as an example of those quite frequent cases in which Mlle. Smith, without knowing the exact translation of the foreign words, nevertheless divines their general signification and comprehends them by their emotional equivalent. "This morning, at a quarter before six, I saw Astané at the foot of my bed. The general sense of his language was at that moment quite clear to my mind, and I give it to you as I understood it—that is, in as clear a manner as possible, having noted it down afterwards:

'How much I regret your not having been born in our world; you would be much happier there, since everything is much better with us, people as well as things, and I would be so happy to have you near me.' That is about what it seemed to me to mean; perhaps some day we may be able to be sure of it."

8 amès	mis	tensée	ladé	si—	amès	ten	tivé	avé
Viens	*un*	*instant*	*vers*	*moi,*	*viens*	*près*	*d'un*	*vieil*
men—	koumé	ié	ché	pélésse—	amès	some	têsé	
ami	*fondre*	*tout*	*ton*	*chagrin:*	*viens*	*admirer*	*ces*	
misaïmé—	ké	dé	surès	pit	châmi—	izâ	méta	ii
fleurs,	*que*	*tu*	*crois*	*sans*	*parfum,*	*mais*	*pourtant*	*si*
borêsé	ti	finaïmé—	iâ	izi	dé	séïmiré		
pleines	*de*	*senteurs!...*	*Mais*	*si*	*tu*	*comprendras!*		

Come towards me a moment, come near an old friend to melt away all thy sorrow; come to admire these flowers, which you believe without perfume, but yet so full of fragrance! But if thou couldst understand.

Auditive and vocal. January 31, 1897 (translated same seance).—Hélène, in hemisomnambulism, sees Astané, who tells her to repeat his words; she replies to him: "But speak plainly . . . I will gladly repeat them . . . but I do not understand very well . . ." Then she pronounces slowly and very distinctly the foregoing text, in groups of words, separated by a moment of silence (marked in the text by the sign—). It is remarked that these groups, with the exception of the sixth, correspond to the hemistiches of the French translation obtained in the same seance. After the sixth group Hélène remains silent for a long time, and finally says: "I cannot understand; " then utters the four last words, which are the reply of Astané to her objection.

9.	ané	éni	ké	éréduté	cé	ilassuné	té	imâ	ni
	C'est	*ici*	*que,*	*solitaire,*	*je*	*m'approche*	*du*	*ciel*	*et*
	bétiné	**chée**	**durée**						
	regarde	*ta*	*terre.*						

It is here that, alone, I bring myself near to heaven and look upon the earth.

Auditive. February 24, 1897 (translated March 14).—Reclining in her easy-chair, after the noonday meal, Hélène hears this sentence, while at the same time she has the vision of a house, constructed by digging into a Martian mountain, and traversed by a sort of air-shafts, and which represents Astané's observatory.

10.	simandini	lé	lâmi	mêné	kizé	pavi	kiz	atimi
	Simandini,	*me*	*voici!*	*amie!*	*quelle*	*joie,*	*quel*	*bonheur!*

Simandini, here I am! friend! what joy! what happiness!

Auditive. March 14, 1897 (translated same seance).—See following text.

11.	i	modé	duméïné	modé	kêvi	cé	mache	povini	
	O	*mère,*	*ancienne*	*mère,*	*quand*	*je*	*peux*	*arriver*	
	poénêzé	**mûné**	**é**	**vi**	**saliné**	**éziné**	**mimâ**	**nikaïné**	**modé**
	quelques	*instants*	*vers*	*toi*	*j'oublie*	*mes*	*parents*	*Nikaïné,*	*mère!*
	—i	**men**							
	—ô	*ami!*							

Oh, mother, former mother, when I can arrive a few instants near thee, I forget my parents Nikaïné, mother!—Oh friend!

Vocal. March 14, 1897 (translated same seance).—From the beginning of this seance Hélène complained of cold hands, then a great desire to weep, and of a buzzing in the ears, which kept increasing and in which she finally heard Astané address to her the Martian words of text 10. Immediately after she passes into full somnambulism; her respirations, very short and panting, rise . to three per second, accompanied by synchronous movements of the left index-finger; then she stops suddenly with a long expiration, immediately followed by a deep inspiration: then her breast heaves, her face assumes an expression of suffering, and the left index-finger announces that it is Esenale (Alexis Mirbel) who is incarnated. After a series of spasms and hiccoughs, Hélène arises, and, placing herself behind Mme. Mirbel, takes her neck in her hands, bows her head upon hers, tenderly pats her cheek, and addresses to her the words of text No. 11 (except the two last words). Then she raises her head, and again, with panting respiration (accelerated to thirty inspirations in sixteen seconds), walks towards M. Lemaître (whose pupil Alexis Mirbel had been at the time of his death). She places her hands upon his shoulders, affectionately grasps his right hand, and with emotion and continued sobbing addresses to him the two words i men! After which she goes through the pantomime of extending her hand to Leopold and of allowing him to conduct her to a couch, where the translation of texts Nos. 10, 11, and 9 is obtained by the customary process, but not without difficulty.

12.	lassuné	ké	nipuné	ani	tis	dé	machir	mirivé		
	Approche,	ne	crains	pas;	bientôt	tu	pourras	tracer		
	iche	manir	sé	dé	évenir	Toué	chi	amiché	zé	forimé
	notre	écriture,	et	tu	posséderas	Dans	tes	mains	les	marques
	ti	viche	tarviné							
	de	notre	langage.							

Approach, fear not; soon thou wilt be able to trace our writing, and thou wilt possess in thy hands the signs of our language.

Auditive. May 23, 1897 (translated same seance).—Shortly after the beginning of the seance, Hélène, still being awake, has a vision of Astané, who addresses her in these words, which she repeats slowly and in a feeble voice. I give the text as it was heard and uniformly noted by several sitters, both at the moment of its utterance and at its subsequent translation. Many corrections, however, would be necessary, in order to make it correspond with the later written texts: **ké nipuné ani**, *et ne crains pas* ("and I am not afraid," or, "and I do not fear") should be changed to **kié nipuné ani**, *ne crains pas* (see text 17); **sé** or **cé** only stands here for *et*, which everywhere else is given as **ni**; **viche** is used in error for **iche** (unless the **v** was added for the sake of euphony, of which there is no other example) and **tis** for **tiche**.

13.	(adèl)	ané	sini	(yestad)	i	astané	cé	fimès	astané	mirâ
		C'est	vous,		ô	Astané	je	meurs!	Astané,	adieu!

It is you, oh Astané, I am dying! Astané, farewell!

Vocal. Same seance as the preceding text, after which Hélène passes into full somnambulism, begins to weep, pants, holds her hand on her heart, and pronounces this sentence, mingling with it the two words *Adèl* and *yestad*, which are not Martian, but belong to the Oriental cycle; they also do not appear in the text as it was repeated at the time of its translation. This intrusion of terms foreign to the Martian dream is explained by the imminence of a Hindoo scene ready to appear, which occupied the latter half of the seance in which the Arab servant, Adèl, plays a leading rôle. The mingling of the two romances is greatly accentuated a few moments later, in a long discourse, devoid of *r*'s and very rich in sibilants, and spoken with so great volubility that it was impossible to gather a single word. At the time of the translation, at the close of the seance, this tirade was repeated with the same rapidity, preventing any notation; according to the French translation which followed, it concerned memories of the life of Simandini which Hélène recalled to Astané and in which there is much mention of the aforesaid Adèl (see Hindoo Cycle, Chap. VII.).

14.	eupié	zé	palir	né	amé	arvâ	nini	pédriné	évaï		
	Eupié,	le	temps	est	venu;	Arva	nous	quitte;	sois		
	diviné	limée	ine	vinâ	té	luné	—	pouzé	men	hantiné	
	heureux	jusque	au	retour	du	jour.	—	Pouzé	ami	fidèle,	
	êzi	vraïni	né	touzé	med	vi	ni	ché	chiré	saïné	— ké
	mon	désir	est	même	pour	toi	et	ton	fils	Saïné.	— Que
	zalisé	téassé	mianiné	ni	di	daziné	—	eupié	—	pouzé	
	l'élément	entier	t'enveloppe	et	te	garde!	—	Eupié!	—	Pouzé!	

Eupié, the time has come; Arva leaves us; be happy till the return of the day. Pouzé, faithful friend, my wish is even for thee, and thy son Saïné.—May the entire element envelop thee and guard thee!—Eupié!—Pouzé!

Auditive. June 18, 1897 (translated June 20).—During a visit I made to Mlle. Smith she has a vision of two Martian personages walking on the shore of a lake, and she repeats this fragment of their conversation which she has heard. According to another text (No. 20), Arva is the Martian name of the sun.

15.	modé	tatinée	cé	ké	mache	radziré	zé	tarvini	va	
	Mère	chérie,	je	ne	puis	pro-noncer	le	langage	où	
	nini	nini	triménên i	ii	adzi	cé	zé	seïmiré	vétiche	i
	nous	nous	compre-nions	si	bien!	Je	le	com-prends	cepen-dant;	ô
	modé	inée	kévi	béri-mir m hed	kévi	machiri cé	di	triné		
	mère	adorée,	quand	reviendra-t-il?	Quand	pour-rai-je	te	parler		
	ti	éstotiné	ni	bazée	animi-na	i	mo dé	cé	méï	ad zi
	de	ma derni ère	et	courte	exis-tence?	O	mér e,	je	t'ai	bi-en
	ilinée	i	modé	inée	cé	ké	lé	nazère	ani	— mir â
	recon-nue,	ô	mère	adorée,	je	ne	me	trompe	pas!	— Adi eu
	modé	itatinée	mirâ	mirâ	mirâ					
	mére	chérie,	adieu,	adieu,	adieu!					

My dearest, I cannot pronounce the language in which we understood each other so well! I understand it, however; oh! adored mother, when will it return? When shall I be able to speak to thee of my last and short existence? Oh! mother, I have well recognized thee, oh! adored mother, I am not mistaken!—Farewell, dearest mother, farewell, farewell, farewell!

Auditive. June 27, 1897 (translated same seance).—Mme. Mirbel being present, Hélène perceives Esenale, who remains in the vicinity of his mother and addresses these words to her. The "adieux" at the close were not spoken at that time, but were uttered by Esenale immediately following and as a complement of the translation; this is the only case (outside of text 36) in which he did not confine himself strictly to the texts already gathered and in which he permitted himself to introduce a new phrase, which otherwise does not contain a single unknown word; **itatinée**, *chérie*, is evidently a slip which should be corrected either to **tatinée**, *chérie*, or to **it atinée**, *ô chérie*. The precise French equivalent of **triménêni** is probably *entretenions*.

* 16.	astané	ésenâle	pouzé	mêné	smandini		mirâ	
	(*Astané,*	*Esenale.*	*Pouzé.*	*Amie*	*Simandini,*		*adieu!*)	

Astané. Esenale. Pouzeé. Friend Simandini, farewell!

Visual. August 22, 1897.—This text, for which there is no need of a translation, constitutes the first appearance of the Martian handwriting. See above, Fig. 21, and the résumé of that seance, pp. 203-205.

* 17.	taniré	mis	méch	med	mirivé	éziné	brima ξ	ti	tès		
	Prends	*un*	*crayon*	*pour*	*tracer*	*mes*	*pa-roles*	*de*	*cet*		
	tensée	**—**	**azini**	**dé**	**améir**	**mazi**	**si**	**somé**	**iche**	**nazina**	
	instant.		*Alors*	*tu*	*vien-dras*	*avec*	*moi*	*admir-er*	*no-tre*	*nou-veau*	
	tranéï.	**—**	**Siman-dini**	**cé**	**kié**	**mach e**	**di**	**pédrin é**	**tès**	**luné**	**ké c é**
	pas-sage.		*Simandi-ni,*	*je*	*ne*	*puis*	*te*	*quitter*	*ce*	*jour.*	*Qu je e*
	êvé	**diviné**	**—**	**pa-trinèz**	**kié**	**ni-puné**	**ani**				
	suis	*heu-reux!*	**—**	*Alors*	*ne*	*crains*	*pas!*				

Take a pencil to trace my words of this moment. Then thou wilt come with me to admire our new passage. Simandini, I cannot leave thee this day. How happy I am!—Then fear not!

Graphic. September 12, 1897 (translated same seance).—See p. 207 and Fig. 23.

* 18. modé   tatinée lâmi   mis mirâ   ti   ché   bigâ   kâ
     Mère   chérie, voici un adieu de   ton   enfant   qui
     ébrinié sanâ   é   vi idé   di   zé   rénir   — zé mess métich kâ é
     pense   tant   à   toi. On   te   le   portera,   le grand homme qui a
     zé   valini iminé — ni   z [é] grani sidiné
     le   visage mince et   le   corps maigre.

My dearest, this is a farewell from thy child, who thinks so much of thee. The big man, who has a thin face and a slender body, will bear it to thee.

Fig. 25. Text No. 18 (October 10, 1897), written in pencil by Mlle. Smith, incarnating Esenale. Reproduction in autotype two-thirds of the natural size.

Auditive, then Graphic. October 10, 1897 (translated same seance).— Hélène has a vision of a Martian landscape, in which Esenale floats discarnate around the plants and speaks these words, which she repeats. (It is understood from the translation that this text was intended for Mme. Mirbel, who was then in the country, but to whom the person very clearly indicated by the final characteristic was about to pay a visit and could carry the message.) I then offer Hélène a pencil in the hope of obtaining this same text in writing; after various tergiversations and grimaces, denoting a state of increasing somnambulism, she finally takes the pencil between her index and middle fingers, tells Esenale that she still sees him and makes him sit down by her side, and then begins to write, completely absent and fascinated by the paper. The left index-finger (Leopold) informs us that it is Esenale himself who is writing by means of Hélène's arm. Twice she interrupts herself in order to say to Esenale, "Oh! do not go yet, stay a little while longer!" She appears nervous and agitated, and often stops writing to stab her paper with her pencil or to make erasures or scribble on it (see Fig. 25); in the **zé** of the last line, she forgets the **é** (this did not prevent Esenale from pronouncing the word correctly at the time of its translation).

Fig. 26. Text No. 26 (August 21, 1898), which appeared in visual hallucination, and was copied by Mlle. Smith. Reproductions in autotype.

19.	m [en]	cé	kié	mache	di	triné	sandiné	téri	
	(Amie,	je	ne	puis	te	parler	longtemps	comme	
	né	êzi	vraïni	zou	réch	mirâ	milé	piri	mirâ
	est	mon	désir;	plus	tard,	adieu			adieu.)

(Friend, I cannot speak to thee a long time, as is my desire; later, farewell, farewell!)

Graphic, then Auditive. October 24, 1897 (there has never been any translation of this text, two words of which are still unknown).—Hélène first sees the table illumined by a green light in which some designs appear which she copies, and which give this text, except the two last letters of the first word, the place of which remains blank. Immediately after she hears Martian spoken, which she repeats. It is the same text; then she has a vision of Astané, Esenale, and a little girl whose name she hears as Niké; but this soon gives way to other non-Martian somnambulisms. (See Fig. 25.)

20	**Siké**	**évaï**	**diviné**	**zé**	**niké**	**crizi**	**capri**	**né**	**am é**		
.	Siké,	sois	heu-reux!	Le	petit	oiseau	noir	est	ve-nu		
	orié	**antéc h**	**é**	**êzé**	**carimi**	**ni**	**êzi**	**érié**	**é**	**nié**	**pa-vinée**	**he d**
	frapper	hier	à	ma	fenêtr e,	et	mon	âme	a	été	joyeus e;	il
	lé	**sadri**	**dé**	**zé**	**véchir**	**tiziné**	**Matê mi**	**mi-saïmé**	**kâ**	**lé**		
	me	chan-ta:	tu	le	verras	de-main.—	Matê mi,	fleur	qui	me		
	amèz	**es-saté**	**Arvâ**	**ti**	**éziné**	**udâniξ**	**amès**	**tès**	**uri**	**amè s**		
	fais	vivre,	soleil	de	mes	songes,	viens	ce	soir ,	vien s		
	sandiné	**ten**	**ti**	**si**	**évaï**	**divinée**		**Romé**	**va**	**né**	**Siké**	
	long-temps	près	de	moi;	sois	heu-reuse!	—	Romé,	où	est	Siké? —	
	atrizi	**ten**	**té**	**taméch**	**épizi**							
	Là-bas,	près	du	"taméch e"	rose.							

Siké, be happy! The little black bird came yesterday rapping at my window, and my soul was joyful; he sang to me: Thou wilt see him to-morrow. Matêmi, flower which makes me live, sun of my dreams, come this evening; come for a long time to me; be happy!—Romé, where is Siké?—Yonder, near the "taméche" rose.

Auditive, then Graphic. November 28, 1897 (translated same seance).—Fragments of conversation heard during the vision of the Martian *fête* described on p. 185. Siké (a young man) and Matêmi (a young girl) form the first couple who pass by and walk off in the direction of a large bush with red flowers (**tamèche**); then a second couple exchange the last words of the text while going to rejoin the first. After this vision, which she contemplated standing and described with much animation, Hélène seated herself and began to write the same Martian phrases. It is ascertained from

Leopold that it was Astané who held her hand (in holding the pencil between the thumb and the index-finger—that is, after the manner of Leopold and not that of Hélène as she had held it in writing text No. 17). The writing being finished, Leopold directs that Hélène shall be made to seat herself on the couch for the scene of translation.

21.	véchêsi	têsée	polluni	avé	métiche	é	vi	ti
	Voyons	*cette*	*question,*	*vieux*	*homme;*	*à*	*toi*	*de*
	bounié	**seïmiré**	**ni**	**triné**				
	chercher,	*comprendre*	*et*	*parler.*				

Now this question, old man; it is for thee to seek, to understand and speak.

Auditive. January 15, 1898 (translated February 13).—Fragment of conversation between two Martian personages seen in a waking vision.

22.	**astané**	**cé**	**amès**	**é vi**	**chée brimi**	**messé téri**
	Astané,	*je*	*viens*	*â toi; ta*	*sagesse grande comme*	
	ché	**pocrimé lé...**				
	ton	*savoir me...*				

Astané, I come to thee; thy great wisdom as well as thy knowledge to me. .

Auditive. About January 25, 1898 (translated February 13).—Vision, at six o'clock in the morning, of a young Martian girl (Matêmi?) traversing a tunnel through a mountain and arriving at the house of Astané, to whom she addresses this utterance, followed by many others which Hélène could not grasp with sufficient distinctness to note them down.

23 [A].		pa-niné	évaï	kirimé	zé	miza	ami	grini		
		Pa-nine,	*sois*	*pru-dent,*	*le*	*"miza"*	*va*	*soulev-er;*		
	ké	chée	éméche	rès	pazé—	[B]	pouzé	tès	lun é	sou-mini
	que	*ta*	*main*	*se*	*re-tire!—*		*Pouzé*	*ce*	*jour*	*riant. .*
	arvâ	ii	cen	zé	primi	ti	ché	chiré	kiz	pavi	luné

—

Arva	si	beau. .	le	revoir	de	ton	fils...	que l	heureux	jour —
[C]	saïné	êzi	chiré	izé	linéï	kizé	pavi	êzi	mané	
	Saïné,	mon	fils,	enfin	debout!	quelle joie!...		Mon	père	
ni	êzé	modé	tiziné	êzi	chiré	êzi	mané	cé	êvé	adi
et	ma	mère. .	Demain,	mon	fils...	Mon	père,	je	suis	bien

anâ

maintenant.

Paniné, be prudent, the "miza" is about to arise; remove thy hand! Pouzé, this laughing day... Arva so beautiful... The return of thy son... What happy day—Saïné, my son, finally standing! What joy!... My father and my mother... To-morrow, my son... my father, I am well now.

Auditive. February 20, 1.898 (translated same seance).—Very complicated Martian vision. First, three small, movable houses, like pavilions or Chinese kiosks, going about on little balls; in one of these, two unknown personages, one of whom puts her hand out of a small oval window, which occasions, on the part of her companion, the observation of the first sentence (A) of the text; at this instant, in fact, these rolling pavilions (**miza**) assume an oscillatory movement, which makes a noise like "tick-tack," and then glide like a train upon rails. They go around a high red mountain and come into a sort of magnificent gorge or ravine, with slopes covered with extraordinary plants, and where they find white houses on an iron framework resembling piles. The two men then alight from their "**miza**," chatting together, but Hélène can only hear fragments (B) of their conversation. A young man of sixteen to eighteen years of age comes to meet them, who has his head tied up in a kind of nightcap, and having no hair on the left side. Martian salutations are exchanged; they mutually strike their heads with their hands, etc. Hélène complains of hearing very confusedly that which they are saying, and can only repeat ends of sentences (C). She has pain in her heart, and Leopold dictates to me by the left index-finger, "*Put her to sleep*," which presently leads to the customary scene of translation of the text.

24.	saïné	êzi	chiré	iée	êzé	pavi	ché	vinâ	ine	ruzzi
	Saïné,	mon	fils,	toute	ma	joie,	ton	retour	au	milieu

ti	nini	né	mis	mess	assilé	atimi...	itéche...
de	nous	est	un	grand,	immense	bonheur...	toujours...
furimir...	nori						
aimera...	jamais.						

Saïné, my son, all my joy; thy return to our circle is a great, an immense happiness... always will love... ever.

Auditive. March 11, 1898 (translated August 21).—"Yesterday morning, on jumping out of bed," wrote Hélène to me, when sending me this text, "I had a vision of Mars, almost the same as that which I had before (at the seance of February 20). I saw again the rolling pavilions, the houses on piling, several personages, among them a young man who had no hair on one side of his head. I was able to note some words. It was very confused, and the last words were caught on the wing, when here and there something a little clear came to me..."

25.	**dé**	**véchi**	**ké**	**ti**	**éfi**	**mervé**	**éni**
	Tu	vois	que	de	choses	superbes	ici.

Thou seest what superb things (are) here.

Auditive. August 21, 1898 (translated same seance).—Waking vision of a river between two rose-colored mountains, with a bridge (like that in Fig. 9) which lowered itself into the water and disappeared in order to allow five or six boats to pass (like that in Fig. 13), then reappeared and was restored to its place. As Hélène describes all this, she hears a voice speaking to her the above Martian words of the text.

26.	**Astané**	**né**	**zé**	**ten**	**ti**	**vi**
	Astané	est	là	près	de	toi.

Astané is there, near to thee.

Visual. August 21, 1898 (translated same seance).—Following the preceding scene: Hélène perceives "in the air" (illumined and red—that of her Martian vision) some characters unknown to her, which she copies (see Fig. 26). I ask her, showing her the word **zé** (which elsewhere always stands for *le*), if she is not mistaken. She verifies it by comparing it with the imaginary model before her and affirms it to be correct.

27.	siké	kiz	crizi	han-tiné	hed	é	ébri-nié	rès	amêr	é			
	Siké,	*quel*	*oiseau*	*fidèle !*	*il*	*a*	*pensé*	*se*	*réu-nir*	*à*			
	nini	éssaté	ti	iche	atimi	matê-mi	han-tiné	hed	né				
	nous,	*vivre*	*de*	*notre*	*bon-heur!*	*— Matê-mi*	*fidèle,*	*il*	*est*				
	han-tiné	êzi	darié	siké	tès	ousti	ké	zé	badêni	las-suné			
	fidèle	*mon*	*cœur!*	*—*	*Siké,*	*ce ba-teau*	*que*	*le*	*vent*	*ap-proche*			
	mazi	trima-zi	hed	é	ti	zi	mazêt	é	po-viné	é	nini	z	priâ é ni
	avec	*force!*	*il*	*a*	*de*	*la*	*peine*	*à*	*ar-river*	*à*	*nous;*	*le flot*	
	é	fou-miné	ivraïni	idé	é	ti zi	mazêté	é	vizêné	zé			
	est	*puis-sant*	*au-jourd'hui;*	*on*	*a*	*de la*	*peine*	*à*	*distin-guer*	*le*			
	chodé												
	"chod é."												

Siké, what (a) faithful bird! he has thought to reunite himself to us, to live of our happiness!—Matêmi faithful, my heart is faithful!—Siké, this boat which the wind brings near with force! it has some difficulty in reaching us; the current is strong to-day; one has some difficulty in distinguishing the "chodé."

Auditive. About the 4th of September, 1898 (translated October 16).— Hélène heard and noted this phrase at the same time at which she had the vision of the two young Martian people who were walking in a kind of flower-garden, and saw a boat arrive, like that in Fig. 13. The meaning of **chodé** has not been ascertained.

Fig. 27. Text No. 28 (October 8, 1898), written by Mlle. Smith, copying a text of Matêmi, seen in a visual hallucination. [The slight tremor of some of the lines is not in the original, but occurred in the copying of the text in the ink, which was written in pencil and too pale for reproduction.]

28	men	mess	Astané	cé	amès	é	vi	itéch	li	tès	
	Ami	grand	Astané,	je	viens	à	toi	toujours	par	cet	
	alizé	néümi	assilé	kâ	ianiné	êzi	atèv	ni	lé		
	élément	mystérieux,	immense,	qui	enveloppe	mon	étre	et	me		
	tazié	é	vi	med	iéeε	éziné	rabriε	ni	tibraε.	men	amès d i
	lance	à	toi	pour	toutes	mes	pensées	et	besoins.	Ami,	viens t s e
	ouradé	ké	Matêmi	uzénir	chée	kida	ni	ké	chée	brizi	pi

souve-nir	que	Matêmi	atten-dra	ta	fa-veur,	et	que	ta	sa-gesse	lui
déza-nir.	évaï	diviné	tès	luné						
répon-dra.	Sois	heu-reux	ce	jour.						

Friend great Astané, I come to thee always by this element, mysterious, immense, which envelops my being and launches me to thee by all my thoughts and desires. Friend, come thou to remember that Matêmi will await thy favor, and that thy wisdom will answer him. Be happy to-day.

Visual. October 3, 1898 (translated October 16).—At a quarter before nine in the evening Mlle. Smith, desiring to obtain a communication from Leopold for herself and her mother, sat down in an easy-chair and gave herself up to meditation. Presently she hears the voice of Leopold telling her that he cannot manifest himself that evening, but that something much more interesting and important is being made ready. The room seems to her to become completely obscured, except the end of the table at which she is sitting, which is illumined with a golden light. A young Martian girl in a yellow robe and with long tresses then comes and seats herself beside her and begins to trace, without ink or paper, but with a point on the end of her index-finger, black figures on a white cylinder, at first placed on the table, afterwards on her knees, and which is unrolled as she writes. Hélène is near enough to see the characters clearly, and copies them in pencil on a sheet of paper (see Fig. 27), after which the vision vanishes and her mother and the room reappear.

29.	sazêni	kiché	nipunêzé	dodé		né	pit	léziré		bèz	
	Sazeni	pourquoi	craindre?	Ceci		est	sans	souffrance		ni	
	neura	évaï	dastrée	firêzi		zé	bodri	né		dorimé	zé
	danger,	sois	paisible;	certainement	le	os		est		sain,	le
	pastri	tubré	né	tuxé							
	sang	seul	est	malade.							

Sazeni, why fear? This is without suffering or danger, be peaceful; certainly the flesh is well, the blood alone is ill.

Auditive. October 14, 1898 (translated October 16).—Morning vision of an unknown gentleman and lady, the latter having her arm, spotted with red, applied to an instrument with three tubes placed on a shelf fastened to the wall. These words were spoken by the man; the lady said nothing.

30.	modé	ké	hed	oné	chandêné	têsé	mûné	ten	ti
	Mère,	que	ils	sont	délicieux	ces	moments	près	de
	vi	bigâ	va	bindié	idé	ti	zâmé	tensée	zou réche
	toi!—	Enfant,	où	trouve	on		de	meilleurs	instants? plus tard
	med	ché	atèv	kiz	fouminé	zati			
	pour	ton	être	quel	puissant	souvenir.			

Mother, how delightful they are, these moments near to thee!—Child, where finds one better moments? later for thy being what (a) powerful remembrance.

Auditive. October 22, 1898 (translated December 18).—"At a quarter-past six in the morning; vision of a pebbly shore; earth of a red tint; immense sheet of water, of a bluish green. Two women are walking side by side. This was all I could gather of their conversation."

Fig. 28. Text No. 31 (October 27, 1898), written by Mlle. Smith, incarnating Ramié. Natural size.

31	Râmié	bisti	ti	Espênié	ché	dimé	ûni	zi
	Ramié	habi-tant	de	Espênié,	ton	sembla-ble	par	la
	trima-zi	tié	vadâzâȿ	di	anizié	bana	mirâȿ.	Ramié di
	force	des	"vada-	te	en-	trois	adieux	Ramié, t

trinir	tié	zas,"	ti	voie	.		e	
		toumaƺ		bé	animinâ	ni	tiche	di uzir nâmi
parle-ra	des	charmes	de	sa	existence	et	bi-entôt	t di-e ra beau-coup
ti	Espênié	évaï	divinée					
.								
de	Espênié	Sois	heu-reuse!					

Ramié, dweller in Espénié, thy like, by the force of the " vadazas," sends thee three adieux. Ramié will speak to thee of the charms of his existence, and presently will tell thee much of Espénié. Be happy!

Graphic. October 27, 1898 (translated December 18).—"Ten minutes to one in the afternoon. No vision, but a severe cramp in the right arm and a strong impulse to take pencil and paper. I write, I know not why." (It is seen by the translation given two months later that the text refers to the first manifestation of Ramié and is an announcement of the ultra-Martian vision which came a few days later.) See Fig. 28. The term **vadazas**, which has never been explained, has not a Martian appearance, and appears to have been borrowed from the Hindoo cycle. As to *Espénié*, see text No. 6.

32	**anâ**	évaï	maniké	é	bétiné	mis	tié	attanâ	
.	Mainte-nant	sois	attentive	à	regard-er	un	de s	monde s	
	kâ	di	médinié	bétinié	tès	tapié	ni	bée	atèv kavivé
	qui	te	entou-rent.	Re-garde	ce	"ta-pié"	et	ses	être s étranges .
	danda	anâ							
	Silence	mainte-nant!							

Now be attentive to behold one of the worlds which surround thee. Look at that " tapié" and its strange beings. Silence now!

Auditive. November 2, 1898 (translated December 18).—Hélène has a morning vision of a Martian (Ramié) who encircles her waist with one arm and with the other shows her, while speaking these words, a strange tableau (**tapié**) containing extraordinary beings speaking the unknown language of the following text. At the moment the vision is effaced Hélène writes, without perceiving that she has done so, text No. 34. (For further details, see the following chapter on the Ultra-Martian.)

33. BAK	SANAK	TOP		ANOK	SIK	
sirima	**nêbé**	**viniâ-ti-mis-métiche**		**ivré**	**toué**	
rameau	vert	nom		de	un	homme sacré dans p.234
ÉTIP	VANÉ	SANIM		BATAM	ISSEM	TANAK
viniâ-ti-misé-bigâ	**azâni**	**maprinié**		**imizi**	**kramâ**	**ziné**
nom de une enfant	mal	entré		sous	panier	bleu
VANEM	SÉBIM	MAZAK		TATAK	SAKAM	
viniâ-ti-mis-zaki	**datrinié**	**tuzé**		**vâmé**	**gâmié**	
nom de un animal	caché	malade		triste	pleure.	

Branch green—name of a man—sacred—in—name of a child—bad—entered—under—basket—blue—name of an animal—hidden—ill—sad—weeps.

Auditive, as to the non-Martian text (see following chapter) which Hélène heard spoken on the 2d of November by the strange beings of the tableau of the preceding vision. Vocal, as to the Martian translation of this text, which was given by Astané (incarnated in Hélène and speaking the unknown language by her mouth, followed by its Martian equivalent for each word), in the seance of the 18th of December, 1898. Immediately after, Astané yielded his place to Esenale, who in turn repeated the Martian phrase, translating it word for word into French by the customary process.

Fig. 29. Text No. 34 (November 2, 1898), written by Mlle. Smith, incarnating Ramié. Natural size.

34. **Ramié di**		pédrinié	anâ	né	ériné	diviné			
Ramié	*te*	*quitte*	*maintenant,*	*est*	*satisfait,*	*heureux* p. 235			
té	mûné	ten	ti	vi.	hed	dassinié	mis abadâ		ti ché
du	*moment*	*près*	*de*	*toi.*	*Il*	*garde*	*un pelt*		*de ton*
atèv	ni	di	parêzié	banâ mirâ§.		—	évaï divinée		
être	*et*	*te*	*laisse*	*trois adieux.*			*Sois heureuse!*		

Ramié leaves thee now, is satisfied, happy for the moment near to thee. He retains a little of thy being and leaves thee three adieux. Be happy.

Graphic. November 2, 1898 (translated December 18).—Hélène only perceived after its accomplishment that her hand, which she felt "firmly held," had written this text at the close of the preceding vision (see Fig. 29).

35. [A]		attanâ	zabiné	pi	ten té	iche	tarvini	mabûré	
		Monde	*arriéré,*	*très*	*près du*	*nôtre,*	*langage*	*grossier,*	
nubé	téri	zée	atèv	[B]	Astané	êzi	dabé	fouminé	ni
curieux	*comme*	*les*	*être!—*		*Astané,*	*mon*	*maître*	*puissant*	*et*
ié	ti	takâ	tubré	né	bibé	ti	zé	umêzé	
tout	*de*	*pouvoir,*	*seul*	*est*	*capable*	*de*	*le*	*faire.*	

Hidden world, very near to ours, coarse language, curious like the beings.— Astané, my powerful master and all powerful, alone is capable of doing it.

Fig. 30. Text No. 37 (March 24, 1899), written by Mlle. Smith, incarnating Astané. [Collection of M. Lemaître.] Owing to a defect of the stereotype plate a dot is lacking on the first letter.

Auditive. December 5, 1898 (translated December 18).—Working by lamplight at seven o'clock in the morning, Hélène again had a vision of the

Martian (Ramié) who had clasped her waist with one arm while showing her something with a gesture of the other (probably the tableau of the preceding vision, though Hélène did not see it) and uttering the first phrase of it (A). The second phrase (B) is the reply of this same Martian to a mental question of Hélène asking him to translate the strange language of the other day. (She trust, therefore, have understood the meaning of the first phrase in order to have replied to it by her appropriate mental question.)

36 [A]	aé	aé	aé	aé	lassunié	lâmi	rêzé	aé	aé	aé
	Aé,	aé,	aé,	aé!—	Approche;	voici	Rêzá...	aé,	aé,	aé,
aé	niké	bulié	va	né	ozâmié	zitêni	primêni —[B]	ozâmié		
aé,	petit	Bulié...	où	est	Ozamié?	Zitêni ,	Primêni. .	Ozamié,		
viniâ	ti	mis	bigâ	kêmâ	zitêni	viniâ	ti	misé	bigâ	kêmisi
nom	de	un	enfant	mâle;	Zitêni,	nom	de	une	enfant	femelle;
primêni	viniâ	ti	misé	bigâ	kêmisi					
Priméni ,	nom	de	une	enfant	femelle.					

Aé, aé, aé, aé! Approach, here is Rézá, aé, aé, aé, aé, little Bulié. . . where is Ozamié? Zitêni, Primêni. . . Ozamié, name of a male child; Zitêni, name of a female child; Primêni, name of a female child.

Fig. 31. Text No. 38 (March 30, 1899), written by Mlle. Smith copying a text of Ramié, who appeared to her in a visual hallucination. [Collection of M. Lemaître.]

Auditive. March 8, 1899 (translated June 4).—Hélène heard the phrase (A) during the vision of which the description follows. At the translation, as the sitters did not at once understand that the three first words are proper names, Esenale adds the phrase (B) with its French signification. "I was unable to go to sleep yesterday evening. At half-past eleven everything around me was suddenly lighted up, and the vivid light permitted me to distinguish surrounding objects. I arose this morning with a very clear remembrance of that which I then saw. A tableau was formed in that light, and I had more before me than the interior of a Martian house—an immense square hall, around which shelves were fastened, or rather little tables suspended and fastened to the wall. Each of these tables contained a baby, but not at all bundled up; all the movements of these little infants were free, and a simple linen cloth was thrown round the body. They might be said to be lying on yellow moss. I could not say with what the tables were covered. Some men with strange beasts were circulating round the hall; these beasts had large flat heads, almost without hair, and large, very soft eyes, like those of seals; their bodies, slightly hairy, resembled somewhat those of roes in our country, except for their large and flat tails; they had large udders, to which the men present fitted a square instrument with a tube, which was offered to each infant, who was thus fed with the milk of these beasts. I heard cries, a great hurly-burly, and it was with difficulty that I could note these few words [of this text]. This vision lasted about a quarter of an hour; then everything gradually disappeared, and in a minute after I was in a sound sleep."

37.	**Astané**	**bounié**	**zé**	**buzi**	**ti**	**di**	**triné**	**nâmi**	**ni**
	Astané	cherche	le	moyen	de	to	parler	beaucoup	et
	ti	**di**	**umêzé**	**séïmiré**	**bi**	**tarvini**			
	de	to	faire	comprendre	son	langage.			

Astané searches for the means to speak to thee much and to make thee understand his language.

Graphic. March 24, 1899 (translated June 4). "Half-past six in the morning. Vision of Astané. I was standing, about to put on my slippers. He spoke to me, but I could not understand him. I took this sheet of paper and a pencil; he spoke to me no more, but seized my hand which held the pencil. I wrote under this pressure; I understood nothing, for this is as Hebrew to me. My

38.	fédié	amès	Ramié	di	uzénir	tès	luné	amès	zé
	Fédié,	viens;	Ramié	te	attendra	ce	jour;	viens,	le
	boua	trinir							
	frère	parlera.							

Fédié, come; Ramié will await thee to-day; come, the brother will speak.

Visual. March 30, 1899 (translated June 4).—Seated at her toilet-table, at half-past nine o'clock in the evening, Hélène found herself suddenly enveloped in a rose-colored fog, which hid one part of the furniture from her, then was dissipated, allowing her to see, at the farther end of her room, "a strange hall, lighted with rose-colored globes fastened to the wall." Nearer to her appeared a table suspended in the air, and a man in Martian costume, who wrote with a kind of nail fastened to his right index-finger. "I lean towards this man; I wish to place my left hand on this imaginary table, but my hand falls into empty space, and I have great difficulty in restoring it to its normal position. It was stiff, and for some moments felt very weak." Happily the idea occurred to her to take pencil and paper and copy "the characters which the Martian, whom I had seen several times before [Ramié], traced; and with extreme difficulty—since they were much smaller than mine—I succeeded in reproducing them" (the Martian text of Fig. 31). All this lasted about a quarter of an hour. I went immediately to bed, and saw nothing more that evening, nor on the following day."

Fig. 32. Text No. 39 (April 1, 1899), written by Mlle. Smith, incarnating Ramié. [Collection of M. Lemaître.] Natural size.

39. Ramié   pondé acâmi   andélir   téri   antéch

Ramié,	savant	astronome,	apparaîtra	comme	hier			
iri	**é**	**vi**	**anâ.**	**riz**	**vi**	**banâ mirâƺ**	**ti**	**Ramié ni**
souvent	à	toi	maintenant.	Sur	toi	trois adieux	de	Ramié et
Astané.	**évaï**	**divinée**						
Astané.	Sois	heureuse!						

Ramié, learned astronomer, will appear as yesterday often to thee now. Upon thee three adieux from Ramie and Astané. Be happy*!

Graphic. April 1, 1899 (translated June 4).—"Again, on going to bed at five minutes past ten, a new vision of the personage seen day before yesterday [Ramié]. I thought he was about to speak, but no sound issued from his lips. I quickly take pencil and paper, and feel my right arm seized by him, and I begin to trace the strange handwriting attached hereto (see Fig. 32). He is very affectionate; his bearing, his look, everything breathes both goodness and strangeness. He leaves me really charmed."

40	**ramié**	**ébanâ**	**dizênâ**	**zivêni**	**ni**	**bi**	**vraïni**			
.	Ramié,	lente-ment,	profondé-ment,	étu-die,	et	son	désir			
	assilé	**né**	**ten**	**ti**	**rès**	**kalâmé**	**as-tané**	**êzi**	**dabé**	**né zi**
	im-mense	est	près	de	se	accom-plir.	As-tané	mon	maítre	es l t à
	med	**lé**	**godané**	**ni**	**ankôn é**	**évaï**	**bané**	**ziza-zi**	**divinée**	
	pour	me	aider	et	réjouir.	Sois	trois	fois	heu-reuse!	

Ramié, slowly, deeply studies, and his great desire is near to being accomplished. Astané, my master, is there to aid me and to rejoice. Mayst thou be thrice happy!

Auditive. June 4, 1899 (translated same seance).Hemisomnambulism, in which Hélène, without having a vision, hears a voice addressing words to her, from which, with some difficulty, she collected the preceding sentences.

41. To these texts, forming sentences, in order to complete the whole, some isolated words must be added, gathered on various occasions, the meaning of which is obtained with sufficient certainty, either from the French context in which they were framed, or from Hélène's description of the objects which they designated These words are **chèke**, *papier* ("paper"); **chinit**, *bague* ("ring"); **asnète**, *espèce de paravent* ("kind of screen"). **Anini Nikaîné**, proper name of a little girl (see p. 176), probably the Martian sister of Esenale, who floats beside her, invisible to her, and watches over her during an illness, after the fashion of spirit protectors. **Béniel**, proper name of our earth, as seen from Mars (which is called **Durée** in texts 7 and 9).

III. REMARKS ON THE MARTIAN LANGUAGE

Provided the reader has given some attention to the foregoing texts, if only to the two first, he undoubtedly will have been easily satisfied as to the pretended language of the planet Mars, and perhaps will be astonished that I have spent so much time upon it. But, as many of the *habitués* of the seances of Mlle. Smith—and, naturally, Mlle. Smith herself—hold seriously to its authenticity, I cannot absolve myself from stating why the "Martian" is, in my opinion, only an infantile travesty of French. Even in default of the astronomical importance which is claimed for it on the authority of Leopold, this idiom preserves all the psychological interest which attaches to automatic products of subconscious activities of the mind, and it well deserves some minutes of examination.

It is necessary at the start to render this justice to the Martian (I continue to designate it by that name, for the sake of convenience)—namely, that it is, indeed, a language and not a simple jargon or gibberish of vocal noises produced at the hazard of the moment without any stability. It cannot be denied the following characteristics—First: It is a harmony of clearly articulated sounds, grouped so as to form words. Secondly: These words when pronounced express definite ideas. Thirdly, and finally: Connection of the words with the ideas is continuous; or, to put it differently, the signification of the Martian terms is permanent and is maintained (apart from slight inconsistencies, to which I will return later on) from one end to the other of the texts which have been collected in the course of these three years.[1] I will add that in speaking fluently and somewhat quickly, as Hélène sometimes does in somnambulism (texts 4, 11, 15, etc.), it has an acoustic quality altogether its own, due to the predominance of certain sounds, and has a peculiar intonation difficult to describe. Just as one distinguishes by ear foreign languages which one does not understand, the whole dialect possessing a peculiar accent which causes it to be recognized, so in this case one perceives, from the first syllables uttered, whether Hélène is speaking Hindoo or Martian, according to the musical connection, the rhythm, the choice of consonants and vowels belonging to each of the two idioms. In this the Martian, indeed, bears the stamp of a natural language. It is not the result of a purely intellectual calculation, but influences of an æsthetic order, emotional factors, have combined in its creation and instinctively directed the choice of its assonances and favorite terminations. The Martian language has certainly not been fabricated in cold blood during the normal, habitual, French (so to speak) state of Mlle. Smith, but it bears in its characteristic tonalities the imprint of a peculiar emotional disposition, of a fixed humor or psychical Orientation, of a special condition of mind, which may be called, in one word, the *Martian* state of Hélène. The secondary personality, which takes pleasure in linguistic games, seems, indeed, to be the same, at its source, as that which delights in the exotic and highly colored visual images of the planet of red rocks, and which animates the personages of the Martian romance.

A glance at the *ensemble* of the foregoing texts shows that Martian, as compared with French, is characterized by a superabundance of *é*, *ê*, and *i*'s, and a scarcity of diphthongs and the nasal sounds. A more accurate statistical table of sounded vowels which strike the ear in reading aloud the Martian texts on the one hand, and their translation into French on the other, gives me the percentages of Table I., which follows. But it is well known that the vowels are distinguished, from the acoustic point of view,

---

[1] If it is objected that the Martian lacks the essential character of a language—that is to say, a practical sanction by use; by the fact of its serving as a means of communication between living beings—I will not answer, like Mlle. Smith, that after all we know nothing about that, but will simply say that the social side of the question does not concern us here. Even if Volapük and Esperanto are not used, they are none the less languages, and the Martian has, in regard to its artificial construction, the psychological superiority of being a natural language, spontaneously created, without the conscious participation, reflective or willing, of a normal personality.

by certain fixed characteristic sounds, and that they are distributed at different heights in the musical scale.

TABLE I.—STATISTICS OF VOWEL SOUNDS

	MARTIAN	FRENCH
a	% 16.3	13.7
e mute (like those of *casemate*)	" 3.6	20.8
e closed or half-closed (like those of *hébété*, *rêvé*)	" 36.9	14.3
e open (like that of *aloès*)	" 2.1	4.6
i	" 34.3	13.4
o	" 2.3	5.7
u	" 2.3	3.1
Diphthongs and nasals (*ou, oi, eu, an, in, on, un*)	" 2.1	24.5

TABLE II.—GROUPING FROM POINT OF VIEW OF HEIGHT

	MARTIAN	FRENCH
Vowels, high (*i* and *e* sounded)	% 73.3	32.3
Vowels, middle (*a* and *o*)	" 18.6	19.4
Vowels, low or hollow (*u*; diphthongs and nasals; *e* mute)	" 8.0	48.4

i and *é* are the highest, *a* and *o* occupy the middle place, *u* and *ou* are found in the lower part of the scale. In adding to the latter, therefore, the nasals, which are always hollow, and also *e* mute, Table I. divides itself into the three groups of Table II. from the point of view of height and sonorousness. It is, therefore, clear that the Martian is of a general tonality much higher than the French; since, while the two languages have almost the same proportion of middle vowels, the low, hollow, or mute sounds, which constitute almost one-half of the French vowels, amount to scarcely one-twelfth in Martian, in which the high sounds, on the contrary, represent in bulk three-quarters of the vowels, against one-third only in the French. On the other hand, researches in the field of colored audition have demonstrated that a close psychological connection exists, based on certain emotional analogies and an equivalence of organic reactions, between the high sounds and the bright or vivid colors, and the low or hollow sounds and the sombre colors. But this same correlation is found in the somnambulistic life of Mlle. Smith, between the brilliant, luminous, highly colored visions which characterize her Martian cycle and the language of the high and sonorous vowels which gushes forth in the same cycle. It is allowable to conclude from this that it is really the same emotional atmosphere which bathes and envelops these varied psychological products, the same personality which gives birth to these visual and phonetic automatisms. The imagination cannot, however, as is easily understood, create its fiction out of nothing; it is obliged to borrow its materials from individual experience. The Martian tableaux are, therefore, only a reflection. of the terrestrial world, but of that part of it which possesses the most warmth and brilliancy—the Orient; in the same way, the Martian language is only French metamorphosed and carried to a higher diapason.

I admit, then, that Martian is a language, and a natural language, in the sense that it is automatically brought forth in the emotional state, or by the secondary personality, which is the source of all the remainder of the cycle without the conscious participation of Mlle. Smith. It remains for me now to mention some of the characteristics which seem to indicate that the inventor of this subliminal linguistic work had never known any idiom other than French, that it is much more sensible to verbal expression than to logical connection of ideas, and that it possesses in an eminent degree that infantile and puerile character which I have already pointed out in the author of the Martian romance. It now becomes necessary to examine rapidly this unknown language, from the point of view of its phonetics and its writing, its grammatical form, its syntax, and its vocabulary.

1. *Martian Phonetics and Handwriting.*—Martian is composed of articulate sounds, all of which, consonants as well as vowels, exist in French. While on this globe languages geographically our neighbors (not to mention those farther away) differ each from the other by certain special sounds—*ch*, German, *th*, English, etc.—the language of the planet Mars does not permit of similar phonetic originalities. It seems, on the contrary, poorer in this respect than the French. As yet I have not found in it the hissing *j* or *ge* (as in *juger*), nor the double sound *x*. Martian phonetics, in a word, are only an incomplete reproduction of French phonetics.

The Martian alphabet, compared with ours, suggests a remarkable analogy. The graphic form of the characters is certainly novel, and no one would divine our letters in these designs of exotic aspect. Nevertheless, each

Martian sign (with the single exception of that of the plural) corresponds to a French sign, although the inverse is not the case, which indicates that here again we are in the presence of a feeble imitation of our system of handwriting.

The twelve written texts upon which I base my comparison comprise about 300 words (of which 160 are different) and 1200 signs. There are altogether twenty-one different letters, all of which have their exact equivalents in the French alphabet, which also has five others which Martian lacks; *j* and *x*, of which the sounds themselves have not been observed, and *q*, *w*, and *y*, of which there is a double use, with *k*, *v*, and *i*. This reduction of graphic material manifests itself in two other details. First, there are neither accents nor punctuation marks, with the exception of a certain sign, resembling the French circumflex, used sometimes in the shape of a point at the end of phrases. In the second place, each letter has only one form, the diversity of capitals and small letters not seeming to exist in Martian. Of ciphers we know nothing.

There are still three small peculiarities to notice:

1. In default of capitals, the initials of proper names are often distinguished by a point placed above the ordinary character.

2. In the case of double letters the second is replaced by a point situated at the right of the first.

3. Finally, there exists, in order to designate the plural of substantives and of some adjectives, a special graphic sign, answering to nothing in the pronunciation and having the form of a small vertical undulation, which reminds one a little of an amplification of the French s, the usual mark of the plural in French. These peculiarities, outside the ordinary form of the letters, constitute the sum total of ingenuity displayed in Martian handwriting.

It must be added that this handwriting, which is not ordinarily inclined, goes from left to right, like the French. All the letters are of nearly the same height, except that the i is much smaller, and that they remain isolated from each other; their assembly into words and phrases offers to the eye a certain aspect of Oriental hieroglyphic inscriptions.

The Martian alphabet never having been revealed as such, we are ignorant of the order in which the letters follow each other. It would seem as though the letters had been invented by following the French alphabet, at least in great part, if one may judge according to the analogies of form of the Martian characters corresponding to certain series of French letters: compare *a* and *b; g* and *h; s* and *t;* and also the succession *k, l, m, n*.

It is in the phonetic value of the letters—that is to say, in the correspondence of the articulated sounds with the graphic signs—that the essentially French nature of the Martian may be seen. The only notable difference to be pointed out here between the two languages is the much greater simplicity of the Martian orthography, resulting in the employment of no useless letters. All are pronounced, even the final consonants, such as *s, n, z*, etc., which are generally silent in French. This gives the impression that the Martian handwriting is moulded on the spoken language, and is only the notation of the articulated sounds of the latter by the most economical means. In so far it realizes the type of a handwriting truly phonetic—that is to say, where each sign corresponds to a certain elementary articulation, constant and invariable, and vice versa. It is full, on the other hand, of equivocations, of exceptions, of irregularities, which make one and the same letter to have very different pronunciations, according to circumstances, and, reciprocally, which causes the same sound to be written in different ways without our being able to perceive any rational explanation for all these ambiguities—were it not for the fact that the very same thing is to be found in French!

Martian is only disguised French. I will mention only the most curious and striking coincidences, all the more striking from the fact that the field from which I have collected them is very limited, being confined to the dozen texts written and pronounced, which contain only 160 different words.

The simple vowels of the Martian alphabet correspond exactly to the five French vowels, *a, e, i, o, u*, and have the same shades of pronunciation.

The Martian *c* plays the triple part which it also fulfils in French. The *s* has the same capricious character as in our language. It is generally hard, but between two vowels it becomes soft, like *z*.

2. *Grammatical Forms.*—The *ensemble* of the texts which we possess does not as yet permit us to make a Martian grammar. Certain indications, however, warrant the prediction that the rules of that grammar, if it ever sees the light of day, will be only the counterpart of, or a parody upon, those of French.

Here, for example, is a list of personal pronouns, articles, possessive adjectives, etc., which have appeared hitherto:

je **cé**	*me* **lé**, *moi* **si**	*ton* **ché**	*ce* **tès**, *ces* **têsé**	*de* **ti**
tu **dé**	*te* **di**, *toi* **vi**	*ta* **chée**	*cette* **tés**, **têsée**	*des* **tié**
il **hed**	*se* **rès**, *lui* **pi**	*tes* **chi**	*le* (pron.) **zé**	*du* **té**
nous **nini**	*mon* **êzi**	*son* **bi**	*qui* **kâ**, *que* **ké**	*au* **ine**
vous **sini**	*ma* **êzé**	*sa* **bé**	*quel* **kiz**, *quelle* **kizé**	
ils **hed**	*mes* **éziné**	*ses* **bée**	*un* **mis**, *une* **misé**	
on **idé**	*notre* **iche**		*le, la, les* (art.) **zé, zi, zée**.	

There are some texts where the feminine is derived from the masculine by the addition of an *e* mute, and the plural by the small, unpronounced sign, which has all the appearance of being a reminiscence of French *s*.

Between these two languages there is another order of points of contact, of a more special interest, because it shows the preponderating rôle which verbal images have often played in the making of Martian to the prejudice of the intrinsic, logical nature of the ideas. I should say that at all times the Martian translates the French word, allowing itself to be guided by auditive analogies without regard to the real meaning, in such a way that we are surprised to discover in the idiom of the planet Mars the same peculiarities of homonyms as in French. It is also the case that two vocables identical as to pronunciation, but of entirely heterogeneous signification, as the preposition *à* and the *a* of the verb *avoir*, are rendered in Martian by the same word, *é*.

Other curious coincidences are to be noted. In French the conjunction *et* only slightly differs, from the point of view of phonic images, from the verb *est;* in Martian also there is a great analogy between **ni** and **né**, which translate these two words. Between the past participle **nié** of the verb *to be* and the conjunction **ni** there is only the difference of an *é*, just as between their French equivalents *été* and *et*.

It must be admitted that all these coincidences would be very extraordinary if they were purely fortuitous.

3. *Construction and Syntax.*—The order of the words is absolutely the same in Martian as in French. This identity of construction of phrases is pursued sometimes into the minutest details, such as the division or amputation of the negation *ne . . . pas* (texts 15 and 17), and also the introduction of a useless letter in Martian to correspond to a French euphemistic *t* (see text 15), **Kèvi bérimir m hed**, *quand reviendra-t-il?* ("when will he return?")

If it is admitted hypothetically that the succession of words, such as is given us in these texts, is not the natural ordering of the Martian language, but an artificial arrangement, like that of juxtalinear translations for the use of pupils, the very possibility of that correspondence absolutely word for word would remain an extraordinary fact without a parallel, since there is not a single language that I know of in which each term of the French phrase is always rendered by *one* term, neither more nor less, of the foreign phrase. The hypothesis referred to is, moreover, inadmissible, since the Martian texts, of which Esenale gives the literal translation, were not previously arranged by him with that end in view; they are the identical words which Mlle. Smith heard and noted in her visions, often weeks and months before Esenale repeats them for the purpose of translating them, and which constitute the conversation, as such, taken from life, of the Martian personages. We must conclude from this that these in their elocution follow step by step and word by word the order of the French language, which amounts almost to saying that they speak a French the sounds of which have simply been changed.

4. *Vocabulary.*—From an etymological point of view, I have not been able to distinguish any rule of derivation, even partial, that would permit the suspicion that the Martian words had come from French words, according to some law. Apart from the entire first text, where it is difficult to deny that the people of Mars have stolen French terms of politeness, at the same time distorting them, no clear resemblance is to be seen between Martian words and the French equivalents; at most, there are traces of borrowing, like **merve**, *superbe*, which might have been abridged from *merveille* (text 25), and **vechi**, an imitation of voir.

Still less does the Martian lexicon betray the influence of other known languages (at least to my knowledge). A term which suggests such similarity is hardly ever met with—*e.g.*, **modé**, *mère* ("mother"), and **gudé** *bon* ("good"), cause us to think of German or English words; **animina** ("existence") is like *anima;* various forms of the verbs *être* and *vivre* ("to be" and "to live"), **êvé**, **évaï**, **essat**, recall the Latin *esse* or the Hebrew *évé*, and that passage of the Biblical story of the Creation where Eve is called the mother of all living beings. A linguist who happened to be at the same time a savant and a humorist would doubtless succeed in lengthening this list of etymologies, after the mode of the eighteenth century. But, *cui bono?* In that rarity of points of contact between the idioms of our terrestrial sphere and the Martian glossary, an argument might be found in favor of the extra-terrestrial origin of the latter, if, on the other hand, it did not seem to betray the influence of the French language from the fact that a notable proportion of its words reproduce in a suspicious manner the same number of syllables or letters as their French equivalents; note, for example, besides the terms of politeness already mentioned, the words **tarvine**, *langage;* **haudan**, *maison;* **dodé**, *ceci;* **valini**, *visage*, etc., and the great majority of the little words, such as **cé**, *je;* **ké**, *que;* **ti**, *de;* **dé**, *tu;* etc.

With the exception of such examples as these, it must be acknowledged that there is no trace of parentage, filiation, of any resemblance whatever between the Martian and French vocabularies, which forms a singular contrast to the close identity which we have established between the two languages in the preceding paragraphs.

This apparent contradiction carries its explanation in itself, and gives us the key to Martian. This fantastic idiom is evidently the naïve and somewhat puerile work of an infantile imagination, to which occurred the idea of creating a new language, and which, while giving to its lucubrations certain strange and unknown appearances, without doubt caused them to run in the accustomed moulds of the only real language of which it had cognizance. The Martian of Mlle. Smith, in other words, is the product of a brain or a personality which certainly has taste and aptitude for linguistic exercises, but which never knew that French takes little heed of the logical connection of ideas, and did not take the trouble to make innovations in the matter of phonetics, of grammar, or of syntax.

The process of creation of Martian seems to have consisted in simply taking certain French phrases as such and replacing each word by some other chosen at random. That is why, especially in the texts at the beginning, the structure of French words is recognized under the Martian. The author herself was undoubtedly struck by it, and from that time exerted herself to complicate her lexicon, to render her words more and more unrecognizable.

This research of originality—which, however, she has never extended beyond the purely material part of the language, never having an idea that there might be other differences in languages—represents an effort of imagination with which she must be credited. Homage must also be rendered to the labor of memorizing, which the making of a dictionary has necessitated. She has sometimes, indeed, fallen into errors; the stability of her vocabulary has not always been perfect. But, finally, after the first hesitation and independently of some later confusions, it gives evidence of a praiseworthy terminological consistency, and which no doubt in time, and with some suggestive encouragement, would result in the elaboration of a very complete language—perhaps even of several languages, as we may augur from text 33, to which we shall return in the following chapter.

5. *Style.*—It remains to investigate the style. If it is true that "manners make the man"—that is to say, not the impersonal and abstract understanding, but the concrete character, the individual temperament, the humor and emotional vibration—we ought to expect to find in the style of the Martian texts the same special stamp which distinguishes the visions, the sound of the language, the handwriting, the personages—in short, the entire romance, that is to say, the curious mixture of Oriental exoticism and of childish puerility of which the secondary personality of Mlle. Smith, at work in this cycle, seems to be composed. It is difficult to pronounce upon these matters of vague æsthetic impression rather than of precise observation; but, as well as I can judge, there seems to me to be in the phraseology of the texts collected an indefinable something which corresponds well with the general character of the entire dream. As these words are evidently first thought in French—then travesties in Martian by a substitution of sounds, the choice of which, as has been seen, apropos of the high tonality of this language, reflects the general emotional disposition—it is, naturally, under their French aspect that we ought to consider them in judging of their actual style. Unfortunately, we do not know how far the translation given by Esenale is identical with the primitive original; certain details seem to hint that there are divergences sometimes. However that may be, it is clearly to be perceived that the literary form of the majority of the texts (taken in French) is more akin to poetry than to prose. While no one of them is in verse, properly speaking, the large number of hemistiches which are met with, the frequency of inversion, the choice of terms, the abundance of exclamations and of broken phrases, betray a great intensity of sentimental and poetic emotion. The same character is found, with a strong shade of exotic and archaic originality, in

the formulas of salutation and farewell ("be happy to-day," "three adieux to thee," etc.), as well as in many expressions and terms of phrases which rather recall the obscure and metaphorical parlance of the Orient than the dry precision of our language of to-day ("*il garde un peu de ton être; cet élément mystérieux, immense,*" etc.)

If, now, it is recollected that everywhere in literary history poetry precedes prose, imagination comes before reason, and the lyric style before the didactic, a conclusion according with that of the preceding paragraphs is reached. Which is, that, by its figures and its style, the Martian language (or the French phrases which serve it for a skeleton) seems to bring to us the echo of a past age, the reflex of a primitive state of mind, from which Mlle. Smith to-day finds herself very far removed in her ordinary and normal states of mind.

IV. MLLE. SMITH AND THE INVENTOR OF MARTIAN

The preceding analysis of the Martian language furnishes its support to the considerations which the content of the romance has already suggested to us in regard to its author (p. 194). To imagine that by twisting the sounds of French words a new language capable of standing examination could actually be created, and to wish to make it pass for that of the planet Mars, would be the climax of silly fatuity or of imbecility were it not simply a trait of naïve candor well worthy of the happy age of childhood.

The whole Martian cycle brings us into the presence of an infantine personality exuberant of imagination, sharing, as to their light, color, Oriental exoticism, the æsthetic tendencies of the actual normal personality of Mlle. Smith, but contrasting with it outside its puerile character in two points to be noted.

First: It takes a special pleasure in linguistic discussions and the fabrication of unknown idioms, while Hélène has neither taste nor facility for the study of languages, which she cordially detests and in which she has never met with success.

Secondly: Notwithstanding this aversion, Hélène possesses a certain knowledge, either actual or potential, of German—in which her parents caused her to take lessons for three years—whereas the author of Martian evidently knows only French. It is, in fact, difficult to believe that, if that author had only a very slight knowledge of the German language (so different from the French by the construction of its sentences, pronunciation, its three genders, etc.), that some reminiscences of it, at least, would not have slipped into its lucubrations. I infer from this that the Martian secondary personality which gives evidence of a linguistic activity so fecund, but so completely subject to the structural forms of the mother-tongue, represents a former stage, ulterior to the epoch at which Hélène commenced the study of German.

If one reflects, on the other hand, on the great facility which Mlle. Smith's father seems to have possessed for languages (see p. 17), the question naturally arises whether in the Martian we are not in the presence of an awakening and momentary display of an hereditary faculty, dormant under the normal personality of Hélène, but which she has not profited from in an effective manner. It is a fact of common observation that talents and aptitudes often skip a generation and seem to pass directly from the grandparents to the grandchildren, forgetting the intermediate link. Who knows whether Mlle. Smith, some day, having obtained Leopold's consent to her marriage, may not cause the polyglot aptitudes of her father to bloom again with greater brilliancy, for the glory of science, in a brilliant line of philologists and linguists of genius?

Meanwhile, and without even invoking a special latent talent in Hélène's case, the Martian may be attributed to a survival or a reawakening under the lash of mediumistic hypnoses of that general function, common to all human beings, which is at the root of language and manifests itself with the more spontaneity and vigor as we mount higher towards the birth of peoples and individuals.

Ontogenesis, say the biologists, reproduces in abridged form and *grosso-modo* phylogenesis; each being passes through stages analogous to those through which the race itself passes; and it is known that the first ages of ontogenic evolution—the embryonic period, infancy, early youth—are more favorable than later periods and adult age to the ephemeral reappearances of ancestral tendencies, which would hardly leave any trace upon a being who had already acquired his organic development. The "poet who died young" in each one of us is only the most common example of those atavic returns of tendencies and of emotions which accompanied the beginnings of humanity, and remain the appanage of infant peoples, and which cause a fount of variable energy in each individual in the spring-time of his life, to congeal or disappear sooner or later with the majority; all children are poets, and that in the original, the most extended, acceptation of the term. They create, they imagine, they construct—and language is not the least of their creations.

I conclude from the foregoing that the very fact of the reappearance of that activity in the Martian states of Hélène is a new indication of the infantile, primitive nature left behind in some way and long since passed by her ordinary personality, of the subliminal strata which mediumistic autohypnotization with her puts in ebullition and causes to mount to the surface. There is also a perfect accord between the puerile character of the Martian romance, the poetic and archaic charms of its style, and the audacious and naïve fabrication of its unknown language.

THE MARTIAN CYCLE (CONCLUDED).—THE ULTRA-MARTIAN

ALL things become wearisome at last, and the planet Mars is no exception to the rule. The subliminal imagination of Mlle. Smith, however, will probably never tire of its lofty flights in the society of Astané, Esenale, and their associates. I myself, I am ashamed to acknowledge, began, in 1898, to have enough of the Martian romance.

Once having satisfied myself as to the essential nature of the Martian language, I did not desire to make a profound study of it, and since the texts had made their appearance so slowly, for two years, as to threaten to continue during the remainder of my natural existence, as well as that of the medium, without coming to an end; finding, on the other hand, that the texts, considered as simple psychological curiosities, varied but little and were at length likely to become burdensome, I decided to try some experiment which, without drying up their source, might at least break through this monotony. Up to that time, without giving a positive opinion as to the Martian, I had always manifested a very real interest in these communications, as well as in Mlle. Smith in her waking state, and in Leopold in his incarnations. Both of these showed themselves fully persuaded of the objective verity of this language, and of the visions which accompanied it. Leopold had not ceased, from the first day, to affirm its strictly Martian authenticity. Hélène, without maintaining absolutely that it came from Mars rather than from any other planet, shared the same faith in the extra-terrestrial origin of these messages; and, as appeared from many details of her conversations and conduct, she saw in it a revelation of the loftiest import, which might some day cause "all the discoveries of M. Flammarion" to sink into insignifance. What would happen if I made up my mind to strike this strange conviction a telling blow, and demonstrate that the pretended Martian was only a chimera, a product, pure and simple, of somnambulistic autosuggestion?

My first tentative experiment, addressed to Leopold, had no appreciable influence on the course of the Martian cycle. It was at the seance of February 13, 1898. Hélène was profoundly asleep, and Leopold was conversing with us by gestures of the arm and spelling on the fingers. I categorically informed him of my certainty that the Martian was of terrestrial fabrication, and that a comparison with the French proved it so to be. As Leopold responded by emphatic gestures of dissent, I detailed to him some evidences, among others the accord of the two languages as to their pronunciation of *ch*, as to the homonym of the pronoun and article *le*. He listened to me, and seemed to understand my arguments, but he refused to admit the force of these characteristic coincidences, and said: "There are some things more extraordinary," and was unwilling to give up the authenticity of the Martian. We stood by our respective opinions, and the later texts do not show any trace of our interview. It seemed, therefore, that it was not through the intervention of Leopold that a modification of the Martian romance was to be suggested.

I allowed some months to pass, then tried a discussion with Hélène while she was awake. On two occasions, in October, 1898, I expressed to her my utter skepticism as to the Martian. The first time, on the 6th of October, in a visit which I made to her outside of any seance, I confined myself to certain general objections to it, to which she replied, in substance, as follows: First, that this unknown language, by reason of its intimate union with the visions, and in spite of its possible resemblances to the French, must necessarily be Martian, if the visions are. Then nothing seriously opposes that actual origin of the visions, and, consequently, of the language itself; since there are two methods of explaining this knowledge of a far-off world—namely, communications properly *spiritistic* (*i.e.*, from spirits to spirits, without material intermediary) the reality of which cannot be held to be doubtful; and clairvoyance, that faculty, or undeniable sixth sense, of mediums which permits them both to see and hear at any distance. Finally, that she did not hold tenaciously to the distinctly Martian origin of that strange dream, provided it is conceded that it comes from somewhere outside herself, it being inadmissible to regard it as the work of her subconsciousness, since she had not, during her ordinary life, absolutely any perception whatever, any sentiment, not the shadow of a hint of that alleged interior work of elaboration to which I persisted in attributing it against all the evidence and all common-sense.

Some days later (October 16th), as Mlle. Smith, perfectly awake after an afternoon seance, passed the evening at my house, and seemed to be in the fulness of her normal state, I returned to the charge with more of insistence.

I had until then always avoided showing her the full translation of the Martian texts, as well as the alphabet, and she only knew by sight, so to speak, the Martian handwriting, and was ignorant of the value of the letters.

This time I explained to her in detail the secrets of the language, its superficial originalities and fundamental resemblances to French: the frequent occurrence of *i* and *e*, its puerile construction, identical with French, even to the slipping in of a superfluous euphonic **m** between the words **bérmier** and **hed** in order to imitate the expression *reviendra-t-il?* its numerous caprices of phonetics and homonyms, evident reflexes of those to which we are accustomed, etc. I added that the visions seemed to me to be also suspicious through their improbable analogies with that which we see on our globe. Supposing that the houses, the vegetation, and the people of Mars were constructed on the same fundamental plan as those here below, it was nevertheless very doubtful whether they had the same proportions and typical aspect; in short, astronomy teaches us that on Mars the physical conditions—the length of the year, the intensity of weight, etc.—are all other than with us: the last point, in particular, should act on all the products, natural and artificial, in such a way as to alter greatly the dimensions as well as the proportions of height and size which are familiar to us. I observed, again, that there are doubtless on Mars, as on the earth, a great variety of idioms, and the singular chance which made Esenale speak a language so similar to French was very astonishing. I concluded, finally, by remarking that all this was easily explicable, as well as the Oriental aspect of the Martian landscapes and the generally infantile character of that romance, if it were regarded as a work of pure imagination, due to a secondary personality or to a dream state of Mlle. Smith herself, who recognized having always had "great taste for that which is original and connected with the Orient."

For more than an hour Hélène followed my demonstration with a lively interest. But to each new reason, after having appeared at first a little disconcerted by it, she did not hesitate to repeat, like a triumphal refrain and as an unanswerable argument, that science is not infallible; that no scientist has yet been on Mars; and that consequently it is impossible to affirm with any certainty that affairs there are not conformable to her visions. To my conclusion she replied that, as far as concerns Mars or anything else, her revelations did not, in any case, spring from sources within herself, and that she did not understand why I was so implacable against that which is the most simple supposition, that of their authenticity, or why I should prefer to it this silly and absurd hypothesis of an underlying self plotting in her, unknown to her, this strange mystification.

Maintaining all the while that my deductions appeared to me strictly correct, I felt bound to admit that science is not infallible, and that a voyage to Mars could alone solve all our doubts as to what takes place there. We parted good friends, but that conversation left me with a very clear impression of the complete uselessness of my efforts to make Mlle. Smith share my conceptions of the subliminal consciousness. But this, however, neither surprises nor grieves me, since from her point of view it is perhaps better that she thus believes.

The following shows, however, that my reasonings on that evening, sterile in appearance, were not without effect. If they have not modified Mlle. Smith's conscious manner of seeing, and, above all, the opinion of Leopold, they have nevertheless penetrated to the profound strata where the Martian visions are elaborated, and, acting there as a leaven, have been the source of new and unexpected developments. This result brilliantly corroborates the idea that the whole Martian cycle is only a product of suggestion and autosuggestion. Just as formerly the regret of M. Lemaître at not knowing that which passes on other planets had furnished the first germ of that lucubration, so now my criticisms and remarks on the language and peoples of that upper world served as a point of departure for new circuits of Hélène's subliminal imagination. If, in fact, the content of our discussion of the 16th of October, which I have above briefly summed up, is compared with the visions of the following months (see beginning with text 30), it is clear that these latter contain an evident beginning of an answer, and are an attempt to satisfy the questions which I raised. A very curious attempt is there made, naïve and infantine, like the whole Martian romance, to escape the defects of which I complained on that occasion, not by modifying and correcting it—that would have been to reverse and to contradict herself—but by going beyond it in some sort, and by superposing upon it a new construction, an *ultra-Martian* cycle, if I may be permitted that expression, hinting at the same time that it unfolds itself on some undetermined planet still farther away than Mars, and that it does not constitute an absolutely independent narrative, but that it is grafted on the primitive Martian romance.

The suggestive effect of my objections of the 16th of October was not immediate, but became a work of incubation. Text 30, coming the following week, differed but slightly from the preceding, save for the absence of a euphonic letter, which, however, had been better in place between the words **bindié idé**, *trouve-t-on*, than in the **bèrimir m hed** of text 15, to which I had attracted Hélène's attention; possibly it is allowable to regard this little detail as a first result of my criticisms. The apparition, a little later, of a new Martian personage, Ramié, who promised Hélène some near revelations as to a planet not otherwise specified (text 31), proves that the ultra-Martian dream was in process of subconscious ripening, but it did not burst forth until the 2d of November (seventeen days after the suggestion with which I connect it), in that curious scene in which Ramié reveals to Mlle. Smith an unsuspected and grotesque world, the language of which singularly differs from the usual Martian. The detailed description of that strange vision, which Hélène sent me, is worth the trouble of citing (see also texts 32 to 35):

"I was awakened, and arose about twenty minutes ago. It was about a quarter-past six in the morning, and I was getting ready to sew. Then, for an instant, I noticed that my lamp was going out, and I ended by not seeing anything more. At the same moment I felt my waist clasped, strongly held by an invisible arm. I then saw myself surrounded by a rose-colored light, which generally shows itself when a Martian vision is coming. I quickly took paper and pencil, which are always within reach on my toilet-table, and placed these two things on my knees, in case some words should come to be noted.

"Hardly were these preparations concluded when I saw at my side a man of Martian visage and costume. It was, in fact, the personage [Ramié] who had clasped my waist with his left arm, showing me with his right hand a tableau, at first indistinct, but which finally outlined itself quite clearly. He spoke also some sentences, which I can note very well, it seems to me [text 32, where Ramié attracts the attention of Hélène to one of the worlds which surround him and makes her see strange beings.]

"I saw then a section of country peopled by men altogether different from those which inhabit our globe. The tallest of all were three feet high, and the majority were an inch or two shorter. Their hands were immense, about ten inches long by eight broad; they were ornamented with very long black nails. Their feet also were of great size.

"I did not see any tree, any bit of verdure. I saw a medley of houses, or rather cabins, of the most simple style, all low, long, without windows or doors; and each house had a little tunnel, about ten feet long [see Fig. 33] running from it into the earth.

Fig. 33. Ultra-Martian houses. Drawn by Mlle. Smith after her vision of November 2, 1898.

"The roofs were flat, supplied with chimneys, or tubes. The men, with arms and bodies bare, had for all clothing only a sort of skirt reaching to the waist and supported by a kind of suspenders thrown over the shoulders, which were apparently very strong. Their heads were very short, being about three inches high by six inches broad, and were close shaven. They had very small eyes, immense mouths, noses like beans. Everything was so different from what we are accustomed to in our world that I should have almost believed it to be an animal rather than a man I saw there, had there not suddenly issued from the lips of one of them some words, which, fortunately—I hardly know how—I was able to note down. This vision lasted a quarter of an hour. Then I found my waist liberated, but my right hand was still firmly held, in order to trace strange characters on the paper" (text 34, adieux of Ramié to Hélène).

A little later there was a continuation, or an abortive repetition, of the same vision; the table did not appear distinctly, and Ramié (text 35) contented himself with teaching Hélène things concerning a world beyond, a near neighbor to Mars, and a coarser language, of which Astané alone could furnish a translation. This is, in effect, what took place two weeks later: Astané incarnated himself with gestures and peculiar spasmodic movements, and repeated (in Hélène's ordinary voice) the barbaric text, followed word by word by its Martian equivalents, which Esenale, in turn, succeeding Astané, interpreted in French, in his customary manner. Leopold also informed us, in reply to a question of one of the sitters, that this uncouth and primitive world was one of the smaller planets; but it is to be presumed that he would also have answered in the affirmative if he had been asked if it were called Phobos or Deimos; and, in short, one of the satellites of Mars would answer better than the asteroids to the globe "very near to ours," of which Ramié spoke.

Up to this point the ultra-Martian messages were confined to the preceding. The last texts obtained (37 to 40) seem to announce that the end has not been reached on that side, and cause us to hope for new revelations, when the astronomer Ramié, as the result of his having studied under the skilful direction of his master Astané, shall be in a position to make further discoveries in the Martian sky. Psychologically speaking, this amounts to saying that the process of latent incubation continues; a new ultra-Martian language is in a state of development in the subliminal depths. If it bursts forth some day, I shall hasten to bring it to the knowledge of the scientific world—in another edition of this book. For the present I limit myself to remarking how much the little ultra-Martian we possess already indicates the wish to answer my questions of the 16th of October.

I had accused the Martian dream of being a mere imitation, varnished with brilliant Oriental colors, of the civilized environment which surrounds us— and here is a world of terrifying grotesqueness, with black soil, from which all vegetation is banished, and the coarser people of which are more like beasts than human beings. I had insinuated that the people and things of that upper world ought really to have other dimensions and proportions than with us—and here are the inhabitants of that farther world veritable dwarfs, with heads twice as broad as they are high, and houses to match. I had made allusion to the probable existence of other languages, referred to the superabundance in Martian of *i* and *e*, impeached its syntax and its *ch*, borrowed from the French, etc.—and here is a language absolutely new, of a very peculiar rhythm, extremely rich in *a*, without any *ch* at all up to the present moment, and of which the construction is so different from the French that there is no method of discovering it.

This latter point, above all, seems to me to present in its apogee the character of childishness and puerility which clearly shows itself in that unexpected appendix to the Martian cycle, as in the entire cycle itself. Evidently the naïve subliminal philologist of Mlle. Smith has been struck by my criticisms on the identical order of the words in Martian and in French, and has endeavored to avoid that defect in her new effort at an unknown language.

But not knowing in just what syntax and construction consist, she has found nothing better to suit her purpose than the substitution of chaos for the natural arrangement of the terms in her thought, and the fabrication of an idiom which had decidedly nothing in common with the French in this respect. Here is where the most beautiful disorder is practically a work of art. It has, moreover, succeeded, since, even with the double translation, Martian and French, of text 33, it is impossible to know exactly what is meant.

It is possibly the little girl *Etip* who is sad, and who *weeps* because the man *Top* has done *harm* to the *sacred* animal *Vanem* (which had *hidden, sick, under* some *green branches*), wishing to *enter in* to a *blue basket*. At least it could not have been the *branch*, the *man*, or the *basket* which was *sacred*, the child *sick*, etc.

The green branch is out of harmony with a world in which, according to Hélène's vision, there were neither trees nor verdure; but Esenale has not specified whether it means *vert* or *ver, vers*, etc., nor whether *caché* and *entré* are participles or infinitives. I leave this rebus to the reader and come to my conclusion, which will be brief, since it accords with the considerations already given at the end of the two preceding chapters.

The whole Martian cycle, with its special language and its ultra-Martian appendix, is only, at bottom, a vast product of occasional suggestions on the part of the environment, and of autosuggestions which have germinated, sprouted, and borne abundant fruit, under the influence of incitement from the outside, but without coming to amount to anything but a shapeless and confused mass, which imposes on one by its extent much more than its intrinsic worth, since it is supremely childish, puerile, insignificant in all aspects, save as a psychological curiosity. The author of this lucubration is not the real adult and normal personality of Mlle. Smith, who has very different characteristics, and who feels herself, in the face of these automatic messages, as though in the presence of something foreign, independent, exterior, and finds herself constrained to believe in their objective reality and in their authenticity. It seems, indeed, rather a former, infantine, less evolved state of Hélène's individuality, which has again come to light, renewed its life, and once more become active in her Martian somnambulisms.

It is hardly necessary to add, in conclusion, that the whole spiritistic or occult hypothesis seems to me to be absolutely superfluous and unjustified in the case of the Martian of Mlle. Smith. Autosuggestibility set in motion by certain stimulating influences of the environment, as we come to see through the history of the ultra-Martian, amply suffices to account for this entire cycle.

THE HINDOO CYCLE

WHILE the Martian romance is purely a work of fantasy, in which the creative imagination was able to allow itself free play through having no investigation to fear, the Hindoo cycle, and that of Marie Antoinette, having a fixed terrestrial setting, represent a labor of construction which was subjected from the start to very complex conditions of environments and epochs. To keep within the bounds of probability, not to be guilty of too many anachronisms, to satisfy the multiple demands of both logic and æsthetics, formed a particularly dangerous undertaking, and one apparently altogether beyond the powers of a person without special instruction in such matters. The subconscious genius of Mlle. Smith has acquitted itself of the task in a remarkable manner, and has displayed in it a truly wonderful and delicate sense of historic possibilities and of local color.

The Hindoo romance, in particular, remains for those who have taken part in it a psychological enigma, not yet solved in a satisfactory manner, because it reveals and implies in regard to Hélène, a knowledge relative to the costumes and languages of the Orient, the actual source of which it has up to the present time not been possible to discover. All the witnesses of Mlle. Smith's Hindoo somnambulisms who are of the same opinion on that subject (several refrain from having any) unite in seeing in it a curious phenomenon of cryptomnesia, of reappearances of memories profoundly buried beneath the normal waking state, together with an indeterminate amount of imaginative exaggeration upon the canvas of actual facts. But by this name of cryptomnesia, or resurrection of latent memories, two singularly different things are understood. For me it is only a question of memories of her present life; and I see nothing of the supernormal in that. For while I have not yet succeeded in finding the key to the enigma, I do not doubt its existence, and I will mention later certain indications which seem to me to support my idea that the Asiatic notions of Mlle. Smith have a wholly natural origin.

For the observer inclined towards spiritism, on the contrary, the sleeping memory which is awakened in somnambulism is nothing less than that of a previous existence of Mlle. Smith, and that piquant explanation, which was first given by Leopold, profits in their eyes from the impossibility which I find in proving that it is anything else.

Doubtless, if one was familiar with all the incidents of Hélène's life from her earliest childhood, and if it were absolutely certain that her knowledge of India had not been furnished her from the outside, through the normal channel of the organs of sense, it would be necessary to seek elsewhere for the solution of the riddle, and to choose between the hypothesis of an atavic memory, hereditarily transmitted across fifteen generations, and actual telepathic communication with the brain of some Indian savant, or a spiritistic reincarnation. But we do not find ourselves in that position. There is nothing less known, in its details, than the daily life of Mlle. Smith in her childhood and youth. But, when all the feats of which the subconscious memory of our present life is capable are considered, it is not scientifically correct to have recourse to a pretended "anteriority," of which the only guarantee is the authority of Leopold, in order to explain the somnambulistic apparitions of facts of which Mlle. Smith in her waking state has no remembrance, I admit, but the origin of which may well have been hidden in the unknown recesses of her past life (reading, conversation, etc.).

The plot of the Hindoo romance, which I have already briefly hinted at on divers occasions, is as follows:

Hélène Smith was, at the end of the fourteenth century of our era, the daughter of an Arab sheik, possibly named Pirux, whom she left in order to become, under the name of Simandini, the eleventh wife of Prince Sivrouka Nayaka, of whom I have the honor to be the actual reincarnation. (I pray the reader once for all to pardon me the immodest rôle which has been imposed upon me in this affair against my will.)

This Sivrouka, who reigned over Kanara, and built there, in 1401, the fortress of Tchandraguiri, does not seem to have been a very accommodating person; although not bad at heart, and quite attached to his favorite wife, he had a wild humor and very uncouth manners. More could not be expected of an Asiatic potentate of that epoch. Simandini, nevertheless, passionately loved him, and at his death she was burned alive on his grave, after the fashion of Malabar.

Around these two principal personages are grouped some secondary figures, among others a faithful domestic named Adèl, and a little monkey,

Mitidja, which Simandini had brought to India with her from Arabia; then the fakir Kanga, who occupies a much more important place in the Martian romance, in which we have seen him reincarnated as Astané, than in the Hindoo cycle.

Some other individuals, all masculine—Mougia, Miousa, Kangia, Kana—appear in obscure rôles, concerning which nothing certain can be said.

The hypnoid states, in which this romance has manifested itself with Hélène, present the greatest variety and all degrees, from the perfect waking state (apparently), momentarily crossed by some visual or auditive hallucination, the memory of which is preserved intact and allows a detailed description, up to total somnambulism, with amnesia upon awakening, in which the most striking scenes of ecstasies or incarnations are unfolded. We shall see divers examples in the following pages.

I. APPARITION AND DEVELOPMENT OF THE ORIENTAL CYCLE

Without recurring to the strange and little-known visions which already haunted the childhood and youth of Mlle. Smith (see pp. 20-25), I will retrace the principal stages of her Asiatic romance from the birth of her mediumship.

During the three first years there were but few manifestations of this sort, in the seances, at least, while as to the automatisms which developed at other times, especially at night, or in the hypnagogic state, we know nothing.

In November, 1892, two seances of the N. group are occupied with the apparition of a Chinese city—Pekin, according to the table—in which a disincarnate spirit, a parent of one of the group, is found performing a mission to a sick child.

In her seances of 1894, Hélène had on several occasions detached visions belonging to the Orient, as appeared from their content, or hints dictated by the table. She also saw Teheran; then the cemetery of the missions at Tokat (June 12th); a cavalier with a white woollen cloak and a turban bearing the name of Abderrhaman (September 2d); and, finally, an Oriental landscape, which depicted a ceremony of Buddhist aspect (October 16th). This latter vision, more especially, seemed to be a forerunner of the Hindoo romance, since the records of the seances of that period show an *ensemble* of characteristic traits which will be again met with in the later Hindoo scenes—*e.g.*, an immense garden of exotic plants, colonnades, rows of palm-trees, with enormous stone lions at the head; rugs of magnificent design, a temple surrounded by trees, with a statue, apparently that of Buddha; a procession of twelve women in white, who kneel, holding lighted lamps; in the centre another woman, with very black hair, detaches herself from the procession, balances a lamp, and burns a powder which expands into a white stone (the continuation of the romance shows this woman to be Simandini, of whom this was the first appearance).

February 17, 1895.—At the end of a rather long seance, the table dictates *Pirux sheik*, and replies to our questions that it refers to an Arab sheik of the fifteenth century. At this moment Hélène awakes, saying that she had seen a man with a black mustache and curly hair, wearing a cloak and a turban, who seemed to be laughing at and mocking her. The spelling out of Pirux was not very clear, and Leopold, when interrogated later, neither affirmed categorically, nor did he deny, that this name was that of the sheik, father of Simandini.

March 3.—Seance with six persons present, all having their hands upon the table. After a brief waiting, Hélène is surprised at no longer being able to see my left middle finger, while she can see all my other fingers quite clearly. My bunch of keys, which I then place upon my middle finger, likewise disappears from her view. This very limited, systematic, visual anæsthesia authorizes the prediction, following numerous examples of former seances, that the phenomena about to appear will concern me. Presently begins a long vision, consisting of scenes which Hélène believes she has already partially seen before.

She describes a pagoda, which she draws with her left hand, with a few strokes of her pencil; then an avenue of palms and statues, a procession, and ceremonies before an altar, etc.

The principal rôles are played by a personage in sandals, a great yellow robe, a helmet of gold, ornamented with precious stones (first appearance of Sivrouka) and by the woman with black hair and white robe, already seen on the 12th of October (Simandini).

In the first part of the vision, Hélène, who follows that woman with ecstatic gaze, describing her to us, sees her coming towards me, but at that moment the invisibility of my finger was extended to my entire person, and Hélène neither sees nor hears me. While she was fully conscious of the other sitters, she was astonished at seeing this woman make "on the empty air" certain gestures of laying-on of hands and benediction, which were made upon my head. On several occasions I change my place, and seat myself in different parts of the room. Each time, after a few seconds, Hélène turns towards me, and, without perceiving me, sees the woman with black hair place herself behind my seat and repeat her gestures of benediction in space, at a height corresponding to that of my head.

As the vision continues, I do not play any further rôle, but it has to do with a ceremony during which the Hindoo woman with a diadem on her head burns incense in the midst of her twelve companions, etc.

During all this time the table, contrary to its custom, gave no explanation; but Hélène, having herself asked some questions, remarks that the imaginary woman replies to her by certain signs of her head and reveals to her many things that she had known in a former existence. At the moment of the disappearance of the vision, which had lasted more than an hour, Mlle. Smith hears the words ("Until presently"). The continuation, in fact, was not long delayed.

March 6.—Repetition and continuation of the preceding seance, with this degree of progress—viz., that the visual hallucination of the woman with the black hair was changed into a total cœnæsthetic hallucination—*i.e.*, instead of a simple vision an incarnation was produced. After a very impressive scene of benediction, Hélène gave herself up to a succession of pantomimes in which she seemed to take part in a fearful spectacle and to struggle with enemies (scene of the funeral pile). She ended by seating herself on the divan when she recovered her normal state, after a series of psychical oscillations, various attitudes, etc. The last of her phases of mimicry was to tear off and throw away all the ornaments which an Asiatic princess could wear—rings on all her fingers, bracelets on her arms and wrists, a necklace, diadem, ear-rings, girdle, anklets. Once awake, she had no recollection of the scene of benediction, but recalled quite distinctly the dreams corresponding to the other pantomimes. She saw again the black-haired woman, the Oriental landscape of the preceding seance, etc. In the course of her description the passage of the simple vision into the scene of incarnation was reflected in a change of the form of her narrative; she spoke to us of the woman in the third person, then suddenly adopted the first person, and said "I" in recounting among other things that she—or the black-haired woman—saw a corpse on the funeral pile, upon which four men, against whom she struggled, endeavored to force her to mount. When I drew her attention to this change of style, she replied that, in fact, it seemed as though she herself was that woman.

Independently of the Hindoo romance, these two seances are interesting from a psychological point of view, because the change from a visual, objective hallucination into total cœnæsthetic and motor hallucination occurs in it, constituting a complete transformation of the personality. This generalization of partial automatism at the beginning, this subjugation and absorption of the ordinary personality by the subliminal personality, does not always produce amnesia with Hélène, that unique impression which she might describe on awakening as being herself and some one else at the same time. (Compare, p. 119.) It must be noted that in the particular case of the identification of the black-haired Hindoo woman with Mlle. Hélène Smith of Geneva, the problem of the causal connection is susceptible of two opposite solutions (and the same remark will be equally appropriate in the case of Marie Antoinette).

For the believing spiritist it is because Mlle. Smith is the reincarnation of Simandini—that is to say, because these two personages, in spite of the separation of their existences in time and space, are substantially and metaphysically identical—that she really again becomes Simandini, and feels herself to be a Hindoo princess in certain favorable somnambulistic states. For the empirical psychologist it is, on the contrary, because the visual memory of a Hindoo woman (her origin is of no importance) grows like a parasite and increases in surface and in depth like a drop of oil, until it invades the whole impressionable and suggestible personality of the medium—this is why Mlle. Smith feels herself becoming this woman, and concludes from it that she formerly actually was that person (see p. 28-30). But we must return from this digression to the Hindoo dream.

March 10.—After various waking visions relating to other subjects, Hélène enters into somnambulism. For twenty minutes she remains seated with her hands on the table, by means of raps struck upon which Leopold informs us that a scene of previous existence concerning me is being prepared; that I was formerly a Hindoo prince, and that Mlle. Smith, long before her existence as Marie Antoinette, had then been my wife, and had been burned on my tomb; that we should ultimately know the name of this Hindoo prince, as well as the time and place of these events, but not this evening, nor at the next seance. Then Hélène leaves the table, and in a silent pantomime of an hour's duration, the meaning of which, already quite clear, is confirmed by Leopold, she plays, this time to the very close, the scene of the funeral pile as outlined in the preceding seance.

She goes slowly around the room, as if resisting and carried away in spite of herself, by turns supplicating and struggling fiercely with these fictitious men who are bearing her to her death.

All at once, standing on tiptoe, she seems to ascend the pile, hides, with affright, her face in her hands, recoils in terror, then advances anew as though pushed from behind. Finally she falls on her knees before a soft couch, in which she buries her face covered by her clasped hands. She sobs violently. By means of her little finger, visible between her cheek and the cushion of the couch, Leopold continues to reply very clearly by yes and no to my questions. It is the moment at which she again passes through her agony on the funeral pile: her cries cease little by little; her respiration becomes more and more panting, then suddenly stops and remains suspended during some seconds which seem interminable. It is the end! Her pulse is fortunately strong, though a little irregular. While I am feeling it, her breathing is re-established by means of a deep inspiration. After repeated sobs she becomes calm, and slowly rises and seats herself on a neighboring sofa. This scene of fatal *dénouement* lasted eight minutes. She finally awakens, remembering to have seen in a dream the dead body of a man stretched on a funeral pile, and a woman whom some men were forcing to ascend the pile against her will.

There was nothing Oriental in the succeeding seances, and the Hindoo dream did not appear again until four weeks later.

April 7.—Mlle. Smith went quickly into a mixed state, in which the Hindoo dream was mingled and substituted, but only so far as concerns me, for the feeling of present reality. She believes me absent, asks other sitters why I have gone away, then rises and begins to walk around me and look at me, very much surprised at seeing my place occupied by a stranger with black curly hair and of brown complexion, clothed in a robe with flowing sleeves of blue, and with gold ornaments. When I speak to her she turns around and seems to hear my voice from the opposite side, whither she goes to look for me; when I go towards her she shuns me; then, when I follow her, she returns to the place I had just left. After some time occupied in these manœuvres she ceases to be preoccupied with me and my substitute in the blue robe, and falls into a deeper state. She takes on the look of a seeress, and describes a kind of embattled château on a hill, where she perceives and recognizes the before-mentioned personage with the curly hair, but in another costume and surrounded by very ugly black men, and women "who are good looking."

Interrogated as to the meaning of this vision, Leopold replies: "*The city of Tchandraguiri in Kanaraau*" (*sic*); then he adds, a moment later, "*There is a letter too many in the last word*," and ends by giving the name *Kanara*, and adding the explanation "*of the fifteenth century*." Upon awaking from this somnambulistic state, which lasted two hours, Hélène recalls having had a dream of a personage with curly hair, in a blue robe, richly ornamented with precious stones, with a cutlass of gold, bent backward, suspended from a hook. She recollects having held a long conversation with him in a strange language which she understood and spoke very well herself, although she no longer knows the meaning of it.

April 14.—Very soon passing into a deep sleep, Mlle. Smith leaves the table and gives herself up to a silent pantomime, at first smiling, then finishing in sadness and by a scene of tears.

The meaning of this is explained by Leopold as follows: Hélène is in India, in her palace of Tchandraguiri, in Kanara, *in 1401*, and she receives a declaration of love from the personage with the curly hair, who is the Prince Sivrouka Nayaka, to whom she has been married for about a year. The prince has flung himself upon his knees, but he inspires in her a certain fright, and she still regrets having left her native country in order to follow him. Leopold affirms that she will remember, on awaking, in French, all that the prince has said to her in Sanscrit, and that she will repeat to us a part of it, but not all, because it is too private. After awaking she seems in reality to recall clearly her entire dream, and tells us that she found herself on a hill, where they were building . that it was not exactly a city, nor even a village, since there were no streets; that it was rather an isolated place in the country, and that which was being built was not in the form of a house; it had holes rather than windows (a fortress and loop-holes).

She found herself in a fine palace, very beautiful as to its interior, but not its exterior. There was a great hall, decorated with greens, with a grand staircase at the end, flanked by statues of gold. She held a long conversation there, not in French, with the swarthy personage with the black curly hair and magnificent costume; he finally ascended the staircase, but she did not follow him.

She appeared to recall well the meaning of all that he said to her in their conversation in a foreign language, but seemed embarrassed by these memories, and would not consent to relate them to us.

May 26.—In the course of this seance, as Hélène, in a silent somnambulism, incarnates the Hindoo princess, I hand her a sheet of paper and a pencil in the hope of obtaining some text or drawing. After divers scribblings she traces the single word *Simadini* in letters which are not at all like her usual hand (see Fig. 34).

Fig. 34.

Then taking a fresh sheet, she seems to write on it with a happy smile, folds it carefully and thrusts it in her corsage, takes it out again, and rereads it with rapture, etc. Leopold informs us that Simadini is the name of the Hindoo princess, and that she is reading a love-letter from Sivrouka. On awaking she remembers having been "in such a beautiful palace," and of having received there a very interesting letter, but the contents of which she refused to disclose to us, being evidently too confidential.

I intercalate here two remarks apropos of the name Simadini, which is one of the first known examples of a handwriting of Mlle. Smith other than her own normal hand.

First: When, four months later, Leopold began to communicate in writing (pp. 98-103), a certain analogy in the formation of the letters, and the identical way of holding the pencil, caused us to believe that it was he who had already traced the word in Fig. 34. But he has always denied it, and we have never been able to discover the author of it. Secondly: I said above, (p. 204), that there had been divergences in the orthography of this name. Here, in substance, is a fragment of a letter which Mlle. Smith wrote me in the winter following (February 18, 1896), depicting to me the vexatious impressions which she still had concerning it.

". . . I am very sad, and I cannot tell why. I have a heavy heart, and for what reason I do not know myself. It came to such a pass to-day (you are going to laugh) that it seemed to me as though my left cheek had grown perceptibly thinner. I am sure that at this moment you would not recognize Simadini, so piteous and discouraged is her countenance! Think, that at the very moment in which I trace these words, I hear a voice speaking to me in my right ear: "*Not Simadini, but Simandini!* What do you think that can be? It is very strange, is it not? Have we misunderstood that name? Or, perhaps, may it not be I who have misunderstood it? . . . "

Mlle. Smith here forgets that the name did not come to her on the first occasion by auditive hallucination, in which case it might be that she had misunderstood it, but by writing in somnambulism, which excludes any mistake of her ordinary consciousness. We must confine ourselves to registering as a fact, inexplicable hitherto, this correction of a graphic automatism by an auditive automatism at the end of several months. Between the two orthographies, I have adopted the second, which has undergone no further changes, and figures only in the Martian texts (10, 16).

June 16.—Fuller repetition of the scene of the letter of the Hindoo prince. Impossible to learn the contents of it. I suggest to her to remember and to relate them to us upon awakening, but Leopold replies: "*She will not reveal it. Why have you not gained her confidence sufficiently, that she may tell you everything without fear?*" and the suggestion had no effect.

June 30.—Somnambulism with silent pantomime, the meaning of which is given by Leopold: It is the scene of the betrothal of Simandini and Sivrouka at Tchandraguiri. There is first a phase of oppression, with sighs and gestures as of a struggle against various pretenders who wish to seize her; then laughter and ecstasy, provoked by the arrival of Sivrouka, who delivers her and drives off his rivals; finally, joy and admiration on accepting the flowers and jewels which he offers her.

I have reported, too much at length perhaps, though still greatly abridged, these first appearances of the Oriental romance, because they form a continuous series, in the reverse of . the chronological order, conformably to a spiritistic theory which holds that in these memories of previous existences the mediumistic memory goes back and recovers the "images" of the more recent events before those which are more remote. During this first period of four months, the Hindoo cycle made irruption into eight seances. (about one-twentieth of those at which I have been present since I have had knowledge of them), and has manifested itself somewhat like the panorama of a magic lantern, unfolding itself in successive tableaux.

This whole history can be summed up by a few principal tableaux: there was the scene of the death on the funeral pile, prepared in vision in the seance of the 6th of March and executed on the 10th; then the scene of the interior of the palace and the fortress in process of construction (7th and 14th of April); that of the love-letter (26th of May and 16th of June); finally, the betrothal (30th of June). There must be added to these the grand tableau at the beginning, first presented in vision the 3d of March, then realized three days later with the astonishing exclamation Atièyâ Ganapatinâmâ. The meaning of this scene has never been explained by Leopold, but seems to be quite clear. A species of prologue can be seen in it, or even apotheosis, inaugurating the entire romance; it is the Hindoo princess of four centuries ago recognizing her lord and master in flesh and blood, under the unexpected form of a university professor, whom she greets with an emphasis wholly Oriental in blessing him, very appropriately, in the name of the divinity of science and of wisdom—since Ganapati is an equivalent of Ganesâ, the god with the head of an elephant, patron of sages and savants.

It can be easily conceived that these two words of Oriental resonance, spoken aloud at a period at which the Martian was not yet born—and followed by all the conversations unfortunately unheard by us, which at the waking at the subsequent seances Hélène recalled having held in a strange language (in *Sanscrit*, according to Leopold) with the Hindoo prince of her dreams—would excite a lively curiosity and a desire to obtain longer audible fragments of this unknown idiom. It was only in September, 1895, that this satisfaction was afforded us, during a seance at which the Oriental romance, which had given no further sign of life since the month of June, made a new outbreak. Starting from that moment, it has never ceased during these four years to reappear irregularly, and, suffering some eclipses, accompanied on each occasion by words of a *Sanscritoid* aspect. But the plot of the romance has no longer the same clearness that it showed at the beginning. In place of tableaux linking themselves in a regular chronological order, they are often no more than confused reminiscences, memories, without precise bonds between them, which gush forth from the memory of Simandini. As the fragments of our youthful years surge up incoherent and pell-mell in our dreams, Mlle. Smith, too, finds herself easily assailed in her somnambulisms by visions connected with certain episodes, and not forming an entire continuation of supposed Asiatic pre-existence.

Some of these scenes concern her life as a young Arab girl. One sees her there, for example, playing joyously with her little monkey, Mitidja; or copying an Arab text (see Fig. 35, p. 312), which her father, the sheik, surrounded by his tribes, furnishes her; or embarking on a strange boat, escorted by black Hindoos, for her new country, etc. But much the larger number of her somnambulistic trances and her spontaneous visions have reference to her life in India and to the details of her daily existence. Her bath, which the faithful domestic Adèl prepares for her; her walks and reveries in the splendid gardens of the palace, all full of a luxurious vegetation and rare birds of brilliant colors; her scenes of tenderness and of affectionate effusions—always stamped, this is to be noted, with the most perfect propriety—towards the Prince Sivrouka, when he is kindly disposed; scenes of regret also and abundant tears for the memory of her far-off native land, when the capricious and brutal humor of the Oriental despot makes itself too severely felt; conversation with the fakir Kanga; devotions and religious ceremonies before some Buddhist image, etc., all this forms an *ensemble* extremely varied and full of local color. There is in the whole being of Simandini—in the expression of her countenance (Hélène almost always has her large eyes open in this somnambulism), in her movements, in the quality of her voice when she speaks or chants Hindoo—a languishing grace, an abandon, a melancholy sweetness, a something of languor and of charm, which corresponds wonderfully with the character of the Orient, as the spectators conceive it to be, who, like me, have never been there, etc. With all this a bearing always full of *noblesse* and dignity conforms to that which one would expect of a princess; there are no dances, for example, nothing of the *bayadère*.

Mlle. Smith is really very wonderful in her Hindoo somnambulisms. The way in which Simandini seats herself on the ground, her legs crossed, or half stretched out, nonchalantly leaning her arms or her head against a Sivrouka, who is sometimes real (when in her incomplete trance she takes me for her prince), sometimes imaginary; the religious and solemn gravity of her prostrations when, after having for a long time balanced the fictitious brazier, she crosses her extended hands on her breast, kneeling and bowing herself three times, her forehead striking the ground; the melancholy sweetness of her chants in a minor key, wailing and plaintive melodies, which unfold themselves in certain flute-like notes, prolonged in a slow decrescendo, and only dying away at the end of a single note held for fully fourteen seconds; the agile suppleness of her swaying and serpentine movements, when she amuses herself with her imaginary monkey, caresses it, embraces it, excites it, scolds it laughingly, and makes it repeat all its tricks—all this so varied mimicry and Oriental speech have such a stamp of originality, of ease, of naturalness, that one asks in amazement whence it comes to this little daughter of Lake Leman, without artistic education or special knowledge of the Orient—a perfection of play to which the best actress, without doubt, could only attain at the price of prolonged studies or a sojourn on the banks of the Ganges.

The problem, as I have already stated, is not yet solved, and I am obliged still to endeavor to discover whence Hélène Smith has derived her ideas in regard to India. It seems that the more simple method would be to take advantage of the hypnotic state of the seances to obtain a confession from Hélène's subconscious memory, and persuade it to disclose the secret; but my efforts in that direction have not as yet succeeded. It is doubtless incompetency on my part, and I will end, perhaps—or some one better qualified than I—in finding the joint in the armor. The fact is that hitherto I have always run up against Leopold, who will not allow himself to be ejected or ridiculed, and who has never ceased to affirm that the Sanscrit, Simandini, and the rest are authentic. All the trails which I have thought I have discovered—and they are already numerous—have proved false. The reader must pardon me for not going into the details of my failures in this regard.

If it was only a question of the Hindoo pantomime the mystery would not be so great: some recitations at school, newspaper articles concerning the incineration of the widows of Malabar, engravings and descriptions relative to the civil and religious life of India, etc.—in short, the varied sources of information which, in a civilized country and at our epoch of cosmopolitanism, inevitably meet some time or other the eyes or ears of every one of us and form part of the equipment (conscious or unconscious) of every individual who is not altogether uncultured, would more than suffice to explain the scene of the funeral pile, the prostrations, and the varied attitudes. There are, indeed, some well-known examples showing how small a thing a cunning intelligence, furnished with a good memory and a fertile and plastic imagination, needs in order to reconstruct or fabricate out of nothing a complex edifice, having every appearance of authenticity, and capable of holding in check for a considerable length of time the perspicacity even of skilled minds. But that which conscious and reflecting labor has succeeded in accomplishing in the cases referred to, the subliminal faculties can execute to a much higher degree of perfection in the case of persons subject to automatic tendencies.

But two points remain, which complicate the case of the Hindoo romance and seem to defy—thus far, at least—all normal explanation, because they surpass the limits of a simple play of the imagination These are the precise *historical* information given by Leopold, some of which can be, in a certain sense, verified; and the Hindoo *language* spoken by Simandini, which contains words more or less recognizable, the real meaning of which is adapted to the situation in which they have been spoken. But, even if Hélène's imagination could have reconstructed the manners and customs and scenes of the Orient from the general information floating in some way in cosmopolitan atmosphere, still one cannot conceive whence she has derived her knowledge of the language and of certain obscure episodes in the history of India. These two points deserve to be examined separately.

II. SIVROUKA AND M. DE MARLÈS

When Kanara, Sivrouka, Simandini, etc., successively made their appearance, slowly spelled out by Leopold, with the date of 1401, my companions of the seance and I hastened to investigate Brouillet, who brought to mind the province of Malabar in connection with the first of these names, but left us in utter darkness as to the others. The geography of Vivien Saint-Martin revealed the existence of no fewer than three Tchandraguiris—a hill, a river, and a small town in the district of Arcot-Nord (Madras). The latter—or rather its citadel on the summit of the hill—answered quite well to the description given by Hélène in her visions of the 7th and 14th of April, but the construction of this fortress dates back only to 1510, and this locality is very far removed from the Kanara where Leopold locates this entire story (see pp. 286-288).

As to Sivrouka and his surroundings, neither biographical dictionaries nor encyclopædias were able to furnish me the least hint on this subject. Living historians or Orientalists to whom I addressed myself were of a discouraging unanimity in replying that they did not recognize even the names, the historic correctness of which they regarded as doubtful, and they did not at all remember having met with them in works of fiction.

"I have there," said a learned professor of history, showing me a good-sized bookcase, "numerous works on the history of India; but they relate only to the north of the peninsula; and as to what transpired in the south during the period to which you refer, we know almost nothing. Your names are unknown to me and do not recall to my mind any personage, real or fictitious."

"The very name of Sivrouka seems to me improbable as a Hindoo name" replied another, who was unable to give me any more information on the subject.

"I greatly regret," wrote a third, on receipt of Hélène's texts, "not to have succeeded in getting upon the trail of the recollections of your medium. I cannot think of any book which would be likely to furnish the information. Tchandraguiri and Mangalore (where several scenes of the Hindoo cycle are located) are correct, but Madras (*id*.) did not exist in 1401. Its name and foundation do not go further back than the seventeenth century. That region was then a dependency of the kingdom of Vijayanagara, and a naïk in the service of those princes resided successively at Tchandraguiri and at Mangalore. I can make nothing of Sivrouka; the king of Vijayanagara, in 1402, was Bukkha II., or Bukkha called Siribukkha, Tiribukkha. But the naïk who so often changed his residence was evidently not a ruling prince. Was it a romance? Certain details caused me to doubt it. A romancer so careful in regard to local coloring as to introduce into his narrative Indian words, would not have given the title of the prince under the Sanscrit form *Nayaka*, but would have used the vulgar form naïk; he would not have made the wife, in speaking to her husband, call him by his name Sivrouka (as Hélène constantly does in this somnambulism). I have no recollection of having read anything of this kind, and I know of no work of fiction from which the story might have been taken."

It will be readily understood that I was annoyed at not being able to establish clearly my presumed Asiatic previous existence. However, while professional science was administering to me these cold douches, I continued, on my own account, to search the libraries at my disposal, and here one fine day I accidentally came across, in an old history of India, in six volumes, by a man named De Marlès, the following passages:

"Kanara and the neighboring provinces on the side towards Delhi may be regarded as the Georgia of Hindustan; it is there, it is said, that the most beautiful women are to be found; the natives, however, are very jealous in guarding them, and do not often allow them to be seen by strangers."

"Tchandraguiri, which signifies *Mountain of the Moon*, is a vast fortress constructed, in 1401, by the rajah Sivrouka Nayaka. This prince, as also his successors, belonged to the sect of the Djaïns."

At last! With what a beating heart did I fasten my eyes on that irrefutable historic evidence that my preceding incarnation, under the beautiful skies of India was not a myth! I felt new life in my veins. I reread twenty times those blessed lines, and took a copy of them to send to those pretended savants who were ignorant even of the name of Sivrouka, and allowed doubts to be cast upon his reality.

Alas! my triumph was of brief duration. It seems that the testimony of De Marlès is not of the highest order. This author is held in slight esteem in well-informed circles, as may be seen from the following passage in a letter of M. Barth, which merely expresses, in a vigorous and lively manner, an opinion which other specialists have confirmed: [1]

"It is through a letter of M. Flournoy that I learn that there has existed since 1828 in Paris, printed in Roman characters, a history of India by De Marlès containing a statement that the fortress of Candragiri was built in 1401, and that its founder was Sivrouka Nayaka. What new facts there are in books one no longer consults! And that of De Marlès is, indeed, one of those that are no longer consulted. I found it yesterday at the library of the Institute. It would have been impossible to have done worse, even in 1828. But sometimes we find pearls in a dung-hill, and perhaps this Sivrouka Nayaka is one of them. Unfortunately, the author gives no hint as to the sources of his information; and later, in his fourth volume, in which he

---

[1] De Marlès' *General History of India, Ancient and Modern. from the Year 2000 B.C. to our Own Times.* Pp. 268-269. Paris, 1828.

narrates the history of the twelfth to the sixteenth centuries, he does not say a word more either of Candragiri or of Sivrouka."

Here was a terrible blow to my Hindoo existence, which poor M. de Marlès had so well established for me.

Nevertheless, the hope still lingers that his information, although not reproduced by later writers more highly esteemed, may perhaps still be correct. This is quite possible, since science has not yet spoken its last word in this department, hardly even its first, if men still more competent may be believed, beginning with M. Barth himself.

"Up to the present moment," says he, "there is no trustworthy history of the south of the peninsula. . . . The Dravidian languages of India is a domain very unfamiliar to the majority of Indian scholars. . . . There is nothing to draw upon but some works and monographs on the aboriginal chronicles and legendary traditions; and it would be necessary to know the Dravidian languages on the one hand and Arabic on the other, to be able to examine or even consult them with profit. The only works which we are able to follow are those which undertake to make this history by epigraphic documents, but these, thus far, say nothing of Simandini, of Adèl, of Mitidja, or even of Sivrouka."

This silence of epigraphy is certainly to be regretted; but who knows whether it will not some day enlighten us by proving De Marlès to be right—and also Leopold—by narrating to us the true story of the Hindoo princess, the Arabian monkey, and the slave Adèl! It costs nothing to hope! Already, thanks again to M. Barth, I have gained information concerning another Tchandraguiri than the one of the District of North Arcot mentioned by Vivien de Saint-Martin—*i.e.*, a Tchandraguiri, situated in South Kanara, and in the citadel of which a hitherto unknown inscription has been discovered which must date back to the time of King Harihara II., of Vijayanagara, who reigned at the beginning of the fifteenth century. [1] Here is something approaching the somnambulistic revelations of Mlle. Smith. While awaiting their definite confirmation by new archæological discoveries, traces of Sivrouka may be sought for in the earlier works upon which De Marlès must have drawn. Unfortunately these works are not easy to

---

[1] Robert Sewell. *Lists of Antiquarian Remains in the Presidency of Madras*. Vol i. p. 238 (1882.) Citation by M. Barth. I have not been able to consult this work.

find, and are inconvenient to consult. Professor Michel, of the University of Liège, has had the kindness to run through those of Buchanan [1] and of Rennell [2] but without result.

If De Marlès did not invent Sivrouka out of whole cloth, which is hardly supposable, it was very probably in the translation of Ferishta by Dow, [3] that he found his facts. I have, unhappily, not yet been able myself to consult that very rare work, which is not to be found in Geneva, so far as I am aware, nor to obtain accurate information regarding its contents.

The uncertainty which hovers over the historical problem extends, naturally, to the psychological problem also. It is clear that if certain inscriptions, or even some old work, should come some day to tell us not only of Sivrouka, but of Simandini, of Adèl, and the other personages who figure in Hélène's Hindoo romance, but of whom De Marlès does not whisper a word, we should no longer care about the latter author, and the question would then be as follows: Could Mlle. Smith have had cognizance of these early works, and if not, how do their contents reappear in her somnambulism? But in the actual condition of things, and all allowance made for possible surprises in the future, I do not hesitate to regard as the more probable and more rational supposition, that it was really the passage of De Marlès, quoted above, which furnished he subliminal memory of Hélène the precise date of 1401—and the three names of the fortress, the province, and the rajah.

Various other traits of the visions of Mlle. Smith betray likewise the same inspiration. The scene in which she sees them engaged in building, and her description of that which is being built, suggest clearly the idea of a fortress furnished by the text. The translation *Mountain of the Moon* contributed to causing her to locate the scene upon a hill. The beauty of the women of the country, on which De Marlès dwells, has its echo in the remark of Hélène

---

[1] Buchanan. *A Journey from Madras through the Countries of Mysore, Canara, and Malabar*, etc. 3 vols. 4to. London, 1807.
[2] James Rennell. *Description Historique et Géographique de l'Indostan*. Translated from the English. Paris, an. VIII. (5800). 3 vols., 8vo and atlas 4to.
[3] Dow. *History of Hindustan*. Translated from the Persian of Ferishta. London, 1803. M. Michel suggests Wilks's *Historical Sketches of the South of India* (London, 1810) as having possibly served as a source of information for De Marlès. If some learned reader may discover any traces of Sivrouka antecedent to De Marlès, I shall be under great obligation to him if he will communicate the information to me.

that the women whom she sees are "good looking." Finally, the princely character of Sivrouka, mentioned by De Marlès, is found throughout the length of the entire romance, and displays itself in the splendor of his costume, of the palace, of the gardens, etc.

It is possible that the names and the nationality of the other personages—Simandini, Adèl, the monkey, the sheik, etc.—may have been borrowed from some unknown work, which would be, for the Arabian portion of the narrative, the pendant to De Marlès for the Hindoo past.

This may be, but it is not necessary. It is permissible to regard, provisionally, the imaginations built up around Sivrouka, as an ingenious expedient, by means of which Hélène's imagination finds a way of binding to that central figure, and also of blending in a single whole, her other Oriental memories not specifically Hindoo.
The hypothesis which I am about to assume, which connects directly with De Marlès the data of Hélène's Asiatic dream, contained likewise in the work of that author, arouses, nevertheless, two objections. The first is drawn from the slight differences of orthography between the text of De Marlès and the words spoken by Leopold. This difficulty is only insurmountable by elevating the inerrancy of the subliminal memory to the plane of absolute infallibility, though the latter must be admitted to be ordinarily very much superior to that of the conscious memory. But the favorite comparison of the forgotten memories, reappearing in somnambulisms, to unchangeable, absolutely true photographic impressions, causes us readily to exaggerate the fidelity of the unconscious memory-images. The example of certain dreams—in which memories of childhood sometimes return with a startling clearness, but, nevertheless, altered or distorted in some details, conformably to later experiences or to recent events—suffices to show that automatisms of the memory are not always sheltered by influences of the imagination, nor absolutely free from error.

In this particular case there are two divergences between De Marlès and Leopold: the latter has substituted a *k* for the *c* in Nayaca, and has omitted the *n* in Tchandraguiri (compare pp. 286 and 288). Another mistake, which he immediately corrected, consisting in dictating first *Kanaraau*, was evidently a confusion such as frequently occurs in writing, occasioned by a too rapid passing from the word *Kanara* to the information following, and already about to come—"*au* fifteenth century." The spelling Nayaka, instead of Nayaca, is attributable to the termination of the word *Sivrouka*, which precedes it. Identity of pronunciation has produced identity of orthography.

The second objection is of a negative character. It consists in the impossibility of showing where, when, or how Mlle. Smith obtained cognizance of the text of De Marlès.

I admit frankly that I know nothing about it, and I give full credit to Hélène for the indomitable and persevering energy with which she has never ceased to protest against my hypothesis, which has the faculty of exasperating her in the highest degree—and one readily understands that it would naturally do so. For it is in vain that she digs down to the very bottom of her memories; she does not discover the slightest trace of this work. And not only that, but how can one seriously suppose that she has ever had the slightest intimation of it, since she never studied the history of India, has neither read nor heard anything on the subject, the very name of De Marlès having been utterly unknown to her up to the day on which she learned that I suspected that author of being the source of the Hindoo romance? It must-indeed, be admitted that the idea of the passage in question having come before the eyes or ears of Mlle. Smith through any ordinary channel seems a trifle absurd. I only know in Geneva of two copies of the work of De Marlès, both covered with dust—the one belonging to the Société de Lecture, a private association of which none of the Smith family nor any friend of theirs was ever a member; the other in the Public Library, where, among the thousands of more interesting and more modern books, it is now very rarely consulted. It could only have happened, therefore, by a combination of absolutely exceptional and almost unimaginable circumstances that the work of De Marlès could have found its way into Hélène's hands; and how could it have done so and she not have the slightest recollection of it?

I acknowledge the force of this argument, and that the wisest thing to do is to leave the matter in suspense. But if the question must be decided, though there is scarcely any choice, extravagance for extravagance, I still prefer the hypothesis which only invokes natural possibilities to that which appeals to occult causes.

Possibly the work of De Marlès may have been heard of by Mlle. Smith without her normal consciousness taking note of it. Either when among her friends or acquaintances, or with her parents, she might have heard some passages read in her young days, etc. The fact that she has no conscious recollection of it proves nothing against such a supposition to any one who is at all familiar with the play of our faculties.

It goes without saying that my method of reasoning is the inverse of that which generally prevails in spiritistic circles. Witness the celebrated Aksakoff, as a single example, who, discovering that a curious typtological message was found already in print in a book which could not readily have come to the knowledge of the medium, and recognizing the fact that the message came from that book, says: "But in what way could the brain of the medium have been made aware of the contents of the book? There is the mystery. *I refuse to admit that it could have been through natural means. I believe it was by some occult process.*"

Very well! this is plain language, and the frankness of the declaration charms me to such a degree that I cannot resist the temptation to appropriate it for myself in the case of Mlle. Smith and M. de Marlès, transposing only two words: "*I refuse to admit that it could have been through occult means. I believe it was by some natural process.*" Evidently, in doubtful cases (which are in an enormous majority), in which the natural and the occult explanations are in direct opposition, without the possibility of a material demonstration as to which is true in fact, a decision must be reached in accordance with personal taste and feeling. Between these two methodological points of view a reconciliation is scarcely possible. The reader may think what he will. But, right or wrong, I claim the first of these as my opinion, and regard the tendency of the supernatural and occult to substitute themselves, on account of the insufficiency of our knowledge, for the acquired rights of natural hypothesis, as an unjustifiable reversal of rôles.

To those who shall find my hypothesis decidedly too extravagant—or too simple—remains a choice between the multiple forms of occult hypothesis. Shall it be Leopold who, in his all-powerful state of disincarnation, has read in the closed volume of De Marlès? Or has there, indeed, been a telepathic transmission of this passage from the brain of some unknown terrestrial reader to that of Mlle. Smith? Shall it be with her a case of clairvoyance, of lucidity, of intuition in the astral body; or, again, of trickery on the part of some facetious spirit? And if, taking the reincarnationist theory seriously, it is admitted that Sivrouka, 1401, and Tchandraguiri, are indeed really reminiscences of the past life of Simandini, how explain that curious coincidence in their choice and their spelling with precisely the designations used by M. de Marlès?

Verily my brain reels in the midst of all these alternatives, and I hasten to pass to another subject.

III. THE ARAB ELEMENTS OF THE ORIENTAL CYCLE

Here is a problem for the partisans of the Oriental pre-existence of Mlle. Smith: How comes it that, recovering in her trances the use of the Hindoo which she formerly spoke at the court of Sivrouka, she has totally forgotten Arabian, which, however, had been her mother-tongue in that same previous existence, and which she was accustomed to use exclusively up to the time of her departure from her native land, in her eighteenth year?
If the emotions caused by her royal marriage had destroyed all memory of the past, one could understand how the idiom might have become obscured along with the rest in that loss of memory of her life as a young girl.

But such was not the case. She preserved very vivid memories of her father the sheik, of his tents gleaming in the sunlight, of the people, of the camels and landscapes of Arabia. In many seances and spontaneous visions she finds herself carried back to that first half of her Asiatic existence. But then she narrates in French that which is unfolded before her eyes, or gives herself up to a silent pantomime. She has never spoken or written anything at all resembling Arabian. Can it be supposed that already in her Hindoo life she had assimilated the language of her adopted country to the point of losing even the latent memories of her maternal language? That would be contrary to all known psychological analogies.

However, in saying that Hélène has never written or spoken Arabian I exaggerate. On one occasion she spoke four words of it. It is the exception which proves the rule. In fact, not only did she fail to accompany that single text with any pronunciation, but she executed it as a drawing, and apparently copied, without comprehending, a model which an imaginary person presented to her.

Here is a review of that incident:

October 27, 1895.—Shortly after the beginning of the seance Mlle. Smith has an Arabian vision: "Look at those tents! There are no stones here—it is all sand . . . [she counts the tents one by one]. There are twenty of them. That one is beautiful. Don't you find it so, M. Lemaître—that largest one? It is fastened by cords and small stakes. . . ." etc. Then she describes the personages: The one who is smoking, seated in a corner, with his legs crossed; others all black (the table says they are negroes, and that the scene takes place in Arabia); then a man clothed in white, whom Hélène has the feeling of knowing without being able to recognize him; she places her finger upon her forehead, in the attitude of a person trying to remember, and the table (on which she has her left hand) informs us then that she lived in Arabia in her life as Simandini, and that she is trying to recollect those far-distant times. A quite long scene follows, in which her Arab reminiscences alternate and mingle with the consciousness of the real environment, though she neither sees nor hears us. At this point a state of mental confusion ensues, which seems to be very painful to her.

". . . M. Lemaître! M. Flournoy! are you there? Answer me, then. Did I not come here this evening? If only I could . . . however, I am not *en voyage*. . . . I really believe it is Sunday at last . . . I understand nothing more about it. I think my brain is so tired that all my ideas are mixed up . . . however, I am not dreaming. . . . It seems to me that I have also lived with them . . . [the sitters at the table], and with them [the Arabs of her vision]. . . . But I know them—all those men. Tell me, then, who you are! Did you arrive in Geneva lately? [They are, says the table, Arabs who lived five centuries ago, among them the father of Simandini.] Come nearer, then, come here. I want you to speak to me! M. Lemaître! Oh, that pretty little sketch! What is that sketch? [The table having said that it is a drawing which her father is presenting to her, and that she can copy it, a pencil and a sheet of paper are placed before her, the latter of which seems to be transformed into papyrus in her dream.] That green leaf is pretty. Of what plant is it the leaf? I think I have a pencil; I am going to try to make this sketch. . . ."

After the usual struggle between the two methods of holding the pencil (see pp. 100-102), she yields to Leopold's manner of holding it, saying, "So much the worse"; then traces, slowly and with great care, Fig. 35, from left to right, often raising her eyes to her imaginary model, as if copying a drawing. After which she goes profoundly asleep; then other somnambulisms come.

On awaking she recollects the state of confusion through which she had passed. "Wretched evening," said she. "I was unhappy. I felt that I was living here, as I always have, and I saw some things as though I were a foreigner. I was with you, but I was living elsewhere," etc.

This whole scene gives the distinct impression that the Arab phrase only existed in Hélène's recollection as a visual memory, without meaning or any verbal images. It was for her an incomprehensible piece of writing, a simple drawing, like Chinese or Japanese characters would be for us. Evidently it was a text which had come before her eyes at some propitious moment, and, having been absorbed by the subliminal imagination—always on the watch for matters of Oriental aspect—had been incorporated in a scene of the Asiatic dream.

Such, at least, is the supposition which seems to me the most plausible. For, to regard it as a fragment of Arabian, which Hélène could speak and write fluently if she were in an appropriate state of somnambulism—as Leopold pretended one day to be the fact—seems to me an hypothesis still more arbitrary, and little in accord with the other trance phenomena of Mlle. Smith.

Fig. 35. Arabian text drawn from left to right by Mlle. Smith in hemisomnambulism: elqalil men elhabib ktsir, *the little from the friend (is) much.* Natural size.

Occasions have not been wanting to her in the five years during which her exotic romances have been unfolding themselves to make use of her supposed philological reserves by speaking and writing Arabian, if her subliminal memory had so desired.

She has presented all degrees and kinds of somnambulism, and more visions of Arabia than could have failed to awaken by association the corresponding idiom, if it really was slumbering in her. The complete and total isolation of the text given above, in the midst of this flood of Oriental scenes, seems to me, therefore, to testify strongly in favor of my supposition that it has to do with a visual flash, unique in its kind, accidentally encountered and stored up, and that the Asiatic secondary. personality of Mlle. Smith is absolutely ignorant of Arabic.

Concerning the other details of the Arab somnambulisms of Hélène, I have nothing to say; they do not go beyond the ideas which she could unconsciously have gathered from the surrounding environment; and to the other sources of her knowledge must be added whatever she might have heard from her father, who had at one time lived in Algeria.

The proper names connected with the Arab scenes, with the possible exception of Pirux, awaken certain associations of ideas, without making it possible to affirm anything with certainty as to their origin.

IV. THE HINDOO LANGUAGE OF MLLE. SMITH

The nature of the Hindoo language of Hélène is less easy to explain clearly than that of the Martian, because it has never been possible to obtain either a literal translation of it or written texts. Besides, being ignorant of the numberless dialects of ancient and modern India, and not believing it to be incumbent upon me to devote myself to their study solely that I might be able to appreciate at their proper value the philological exploits of an entranced medium, I am not in a situation to allow myself any personal judgment in regard to this matter.

There is not even left to me the resource of placing the parts of the process as a whole before the reader, as I have done in the case of the Martian, for the reason that our ignorance of Hélène's Hindoo, added to her rapid and indistinct pronunciation—a real prattle sometimes—has caused us to lose the greater part of the numerous words heard in the course of some thirty Oriental scenes scattered over a space of four years.

Even the fragments which we have been able to note down present for the most part so much uncertainty that it would be idle to publish all of them. I have communicated the best of them to several distinguished Oriental scholars. From certain information which they have kindly given me, it appears that the soi-disant Hindoo of Hélène is not any fixed idiom known to these specialists; but, on the other hand, there are to be found in it, more or less disfigured and difficult to recognize, certain terms or roots which approach more nearly to Sanscrit than any actual language of India, and the meaning of which often very well corresponds with the situations in which these words have been uttered. I proceed to give some examples of them:

1. The two words, **atiêyâ ganapatinâmâ**, which inaugurated the Hindoo language on the 6th of March, 1895 (see p. 282), and which were invested at that moment, in the mouth of Simandini, with the evident meaning of a formula of salutation or of benediction, addressed to her late husband, inopportunely returned, were articulated in a manner so impressive and so solemn that their pronunciation leaves scarcely any room for doubt.

It is all the more interesting to ascertain the accord of my scientist correspondents upon the value of these two words; the first recalls to them nothing precise or applicable to the situation, but the second is a flattering and very appropriate allusion to the divinity of the Hindoo Pantheon, which is more actively interesting to the professional world.

M. P. Oltramare, to whom I sent these words, without saying anything as to their source, replied: "There is nothing more simple than the word **ganapatinâmâ**; it means, '*who bears the name of Ganapati*,' which is the same as *Ganesa*. . . . As to **atiêyâ**, that word has not a Hindoo appearance; it might perhaps be **atreya**, which, it seems, serves as a designation for women who have suffered an abortion, an explication which, however, I do not guarantee. [In order to affirm more concerning these words, it would be necessary to know] whether they are really Sanscrit, since if they belong to the vulgar languages, I excuse myself absolutely."

M. Glardon, who is more familiar with the vulgar languages and speaks Hindustani fluently, did not hint to me of any other meaning for **atiêyâ** and saw also in the other word "an epithet of honor, literally, '*named Ganapati*,' familiar name of the god Ganesa."

M. de Saussure also found no meaning whatever for the first term, in which he inclines now to see an arbitrary creation of the Martian order, and he remarked that in the second, "the two words, **Ganapati**, well-known divinity, and **nâmâ**, *name*, are constructed together, in some inexplicable manner, but not necessarily false. It is quite curious," adds he, "that this fragment, which is mixed up with the name of a god, may be properly pronounced with a kind of solemn emphasis and a gesture of religious benediction. This denotes, indeed, an intelligent and intentional use."

According to this first brief specimen, therefore, Hélène's Hindoo appears to be a mixture of improvised articulations and of veritable Sanscrit words adapted to the situation. Later specimens only serve to corroborate this impression.

2. The next outbreak of Hindoo took place five months later (September 15, 1895), in the midst of a very long Oriental seance, in which I only refer to points especially interesting to us—to wit, Hélène's supposed Sanscrit, the French interpretation which Leopold gave of it, and the curious evidences of agreement of these two texts.

In one tender scene, with sighs and tears, in connection with Sivrouka, Hélène uttered in an exceedingly sweet voice the following words: **ou mama priva** (or **prira, priya**)—**mama radisivou**—**mama sadiou sivrouka**—**apa tava va signa damasa**—**simia damasa bagda sivrouka**. During the various phases which precede the awaking, I ask Leopold the meaning of these words. He at first refused to give it, saying, "Find it out yourself"; then, as I insist, "I would have preferred that you found it out yourself." I beg him to give at least the correct spelling of an Oriental text furnished us in so uncertain a manner, but he disappeared, saying he was ignorant of Sanscrit. By means of later questions which he answers by "yes" and "no," it is discovered that they are words of love from Simandini to her husband, who was about to leave her for a voyage to his principality. Then suddenly, as the awaking seems to be approaching, Leopold moves the index-finger feverishly, and commences to dictate impatiently: "*Hasten* [to spell] . . . My good, my excellent, my dearly loved Sivrouka, without thee where to find happiness?" His answers to our questions lead us to understand that this is the substantial meaning of all the Sanscrit spoken that evening (and given above), that it is not he, Leopold, who speaks this language to Hélène, because he does not understand it, but that it is indeed he who gives us the French equivalent for it, not by a literal translation of the words themselves, since he does not understand them, but by interpreting the inmost feelings of Mlle. Smith, with which he is perfectly familiar. Shortly afterwards Hélène awakes without recollection.

According to M. de Saussure there are certainly in this text some Sanscrit fragments answering more or less to the interpretation of Leopold. The most clear are **mama priya**, which signifies *my dear, my dearly loved*, and **mama sadiou** (corrected to **sâdhô**), *my good, my excellent*. The rest of the phrase is less satisfactory in its present condition; **tava** could well be *of* *thee*, but **apa tava** is a pure barbarism, if it is intended for *far from thee*. In the same way the syllable **bag** in **bagda** seems to mean, independently of the translation of Leopold, **bhâga**, happiness, but is surrounded by incomprehensible syllables.

3. In a subsequent seance (December 1, 1895), Hélène gave herself up to a varied series of somnambulistic pantomimes representing scenes in the life of Simandini, which were thought to be located at Mangalore, and in the course of which several Hindoo words escaped her, of which, unhappily, no interpretation could be obtained from Leopold. But here again, if one is not too difficult to satisfy, a meaning more or less adapted to the pantomime is finally discovered.

In the midst of a playful scene with her little monkey, Mitidja, she tells him in her sweetest and most harmonious tones (A), **mama kana sour** (or **sourde**) **mitidya . . . kana mitidya** (*ter*). Later, answering her imaginary prince, who, according to Leopold, has just given her a severe admonition (the reason for which is not known), and to which she listened with an air of forced submission, and, almost sneeringly, she tells him (B), **adaprati tava sivrouka . . . . nô simyô sinonyedô . . . on yediô sivrouka**. Returning to a better feeling and leaning towards him, she murmurs with a charming smile (C) **mama plia . . . mama naximi** (or **naxmi**) **sivrouka . . . aô laos, mi sivrouka**.

In the fragment (A), one may suppose the **mama kana** to be a term of affection, taking the **kana** to be equivalent to the Sanscrit *kânta*, "beloved," or *kanistha*, "darling," unless it be translated, as M. Glardon does, **kana** (corrected to **khana**) **mitidya** *to eat for Mitidja*.

In the phrase (B), according to M. de Saussure, "the last words might, with some show of reason, make us think of the word **anyediuh**, *the following day*, or, *another day*, repeated twice; and, on the other hand, the first word might be transformed into **adya-prabhrti**, *starting from to-day;* which, combined with other syllables, themselves conventionally triturated, might give something like: **adya-pra-bhrti tava, sivruka . yôshin . . . na anyediuh, anyediuh**: *from to-day, of thee, Sivrouka, that I am . . . wife . . . not another day, another day*—which, besides (if it has any meaning at all,) has scarcely any connection with the scene."

In the phrase (C) the words **mama plia** evidently mean the same as the words above, **mama priya**, *my beloved;* **naxmi** might be **lakshmî**, *beauty and fortune;* and the last words might contain **asmi**, *I am.*

While, therefore, recognizing some words of pure Sanscrit, the whole appearance of these first texts presents, on the other hand, certain matters quite suspicious, from the point of view of construction, of the order of the words, and possibly also the correctness of the forms.

"*E.g.*," observes M. de Saussure, "I do not remember that one can say in Sanscrit, 'my Sivrouka,' nor 'my dear Sivrouka.' One can well say **mama priya**, *my well beloved*, substantively; but **mama priya Sivruka** is quite another thing: but it is *my dear Sivrouka* which occurs most frequently. It is true," adds my learned colleague, "that nothing can be affirmed absolutely, especially concerning certain epochs at which much bad Sanscrit was made in India. The resource always remains to us of assuming that, since the eleventh wife of Sivrouka was a child of Arabia, she had not had time to learn to express herself without error in the idiom of her lord and master, up to the moment at which the funeral pile put an end to her brief existence."

The misfortune is, in assuming by hypothesis the point of view of the romance, one exposes himself to another difficulty. "The most surprising thing," remarks M. de Saussure, "is that Mme. Simandini spoke Sanscrit, and not Pracrit (the connection of the first with the second is the same as that between Latin and French, the one springing from the other, but the one is the language in which the savants write, while the other is the spoken language). While in the Hindoo drama the kings, the brahmins, and the personages of high degree are observed habitually to use Sanscrit, it is questionable if such was constantly the case in real life. But, under all circumstances, all the women, even in the drama, speak Pracrit. A king addresses his wife in the noble language (Sanscrit); she answers him always in the vulgar language. But the idiom of Simandini, even though it be a Sanscrit very hard to recognize, is not in any case the Pracrit."

The numerous Hindoo speeches of Mlle. Smith during these latter years give rise to certain analogous observations, and do not throw any new light on their origin. I shall confine myself to a few examples, which I have chosen less for the sake of the Sanscritoid texts themselves, which are also always defective and distorted, than for the reason that the varied circumstances in which they have been produced afford a certain psychological interest.

4. Scene of Chiromancy. In the course of a long Arab seance, then Hindoo (February 2, 1896), Hélène knelt down by the side of my chair, and, taking me for Sivrouka, seized and examined my hand, all the while carrying on a conversation in a foreign language (without seeming to notice my actual words). It seems that this conversation contained some expression of anxiety in regard to my health, which had inspired several somnambulisms of Mlle. Smith during the preceding months (an example will be found on pp. 121-122).

At the same time at which she attentively examines the lines of my hand, she pronounces the following fragmentary sentences, separated by silences corresponding to the hallucinatory replies of Sivrouka: "**Priya sivrouka . . . nô** [signifying No, according to Leopold] **. . . tvandastroum sivrouka . . . itiami adia priya . . . itiami sivra adia . . . yatou . . . napi adia . . . nô . . . mama souka, mama baga sivrouka . . . yatou.**" Besides **sivra**, which, Leopold says, is an affectionate name for Sivrouka, we can divine in this text other terms of affection: **priya**, *beloved;* **mama soukha, mama bhâga**, *Oh, my delight, oh, my happiness!*" M. Glardon also calls attention to the word **tvandastroum**, which approaches the Hindustani *tandarast* (or *tandurust*), "who is in good health"—*tandurusti*, "health," coming from the two words *tan*, "physical condition," and *durust*, "good, true," of Persian origin. But he adds that it is possibly only a coincidence, and seems to me doubtful whether he would have thought of the connection if it were not found in a scene of chiromancy.

5. The Hindoo cycle, like the others, makes numerous irruptions into the ordinary life of Mlle. Smith, and affects her personality in most varied degrees, from the simple waking vision of Oriental landscapes or people up to the total incarnations of Simandini, of which Hélène preserves no memory whatever. One frequent form of these spontaneous automatisms consists in certain mixed states, in which she perceives personages who seem to her objective and independent, while continuing to have the feeling of a subjective implication or identification in regard to them, the impression of an indefinable *tua res agitur*. It then easily happens that the conversations she has with them are a mixture of French and a foreign language which she is wholly ignorant of, though feeling the meaning of it. The following is an example:

March 1, 1898.—Between five and six in the morning, while still in bed but wide awake, as she affirms, Hélène had "a superb Hindoo vision." Magnificent palace, with a huge staircase of white stone, leading to splendid halls furnished with low divans without cushions, of yellow, red, and more often of blue materials. In a boudoir a woman (Simandini) reclining and leaning nonchalantly on her elbow; on his knees near her a man with black curly hair, of dark complexion (Sivrouka), clothed in a large, red, embroidered robe, and speaking a foreign language, not Martian, which Hélène did not know, but which, however, she had the feeling of comprehending inwardly, and which enabled her to write some sentences of it in French after the vision. While she *listened* to this man speaking, she *saw* the lips of the woman open, without hearing any sound come from her mouth, in such a way that she did not know what she said, but Hélène had at the same time the impression of answering *inwardly, in thought*, to the conversation of the man, and she noted his reply. (This means, psychologically, that the words of Sivrouka gushed forth in auditive images or hallucinations, and the answers of Simandini-Hélène in psychomotor-spoken images of articulation, accompanied by the usual representation of Simandini effectuating the corresponding labial movements.) Here is a fragment of conversation noted by Hélène in pencil at the outset of the vision, in her ordinary handwriting, but very irregular, attesting that she had not yet entirely regained her normal state.

(Sivrouka.) "My nights without repose, my eyes red with tears, Simandini, will not these touch at last thy **attamana?** Shall this day end without *pardon, without love?*" (Simandini.) "Sivrouka, no, the day shall not end without pardon, without love; the **sumina** has not been launched far from me, as thou hast supposed; it is there—dost thou see?" (Sivrouka.) "Simandini, my **soucca, maccanna baguea**—pardon me again, always!"

This little scrap of conversation, it may be remarked in passing, gives quite correctly the emotional note, which is strong throughout the whole length of the Hindoo dream in the relationship of its two chief personages. As to the Sanscritoid words which are there mingled with the French, they have not an equal value. "**Sumina**," says M. de Saussure, "recalls nothing. **Attamana**, at most **âtmânam** (accusative of **âtmâ**), *l'âme*, 'the soul'; but I hasten to say that in the context in which **attamana** figures one could not make use of the Sanscrit word which resembles it, and which at bottom only signifies (*âme*) 'soul' in philosophical language, and in the sense of '*l'âme universelle*,' or other learned meanings."

6. The apparition of isolated Hindoo words, or words incorporated in a non-Hindoo context, is not very rare with Hélène, and is produced sometimes in auditive hallucinations, sometimes in her writings (see, *e.g.*, Fig. 37, p. 333); sometimes, again, in the course of words uttered in hemisomnambulism more or less marked. The list which has been collected of these detached terms shows the same mixture of pure Sanscrit and unknown words, which can only be connected with that language by some transformation so arbitrary or forced as to destroy altogether the value of such comparison.

To this second category belong, for example, **gava**, **vindamini**, **jotisse**, also spelled by Mlle. Smith. These terms, of whose signification she is absolutely ignorant, struck her ear in the course of a Hindoo vision which occurred in the morning when she first awoke. The last of these words recalls to M. de Saussure the Sanscrit *jyôtis*, "a constellation"; but then he would pronounce it *djiôtisse*, which hardly corresponds to the manner in which Hélène heard and wrote it. There must be added to these examples certain Hindoo words which have made irruptions into some Martian texts.

These are *Adel*, a proper name, and *yestad*, "unknown," in text 13; and (in text 31) *vadasa*, which, according to the rest of the sentence, seems to designate some divinities or some powers, and in which MM. de Saussure and Glardon suspect a mangled reminiscence of the Sanscrit term *dévâ-dâsa*, "slave of the gods."

7. To crown these specimens of the Sanscrit of Hélène, let us cite her "Hindoo chant," which has made half a dozen appearances in the last two years, and of which Leopold deigned, on a single occasion, to outline the translation.

The utterances consist essentially of the Sanscrit word *gaya* "chant," repeated to satiety, with here and there some other terms, badly articulated and offering discouraging variations in the notes taken by the different hearers. I will confine myself to two versions.

One of them is by Hélène herself. In a spontaneous vision (May 18, 1898, in the morning, upon awaking), she perceived a man, richly dressed in yellow and blue (Sivrouka), reclining upon beautiful cushions near a fountain surrounded by palm-trees; a brunette woman (Simandini) seats herself on the grass, sings to him in a strange language a ravishing melody. Hélène gathers the following fragments of it in writing, in which may be recognized the disfigured text of her ordinary song, "**Ga haïa vahaïyami . . . vassen iata . . . pattissaïa priaïa.**"

Fig. 36. Modulation of a Hindoo song. The final *G* of the three variations was held with perfect steadiness during fourteen seconds. The series A was often doubled and trebled before the continuation.

The other version is that of M. de Saussure, very much better qualified than we are to distinguish the Hindoo sounds. He was quite near Hélène, who sang seated upon the ground, whose voice for the moment articulated so badly that several words escaped him, and he does not vouch for the accuracy of his text, which is as follows, as he wrote it to the measure: "**Gaya gaya naïa ia miya gayä briti . . . gaya vaya yâni pritiya kriya gayâni i gâya mamatua gaya mama nara mama patii si gaya gandaryô gâya ityami vasanta . . . gaya gaya yâmi gaya priti gaya priya gâya patisi. . . .**"

It was towards the end of this same seance that Leopold, undoubtedly with the idea of doing honor to the distinguished presence of M. de Saussure, decided, after a scene of Martian translation (text 14, by Esenale), to give us, in Hélène's voice, his interpretation of the Hindoo chant, which follows, *verbatim*, with its mixture of Sanscrit words: "Sing, bird, let us sing! **Gaya!** Adèl, Sivrouka, sing of the spring-time! Day and night I am happy! Let us sing! Spring-time bird, happiness! **ityâmi mamanara priti**, let us sing! let us love! my king! Miousa, Adèl!"

In comparing these translations of the Hindoo text, certain points of resemblance are discovered between them. Outside the two perfectly correct words, **gâya**, *song*, and **vasanta**, *spring-time*, the idea of "*let us love*" is discovered in **priti** and **briti** (Sanscrit *prîti*, the act of loving), and an approximate equivalent of "*my king*" in **mama patii**, recalling the Sanscrit *mama patê*, "my husband, my master."

It is, unfortunately, hardly possible to carry the identification further, except perhaps for *bird*, which, with some show of reason, might be suspected in **vayayâni**, vaguely recalling **vâyasân** (accusative plural of **vâyasa** bird).

As to the melody of this plaintive ditty, M. Aug. de Morsier, who heard it at the seance of the 4th of September, 1898, has kindly noted it as exactly as possible (see Fig. 36).

The preceding examples suffice to give an idea of Hélène's Hindoo, and it is time to conclude.

It apparently does not belong to any actually existing dialect. M. Glardon declares that it is neither ancient nor modern Hindustani, and, after having put forth at the beginning, by way of simple hypothesis, the idea that it might be Tamil, or Mahratta, he now sees in it a *mélange* of real terms, probably Sanscrit and invented words. M. Michel, likewise, is of the opinion that the grotesque jargon of Simandini contains fragments of Sanscrit quite well adapted to the situation. All my correspondents are, on the whole, of exactly the same view, and I could not better sum up their opinion than by quoting the words of M. de Saussure:

"As to the question of ascertaining whether all this really represents Sanscrit, it is evidently necessary to answer, *No*. One can only say:

"First: That it is a medley of syllables, in the midst of which there are, incontestably, some series of eight to ten syllables, constituting a fragment of a sentence which has a meaning (especially exclamatory phrases—*e.g.*, **mama priya**, *mon bien-aimé* ("my well-beloved"); **mama soukha**, *mes délices* ("my delight").

"Secondly: That the other syllables, of unintelligible aspect, never have an anti-Sanscrit character— *i.e.*, do not present groups materially contrary or in opposition to the general figure of the Sanscrit words.

"Thirdly and finally: That the value of this latter observation is, on the other hand, quite considerably diminished by the fact that Mlle. Smith seldom launches out into complicated forms of syllables, and greatly affects the vowel *a;* but Sanscrit is a language in which the proportion of the *a*'s to the other vowels is almost four to one, so that in uttering three or four syllables in *a*, one could hardly avoid vaguely encountering a Sanscrit word."

It follows from this last remark of M. de Saussure that it ought not to be very difficult to fabricate Sanscrit after the mode of Simandini, if only one is possessed of some veritable elements which can serve as a model and give tone to the remainder. And there is no need to know very much of it, either, as M. Barth remarks:

"Has Mlle. Smith been in communication with any person from whom she could have taken some scraps of Sanscrit and of history? That would suffice, in this case, for the original germ, even though it were but slight. Imagination would do the rest. Children are very frequently *onomatopoioi*."

But it is, naturally, Mlle. Smith herself who furnishes us, in her own Martian, the fact most likely to throw light upon her Hindoo. It evidently is not difficult for a subconscious activity capable of manufacturing a language out of whole cloth to make another by imitation and by spinning out some real data. Also, as to the beginning of the Martian (a year later, as we have seen, to that of the Hindoo), M. de Saussure does not hesitate to make this comparison, and explains, *e.g.*, the initial Sanscritoid text, the famous phrase of benediction, **atiêyâ ganapatinâmâ**, by the same process of fabrication which shone forth in the words of Esenale or Astané.

I am not convinced that the general process of replacing word for word the French terms by terms of Oriental aspect, which is certainly the process employed in the fabrication of the Martian, has been made use of in the case of Hélène's Oriental words. Leopold, who has laid so much stress on procuring us a quasi-magical means of obtaining the literal translation of the Martian, has never condescended to do the same thing for the Hindoo, but has confined himself to outlining for us some free and vague interpretations, which scarcely add anything to that which the pantomime permits us to divine. This leads us to think that an entire precise translation of the Hindoo is impossible—in other terms, that Hélène does not fabricate her *pseudo*-Sanscrit by following step by step a French plot, and by maintaining in her neologisms the meaning which has been once adopted, but that she improvises and leaves the result to chance, without reflection (with the exception of some words of true Sanscrit, the meaning of which she knows and which she applies intelligently to the situation).

It is not, then, to the Martian texts proper, in my opinion, that we must compare Hélène's Hindoo, but to that *pseudo*-Martian jargon spoken with volubility in certain seances, and which have never been noted with certainty nor translated by Esenale.

It is understood, too, that while Hélène's subliminal self can safely give itself up to the creation of a definite language in the freedom which the planet Mars affords, where there is no pre-existing system to be conformed to nor any objective control to fear, it would be very imprudent and absurd to repeat the process in connection with India: the few words of pure Sanscrit which were at its disposal kept it from inventing others, the falseness of which would be evident at the first attempt at a literal and verbatim translation. It, therefore, contented itself with these veridical elements, insufficient in themselves alone for the construction of complete sentences, being a jargon devoid of meaning, but in harmony through their dominant vowels with the authentic fragments.

Now how could these authentic fragments have come into the possession of Mlle. Smith, who has no recollection whatever (nor has her family) of ever having studied Sanscrit, or of having ever been in communication with Oriental scholars? This is the problem which my researches have encountered hitherto, and as a solution of which I can think of nothing more likely than that of a fortunate chance, analogous to that which enabled me to discover the passage of De Marlès. I am, for the time being, reduced to vague conjectures as to the extent of Mlle. Smith's latent knowledge of Sanscrit, and the probable nature of its manner of acquisition.

I had long thought that Hélène might have absorbed her Hindoo principally by *auditive* means, and that she had, perhaps, in her infancy lived in the same house with some Indian student, whom she had heard, across the street or through an open window, speaking aloud Sanscrit texts with their French translation. The story of the young domestic without education is well known, who, seized with a fever, spoke both Greek and Hebrew, which had been stored up in her mind, unknown to her, while she was in the service of a German savant. *Se non è vero è ben trovato*. In spite of the just criticisms of Mr. Lang, apropos of its poorly established authenticity, this standard anecdote may be considered as a type of many other facts of the same kind which have since been actually observed, and as a salutary warning to distrust subconscious memories of auditive origin. But Indian scholars are rare in Geneva, and this trail has yielded me nothing.

I am really inclined to admit the exclusively *visual* origin of Hélène's Sanscrit. First, it is not necessary for her to have heard that idiom. Reading of texts printed in French characters coincides very well with a pronunciation so confused and badly articulated as hers; and, further, it alone can account for certain inexplicable errors of pronunciation if Mlle. Smith had acquired that language by ear.

The most characteristic of her errors is the presence in Hindoo of the French sound *u*, which does not exist in Sanscrit, but is naturally suggested by reading if it has not been previously ascertained that that letter is pronounced *ou* in the Sanscrit words in which it appears.

Other observations militate in favor of the same supposition. Never in the seances has Simandini ventured to *write* Sanscrit, and it is in French letters that her name was given (see p. 288).

Fig. 37 Fragment. Final sentence of a letter of Mlle. Smith, finished (or rather remaining unfinished), during the irruption of a spontaneous access of Hindoo somnambulism. Note foreign words, *boulboul* (Persian name for nightingale), *Kana* (Hindoo slave of Simandini), and *radyiva* (Sanscrit name for blue lotus); also the Sanscrit letters *a, e, i, d, r*, taking the place of the French initials. Note also the change of form of the *t*'s.

Still, Hélène subconsciously possesses a part, at least, of the Devanagari alphabet, since sometimes certain characters belonging to it slip into her normal writing. But it is to be noted that her knowledge of this kind does not seem in any way to go beyond that which might have resulted from a rapid glance at a Sanscrit grammar.

In certain cases this irruption of foreign signs (altogether analogous to that which has been seen in the case of the Martian) is connected with an access of spontaneous somnambulism and makes part of a whole troop of images and of Oriental terms.

An interesting example is found in Fig. 37, which reproduces the end of a letter which Hélène wrote me from the country. All the rest of this six-page letter is perfectly normal, both as to handwriting and content, but suddenly, tired by her effort of prolonged attention, she begins to speak of her health, sleep overcomes her, and the last lines show the invasion of the Oriental dream.

Kana, the slave, with his tame birds, and the brilliant plants of the tropics, substitute themselves little by little for the actual room. The letter reached me unfinished and without signature, as is shown in Fig. 37; Hélène closed it mechanically during her somnambulism, without knowledge of this unusual termination, at which she was surprised and annoyed when I showed it to her later.

Examination and comparison of all these graphomotor automatisms show that there are in Hélène's subconsciousness some positive notions, albeit superficial and rudimentary, of the Sanscrit alphabet. She knows the exact form of many isolated characters, and their general value, in the abstract, as it were, but she does not seem to have any idea of their concrete use in connection with other letters.

In a word, these fragments of graphic automatisms betray a knowledge of Hindoo writing such as a curious mind might be able to acquire by perusing for some moments the first two or three pages of a Sanscrit grammar. It would retain certain detached forms; first, the a and the e, which, striking the eye at the commencement of the two first lines (containing the vowels, and usually separated from the following lines containing the consonants) of the standard arrangement of the Hindoo letters in ten groups; then the series of ciphers, occupying a line by themselves and easy to retain; finally, some other simple signs gleaned at hazard; but there will probably not be retained any of the too complicated figures resulting from the union of several characters in order to form words. This supposed genesis entirely corresponds with the extent of the notions as to Sanscrit writing of which Mlle. Smith's subconsciousness gives evidence.

It will suffice in summing up, to account for Mlle. Smith's Hindoo language, that perhaps in the N. group, or in some other spiritistic environment of which I am ignorant, some one, for the sake of curiosity, may have shown her and allowed her to glance over a Sanscrit grammar or lexicon, immediately after a seance, during that state of suggestibility in which the exterior suggestions are registered very strongly in her case, often without leaving traces in her conscious memory. The fact will also be explained that Hélène has no memory whatever of it, is absolutely convinced that she never saw or heard the least fragment of Sanscrit or any other Oriental language.

I ought also to add that the information which I have up to the present time been able to gather has furnished me with no positive indication of the truth of my supposition, while, on the other hand, it has not tended to establish its falsity.

Fig. 38. Examples of Sanscrit characters, automatically substituted for French words and ciphers, in words and figures appearing in the normal writings of Mlle. Smith (*la*me, *ru*bis, 166, *pl*rs, 286/5, 154). Natural size.

V. THE SOURCES OF THE HINDOO DREAM

This paragraph will have no meaning whatever for those who hold the Oriental cycle to be in reality the reappearance in Mlle. Smith's somnambulistic states, of memories belonging to an anterior existence in which she was an Asiatic princess, and I myself naik of Tchandraguiri, Professor Seippel, an Arab slave, etc.

I shall confine myself in this case to an expression of regret that the chance which has united us afresh, after five centuries of separation, did not leave us in the midst of those tropical splendors instead of transporting us to the banks of the Rhône just where the fog is densest in winter. It is a severe punishment for our past misdeeds. But when one pushes his skepticism so far as only to see in the entire Hindoo dream a fantastic product elaborated out of certain scattered facts, as I have done in the preceding paragraphs, one is likewise punished for his want of faith by the obscure problems which are met with on the subject of the sources of this dream. I would say also that it is difficult to understand why the hypnoid imagination of Mlle. Smith gave itself up to such pranks, and distributed as it did the rôles of this comedy.

It is easy to understand how a nature given to subconscious reveries, and such as I have described in the first chapters of this book, has taken pleasure in the fiction of the tragic destiny of Simandini, and also that she felt specially attracted towards the career of Marie Antoinette.

But M. Seippel, whom I quoted above, has nothing about him of the Arab, and still less of the slave, neither in outward appearance nor in character; and as to myself, let us say here, M. F.—if I may be permitted to substitute harmless initials for the always odious "I"—as for M. F., there is generally to be met with in him, under some diffidence, a certain mildness of manner and disposition which would scarcely seem to predestinate him to the energetic and wild rôle of a violent, whimsical, capricious, and jealous Oriental despot.

As to the psychological origins of the Hindoo dream—considered not so much in its Oriental decoration, but in its essential note, which is the relation of Simandini to Sivrouka (the pretended anteriority of M. F.)—two hypotheses can be framed, between which it is difficult to choose.

First. From the point of view of psychopathology I should be tempted to cause this entire somnambulistic romance to be included in that which Freud calls *Abwehrpsychosen*, resulting from a sort of autonomy which frees the normal self from an affective idea incompatible with it; which idea revenges itself by occasioning very diverse perturbations, according to the subjects, from disorders of innervation, coming to disturb the daily life (hysteria by somatic conversion of the affective coefficient of the repulsed idea), up to the case in which the self only escapes the intolerable contradiction between the given reality and the idea which besets it by plunging itself entirely into the latter (mental hallucinatory confusion, delirium, etc.).

Between these varied results may be found that in which the idea excluded from the consciousness becomes the germ of hypnoid developments, the point of departure of a secondary consciousness unknown to the ordinary personality, the centre of a somnambulistic life in which the tendencies which the normal self has driven far away from it may take refuge and give themselves free play.
This is, perhaps, the happiest solution, from a practical and social point of view, since it leaves the individual in a state of perfect equilibrium and free from nervous troubles, outside of the very limited moments in which the underlying processes break out in accesses of somnambulism.

Such may be the case of the Hindoo dream and the origin of the attributing of the rôle of Sivrouka to M. F. Nothing, assuredly, in the normal life or being of Mlle. Smith would cause the suspicion that she had ever consciously felt towards the latter the absurd sentiments which good sense would have condemned in advance; but divers hints of her subliminal life, independently of the Hindoo cycle itself (certain dreams, etc.), have sometimes seemed to betray a latent conflict, which the sane and reasonable self would have quickly gotten rid of by the banishment from the ordinary personality of the affective idea, inadmissible in the given conditions of reality. Hence, with a temperament accustomed to mediumistic doubling of personality and imbued with spiritistic doctrines, the birth and development, underneath the level of the normal consciousness, of this romance of a former existence, in which emotional tendencies incompatible with the present life have found on occasion a sort of theoretic justification and a free field for expansion.

Secondly: It may also be presumed, and I prefer to admit, that the sentiments of Simandini towards her fictitious rajah, far from being the reflection and somnambulic transposition of an impression really felt by Mlle. Smith in regard to some one real and determined, are only a fantastic creation—like the passion with which juvenile imaginations are sometimes inflamed for an ideal and abstract type while awaiting the meeting with a concrete realization more or less like it—and that the assimilation of Sivrouka to M. F. is only a coincidence due to the simple chance of Mlle. Smith having made the acquaintance of M. F. at the time when the Hindoo dream was about to begin. Two points strengthen this hypothesis of a contingent and superficial confusion between M. F. and Sivrouka. First, the Hindoo dream was evidently begun by a characteristic vision in which Simandini appeared, almost two months before the admission of M. F. to the seances (see pp. 279-281). Instead of supposing that the subconsciousness of Mlle. Smith foresaw already the probable arrival of this new spectator, and reserved for him in advance a leading rôle in the romance of former existence which she was in process of elaborating (which is not altogether impossible, it is true), it hardly seems as though M. F. could have stood for anything in the dream-personage of Sivrouka. In the second place, it is only in the light somnambulisms and her mixed or crepuscular states that Mlle. Smith happens to take M. F. for the Hindoo prince and to seat herself at his feet in attitudes of tenderness and abandon (without otherwise ever departing from the bounds of perfect propriety); as soon as the trance becomes profound and the Hindoo somnambulism complete, M. F. ceases to exist for her, as well as the others present, and she then is concerned only with an absolutely hallucinatory Sivrouka. This is the place to state that Hélène has never presented any phenomenon similar to—far from it—certain cases in which have been seen the awakening in the hypnotic subject of gross and more or less bestial tendencies, for which the subjects would have blushed in their waking state. There is nothing of that nature in Mlle. Smith. Somnambulism does not detract in any way from the elevation of her moral sense. The same is true of her deepest trances or when she "incarnates" personages very different from her ordinary character—she never departs from that real dignity which is a trait of her normal personality.

To sum up—the hypothesis of a purely accidental identification, a kind of association by simple contiguity between the Hindoo prince and M. F., seems to me, on the whole, the most natural. It releases the latter, besides, from all responsibility (altogether involuntary, however) for the sentiments so profound, so disinterested, so worthy of a less tragic fate, which the imaginary personage of Sivrouka Nayaka inspires in the poor Princess Simandini.

THE ROYAL CYCLE

IF I were obliged to give this cycle a place proportioned to that which it occupies in the somnambulic life of Mlle. Smith, a hundred pages would not suffice. But permit me to pass rapidly over facts concerning which I should only be obliged to repeat the greater part of the observations called forth by the preceding romances, which apply equally well, *mutatis mutandis*, to the personification of Marie Antoinette by Hélène.

The choice of this rôle is naturally explained by the innate tastes of Mlle. Smith for everything that is noble, distinguished, elevated above the level of the common herd, and by the fact that some exterior circumstance fixed her hypnoid attention upon the illustrious queen of France in preference to the many other historic figures equally qualified to serve as a point of attachment for her subconscious megalomaniac reveries.

In default of absolutely certain information on this point, I strongly suspect the engraving from the *Memoirs of a Physician*, representing the dramatic scene of the decanter between Balsamo and the Dauphiness, of having given birth to this identification of Hélène with Marie Antoinette, as well as to that of her secondary personality of Leopold with Cagliostro.

We have, in fact, seen that this engraving (pp. 94-95), so well calculated to impress the imagination, was shown to Mlle. Smith by Mme. B. at the end of a seance—that is, at a moment when one is never sure that Hélène's return to her normal state is complete, and in which her hypnoid personality, still on a level with consciousness, so to speak, is very prone to absorb the interesting suggestions which the environment may furnish. It was several months—a year and a quarter, possibly—after this incident (the precise date of which, in 1892 or 1893, it is impossible to determine) that announcement was made by the table, on the 30th of January, 1894, that Hélène was the reincarnation of Marie Antoinette. It is to be recollected that in the interval she had for some time believed herself to be the reincarnation of Lorenza Feliciani; it is, however, to be noted that these two successive identifications did not have the same guarantee or psychological signification. In fact, it was Mlle. Smith, in the waking state—that is, in her normal personality—who accepted the supposition of Mme.

B., that she was the reincarnation of Lorenza; but the table—*i.e.*, her subconsciousness—always remained silent on this point. On the contrary, the idea of having been Marie Antoinette does not seem to have occurred to Hélène's ordinary consciousness up to the time at which Leopold revealed this secret by the table. If any conclusion may be drawn from this, it is that, under the multiple suggestions of the engraving from Dumas' works and the suppositions of Mme. B., the hypnoid imagination of Mlle. Smith at first preferred to the rôle of Lorenza that of Marie Antoinette, which is undoubtedly more flattering and more conformable to Hélène's temperament, and then elaborated and matured it, very slowly, it is true, but not excessively so, in comparison with other examples of subliminal incubations of Mlle. Smith.

From the point of view of its psychological forms of manifestation, the Royal cycle from that time followed an evolution analogous to that of its congeners described in the preceding chapters. After some months, during which it unfolded itself in visions described by Hélène and accompanied by typtological explanations dictated by the table, the trance became more profound. Mlle. Smith began to personate the queen in pantomime, of which Leopold gave the exact signification by digital indications. Speech was added the year following, at a date which I cannot fix, but the first occasion on which I was a witness to it was on the 13th of October, 1895. Handwriting only made its appearance, as far as I am aware, two years later (November 1, 1897, see Fig. 39), when the royal incarnation attained its apogee and Hélène was in the habit of retaining in memory the somnambulistic rôle of Marie Antoinette for several hours. Since then the rôle has maintained itself at a very remarkable level of perfection, but it scarcely seems to me progressing, and seems likely to become stereotyped. The objectivity of the general type of queen must be distinguished in this brilliant personality, or at least that of a lady of great distinction, as well as a realization of the individual characteristics of Marie Antoinette of Austria. As to the first point there is almost nothing left to be desired. Mlle. Smith seems by nature to possess all that this rôle demands, and hypnoid autosuggestion finds no lack of material upon which to work.

When the royal trance is complete no one can fail to note the grace, elegance, distinction, majesty sometimes, which shine forth in Hélène's every attitude and gesture.

Je n'ai pas dormi une seule minute et il paroitrait que sans que je m'en sois doutée un seul instant, la voix de Marie-Ant. s'est long-temps fait entendre.

Plus-tard également, et encore toujours sans m'en douter, j'ai parlé sanskrit et cela pendant de longs instants.

Léopold est venu seulement deux ou trois minutes, et la séance a été close sans qu'il soit venu nous dire adieu.

M.ʳ Quendet m'a monté hier tout l'alphabet martien que M.ʳ Flournoy lui aurait envoyé n° ce qu'il dit.

Fig. 39. First known example of automatic irruption of the orthography and handwriting called that of Marie Antoinette among the normal writings of Mlle. Smith. Fragments of a letter of Helen of November 1, 1897, narrating a seance during which she had successfully incarnated the queen of France and the Hindoo princess. [Collection of M. Lemaitre.] See also p

She has verily the bearing of a queen. The more delicate shades of expression, a charming amiability, condescending hauteur, pity, indifference, overpowering scorn flit successively over her countenance and are manifested in her bearing, to the filing by of the courtiers who people her dream. The play of her hands with her real handkerchief and its fictitious accessories, the fan, the binocle with long handle, the scent-bottle which

Fig. 40. Writing of Mlle. Smith incarnating Marie Antoinette. Seance of November 7, 1897. Beginning of a letter, written in ink and addressed to Philippe d'Orléans (M. Aug. de Morsier, who was not present at the seance). After the ink-stains of the last line, Hélène threw down her pencil, then began again and finished her letter in pencil in a still more regular and slanting hand than the above.

Fig. 41. Writing and signature of Marie Antoinette. Fragment of a letter written from the Temple to General de Jarnayes, and reproduced in the *Isographie des Hommes célèbres*. [Collection of fac-similes published under the direction of Duchesne, Sr., Paris, 1827-30.]

she carries in a pocket in her girdle; her curtseying, the movement, full of grace and ease, by which she never forgets at each turning around, to throw back her imaginary train; everything of this kind, which cannot be described, is perfect in its ease and naturalness. Special personification of the unhappy Austrian wife of Louis XVI. is of a less evident, and moreover doubtful, accuracy. To judge of it from the only objective point of comparison at our disposal, the handwriting (see Figs. 39 to 41), the Marie Antoinette of Hélène's somnambulisms little resembles her supposed prototype, for there is less of difference between the autographs of Cagliostro and of Leopold (see p. 109) than there is between that of the real queen and that of her pretended reincarnation in Mlle. Smith, the latter having a rounded, inclined calligraphy, much more regular than in her normal state, instead of the angular and illegible writing which was characteristic of the queen of France, to say nothing of the glaring differences in formation of many letters. Some orthographic analogies (Hélène writes *instans*, *enfans*, *étois*, etc.) have nothing specific about them, and simply recall the general habits of the last century (see p. 112).

Not having discovered any indication as to Marie Antoinette's manner of speaking, I do not know whether the hypnoid imagination of Hélène has succeeded better than with the handwriting in adopting in her royal incarnations certain intonations and a pronunciation which have nothing of German in them, and would rather recall the English accent. The timbre of her voice does not change, but her speech becomes trailing, with a slight rolling of the *r*'s, and takes on something precise and affected, very pretty, but slightly irritating by its length. We already know that there is not an absolute wall of separation between Hélène's various trances. Just as is the case with the Martian and the Hindoo, the handwriting or the spelling of the queen sometimes slips into the correspondence of Mlle. Smith (see Fig. 39), and she also sometimes assumes the accent of Marie Antoinette, if not in the ordinary waking state (I do not know whether that is ever the case), at least outside her Royal cycle, especially in the phases of transition in which she begins or ends by incarnating Leopold, the Martians, etc. (see, for example, p. 56).

From the point of view of its content, the Royal cycle forms a collection of scenes and varied tableaux, like the Martian dream, lacking any continuous plot, and in which marked historic events scarcely hold a place—*e.g.*, in it the queen is never seen to mount the scaffold as Simandini ascends her funeral pile. One does not always even know whether the spectacle before our eyes is supposed to be the repetition, the exact recollection, of unknown but real episodes in the life of Marie Antoinette, or indeed whether it has to do with new, actual incidents passing now between the reincarnated queen and her old acquaintances whom she discovers in the persons present at the seance or in the disincarnate spirits in mediumistic relationship with her. That depends on the case—*e.g.*, on the 25th of December, 1896, Mlle. Smith, entranced, addresses touching exhortations to a lady present whom she took for the Princess Lamballe, which, according to Leopold, is a reproduction of the last evening which the unhappy queen, sustained by her companion in captivity, passed in this world. (It is true that at Christmas, 1792, the princess had already, three months previously, fallen a victim to the massacres of September.) Again the Abbé Grégoire dictates by the table, which bows significantly to Hélène, "*I desired to save you, but I was not able*"; or the sinister Hébert says to her by the same process, "*I was the cause of your death . . . I suffer; pray for me*." Ought we to consider real the homage and the posthumous remorse which these two disincarnate spirits bring after the lapse of a century to their sovereign, finally recognized in the person of Mlle. Smith?

Generally it is impossible to decide whether the incident transpiring pretends simply to republish the past or constitutes a new fact.

The location of the royal scenes and visions is often undetermined. Many are located in the gardens or the apartments of the Petit Trianon, and the furniture which Hélène describes there is, indeed, always pure Louis XVI. More rarely Marie Antoinette is found at the Temple, or at certain rendezvous—innocent, but very imprudent—in some secret abode in Paris. She is never seen in Austria, since, unlike the Hindoo princess still filled with her Arab memories, she seems to have completely lost sight of her past as a young girl.

In the surroundings of the queen, the king is conspicuous by his absence; very rarely she makes some allusions to him with a marked indifference. The greater part of the personages known to that epoch, whom I refrain from enumerating, figure in it incidentally, but there are three who continually reappear and hold the first rank. There is, first, the Count of Cagliostro, "*mon sorcier*," or "*ce cher sorcier*," as the queen familiarly calls him, who never has enough of his visits and his conversations, which are very varied, including the discussion of philosophic subjects, such as the future life and the existence of God as well as the gossip of the last *fête* at Versailles. There is, secondly, Louis Philippe d'Orléans (Equality); while the third is the old Marquis de Mirabeau; all of whom, especially the first, have served as hallucinatory interlocutors towards Hélène in numerous scenes— up to the time at which, to the great amusement of the sitters, the somnambulistic monologue was transformed into real and lively conversation, in consequence of the introduction into the seances of M. Eugène Demole, then of M. Aug. de Morsier, in whom Marie Antoinette immediately recognized the two personages last above mentioned.

Since this unexpected meeting with her two contemporaries, reincarnated, like herself, the somnambulistic queen freely permits herself, on occasion, the pleasure of renewing the little suppers and joyous evenings of long ago. When a seance which has lasted from four o'clock until seven in the afternoon seems to have come to an end, and Mlle. Smith, after having awakened from a long series of Hindoo, Martian, and other scenes, has been invited to dine and refresh herself before taking up her household duties, it often happens that, perceiving M. Demole or M. de Morsier among the persons present, she gives a slight start, with a change of countenance, sometimes barely perceptible, but which there is no mistaking; then, in her very characteristic accent of Marie Antoinette, exclaims, "Oh, marquis, you have been here, and I had not noticed you before!" And then follows a somnambulistic vigil which may be prolonged until nearly ten o'clock in the evening, maintained by means of the suggestive amiability of her improvised companions in sustaining their rôles of Mirabeau or Philippe d'Orléans.

They descend to the dining-room. The queen takes her place at the table alongside of the marquis (or of Philippe). She has eyes and ears for him alone, the other guests and the servants remaining shut out from her dream. She eats and drinks only that which he sets before her, and it is no sinecure to supply the wants of this august neighbor, since she possesses a truly royal appetite. The amount of food which she devours and the goblets of wine which she drinks off one after another, without suffering any inconvenience, are astounding, as in her normal state Mlle. Smith is sobriety itself and eats very little. After dinner they pass into the salon, with many compliments and obeisances, and Marie Antoinette takes coffee. On the first occasions of this kind, she also accepted a cigarette from Philippe and smoked it—Mlle. Smith never smokes in her waking state—but the remarks of the persons present upon the historical untruthfulness of this feature must have been registered, and bore fruit, since at the following seances she did not seem to understand the use of tobacco in that form; she accepted, on the other hand, with eagerness, a pinch of imaginary snuff, which almost immediately brought about by autosuggestion a series of sneezes admirably successful.

The evening passes in most varied conversation, until, evidently feeling fatigue, the queen becomes silent, closes her eyes, and goes to sleep in an easy-chair. At that instant Leopold, who gives no sign of life, and from whom no response can be obtained during the royal somnambulism, reappears and answers by the fingers or manifests himself in spontaneous gestures. Hélène's hand, *e.g.*, is raised, and makes passes on her forehead to accentuate the restorative sleep which is about to bring her back to her normal state. At the end of some time—half an hour or more—she awakes without any recollection of the evening, believing that she has not yet dined, and complaining of hunger and thirst, as if her stomachic sensibility participated in the amnesia and other modifications which accompany the change of personality. Nevertheless, at such times I have never seen her accept anything more than a couple of glasses of water, after which she feels wide awake.

In escorting her home, I was witness on one occasion to a return of the royal somnambulism. She was exceedingly desirous of going to the house of a well-known personage (whom she had perceived in her vision during the seance), who had been received at the court of Marie Antoinette, and who died in Geneva in the first quarter of this century; it was only upon arriving before the house in which he had lived, and as she was upon the verge of entering it, that I finally succeeded in awakening and restoring her to herself, without memory of the incident, and very much astonished at the unaccustomed streets in which we found ourselves.

It is useless to give a more circumstantial narration of these dinners and *soirées* of Marie Antoinette. They are very entertaining for the spectators, but lose much of their interest when related in their entirety. Their details are exactly what might be expected of a lively subliminal imagination, alert and full of verve, abundantly supplied, on account of the illustrious queen, with notions still more easily explicable, thanks to the intellectual atmosphere of France, than those of the Hindoo cycle.

Numerous anachronisms, however, slip into them, and her Majesty sometimes falls into the snares which the marquis or Philippe take a malicious pleasure in setting for her. She often escapes them when they are too clumsy, and, with a most comical display of temper, is at first confused, then curiously questions, or manifests uneasiness in regard to the mental state of her interlocutors when they introduce the telephone, the bicycle, steamships, or the modern scientific vocabulary into their eighteenth-century conversation. But, on the other hand, she herself employs terms still more malapropos, such as, "to derail" (figuratively), "metre" and "centimetre," etc. Certain words, such as "tramway" and "photography," have occasioned serious conflicts. Marie Antoinette first allows the treacherous word to pass unnoticed, and it is evident that she perfectly understood it, but her own reflection, or the smile of the sitters, awakens in her the feeling of incompatibility; she returns to the word just used, and pretends a sudden ignorance and astonishment in regard to it. Spiritism explains these blunders by accusing the Machiavellian companions of the queen of grossly abusing the suggestibility attached to the trance state by jumbling her ideas and throwing her into confusion. Psychology is not surprised that the subliminal imitation, however remarkable it may be, presents some little defects, and every one is in accord in regard to her thoughtless manner of expressing herself, in attributing these anachronisms to an accidental mingling of the memories of her ordinary personality and of the present life with those of the royal personality revived during the somnambulism. In her rôle as queen, Mlle. Smith gives evidence of a great deal of ingenuity. She is full of witty repartees, which disconcert her interlocutors, the style of which is sometimes perfectly after the manner of the epoch.

This ease and readiness of dialogue, excluding all reflective or calculating preparation, denote a great freedom of mind and a wonderful facility for improvisation. There are mixed with these, on the other hand, some witticisms and episodes which are not at all impromptu, but are the evident result of a preliminary elaboration in the course of the subconscious reveries and various automatisms which the royal romance causes to surge up in Hélène's ordinary life.

There are some scenes whose development or repetition can be followed in a series of seances and spontaneous visions as it passes through the other cycles. The following is one example among many:

At the end of a seance at which M. de Morsier was present (October 10, 1897), Mlle. Smith enters into her dream of Marie Antoinette. During dinner she makes several allusions to her son, the Dauphin, speaks of her daughter, tells of having demanded of her sorcerer the sex of her next child, etc.—matters all foreign to the conversation of Philippe, and which seem to announce some underlying scene ready to break forth. In fact, in the middle of the *soirée* the queen becomes absorbed and distrait, and finally falls on her knees in a dark corner of the *salon;* her monologue indicates that she is before the cradle where the little Dauphin and his sister are lying asleep. Presently she returns to seek Philippe and to conduct him to admire the sleeping children, to whom, in a very soft voice, she sings an unknown nursery rhyme ("Sleep in peace," etc.) of a plaintive melody analogous to that of the Hindoo chant; the tears gush from her eyes; tender kisses upon the imaginary cradle and a fervent prayer to the Virgin terminate this extremely touching maternal scene.

Several weeks after (the 1st of December), a new romance makes its appearance in a spontaneous access of visual, auditive, and graphic automatism, the recital of which Hélène sent me the following day. That evening, while alone with her mother, she had interrogated Leopold upon an affair in which she was greatly interested, and had obtained from him an answer: "As soon as his communication was ended, I saw everything disturbed around me; then at my left, at a distance of about thirty feet, a Louis XVI. *salon*, not very large, was outlined, in the middle of which was a square piano, open. Before this piano was seated a woman, still young, the color of whose hair I could not distinguish. Whether it was blond or gray I could not clearly see. She played and sang at the same time. The sounds of the piano, the voice even, reached me, but I could not catch the words of the song. A young girl and a boy stood on either side of the piano. Not far from them was seated a young lady holding an infant on her lap.[1] This charming vision lasted a very short time, not longer than ten minutes."

After the disappearance of the vision, Hélène had the idea of taking up her pencil. " With pencil in hand, I was asking myself what I should write, when all at once I heard again the melody; then, this time very distinctly, the words, but without any vision. The whole passed into my head, into my brain, and instinctively I pressed my hand to my forehead in order to hear and understand better. I felt myself compelled to hold the pencil in a manner different from my habitual way of holding it. Here are the words of the song heard and traced at that instant. As you see, the handwriting is not like mine; there are also some very glaring errors of orthography.

"Approchez-vous approchez-vous | enfans chéris approchez-vous | quand le printemps sur nous ramène | ses frais parfums ses rayons d'or | venez

---

[1] It will be readily understood that this vision represents Marie Antoinette with her three children and Madame Elizabeth.

enfans sous son haleine | gazouiller bas mes doux trésors | approchez-vous approchez-vous | enfans chéris approchez-vous | êtres chéris enfans bénis—approchez-vous de votre mère | son doux baiser petits amis | calme et guérit toutes misères | approchez-vous approchez-vous | enfans chéris approchez-vous." [1]

Some months later the two preceding scenes were reproduced, with variations of detail, on the same evening, during which Marie Antoinette first conducts Philippe towards the fictitious cradle of her cherubs and sings to them her first song: "Sleep in peace," etc. Then she leads him to the piano, and, displaying an imaginary sheet of music beneath his eyes, obliges him to accompany her while she sings the "Song of Elizabeth."

M. de Morsier, who, fortunately, is not easily embarrassed, improvised an accompaniment to which the queen accommodated herself after some criticism, and to which she sings in a very sweet, pure voice some words which were found to be, word for word, identical with those automatically written by Hélène on the preceding 1st of December. In this example is seen the mixture of preparation, of repetition, and of impromptu, which are inferred from the varied incidents which constitute the royal *soirées*.

It is probable that if it were possible to be a witness of, or if Mlle. Smith could remember all the spontaneous automatisms which aid in nourishing the royal romance, nocturnal dreams, hypnagogic visions, subconscious reveries during the waking state, etc., there would be presented interminable imaginary conversations with the marquis, Philippe, Cagliostro, and all the fictitious personages who occasionally make their appearance in the somnambulistic scenes of Marie Antoinette.

It is by this underlying and unknown work, perhaps never interrupted, that the personality of the queen of France is slowly prepared and elaborated, and which shines forth and displays itself with so much of magnificence in the soirées with Philippe d'Orléans and the Marquis de Mirabeau.

---

[1] I have respected the orthography as well as the complete absense of punctuation of this bit of automatic writing, confining myself to marking by vertical bars its evident separation into verses of eight feet. It is written in the inclined and regular hand called that of Marie Antoinette (like that of Fig. 40), but with a pencil too pale to permit its reproduction.

I have stated that, except these two gentlemen, who always form part of the royal dream when they are present (and even sometimes when absent), the others present at the seances are excluded. It is understood that they do not pass unperceived on this account.

In the same manner as in the negative hallucinations or systematic anæsthesia of hypnotized subjects, that which seems to be not felt is nevertheless registered; so, in like manner, it is altogether probable that nothing of that which passes around her escapes the fundamental individuality of Mlle. Smith. The royal personality which occupies the foreground of the scene and finds itself in an elective rapport, limited to Philippe and the marquis, merely causes the other personalities to be relegated to the background without breaking their connection with the environment. There are many proofs of this. For example, in walking, Marie Antoinette never runs against any of the others present. The remarks and criticisms of the latter are not lost upon her, since very frequently her conversation betrays their influence after some minutes. At the same time, if any one pinches her hand or tickles her ear, her lips, her nostrils, she seems anæsthetic; still, at the end of a few seconds she turns her head away, and if the tickling is persisted in, she experiences a kind of agitation accommodated to the circumstances of her dream, changes her position on some pretext, etc.

It is manifest, in short, that the excitations to which she seems to be insensible at the moment, far from having no effect, are stored up and produce, by their sum total, reactions which are retarded for some minutes and which are intelligently adapted to the somnambulistic scene, but with an intensity much more exaggerated than diminished by this period of latency.

Music also affects her, precipitating her out of the dream of Marie Antoinette into a common hypnotic state, in which she assumes passionate attitudes, which have in them nothing of the regal, and which conform to the varied airs which follow each other upon the piano.

In her phases as Marie Antoinette, Hélène has an accent characteristic of it; she recognizes me vaguely; she has some allochiria, a complete insensibility of the hands, and a large appetite; she does not know who Mlle. Smith is; if she is asked to give the actual date, she replies correctly as to the month and day, but indicates a year of the last century, etc. Then all at once her state changes; the royal accent gives way to her ordinary voice, she seems wide awake, all mental confusion has disappeared, she is perfectly clear as to persons, dates, and circumstances, but has no memory of the state from which she has just emerged, and she complains of a sharp pain in her finger (where I had pinched it while in her preceding phase). I took advantage one day of these alternations to offer her a pencil, and dictated to her the sentence of Fig. 42. In her normal moments she holds the pencil in her accustomed manner, between the index and middle fingers, and writes in her usual hand; during the returns of the royal somnambulism she holds it between the thumb and index-finger and assumes her handwriting and orthography known as that of Marie Antoinette, exactly as her voice is invested with the accent. It is to be presumed that all her other functions, if one could examine them, would show parallel analogous variations, the changing of the personality being naturally accompanied by connected changes not only of the memory and the sensibility, but of motility of the emotional disposition—in brief, of all the faculties of the individuality.

I must add that in each of her states Hélène has the memory of preceding periods of the same kind, but not of another state: it was, for example, necessary to dictate anew, for the second test, the sentence of , which she did not remember having heard or written a few minutes previously. This separation into distinct memories is not, however, absolute, nor very profound: the personality of Marie Antoinette is, in short, a modification— of an intensity and extent which vary greatly with the seances—of the ordinary personality of Mlle. Smith, rather than an alternating and exclusive personality, of which so many striking cases have been observed.

Fig. 42. Differences of handwriting of Mlle. Smith at the end of an incarnation of Marie Antoinette, according to whether she is in her normal state (upper lines, in her usual handwriting), or in a return of the royal dream (lower lines; note the word *foisoit*). Natural size. The tremor of some of the strokes is not in the original, but occurred in the reproduction in ink.

For the mere spectators, the royal somnambulism is perhaps the most interesting of all of Hélène's cycles, on account of the brilliancy and life of the rôle, the length of time during which it may be sustained, the unexpected happenings which the presence of other real persons brings into it. It is truly a comedy.

But for the lovers of the supernormal it is the least extraordinary of the subliminal creations of Mlle. Smith, because the general environment, being in France, is so imbued with historic or legendary memories of the illustrious and unfortunate queen that there is nothing surprising in the hypnoid reconstruction of a personage so well known.

Finally, the psychologist and moralist who undertakes to reflect on the inner meaning of things cannot escape the impression of sharp contrast as compared with reality which this sparkling romance affords.

In themselves, Mlle. Smith's royal somnambulisms are almost always gay and joyous; but, considering their hidden source, in so far as they are the ephemeral and chimerical revenge of the ideal upon the real, of impossible dreams upon daily necessities, of impotent aspirations upon blind and crushing destiny, they assume a tragic signification. They express the sensation lived through, felt, of the bitter irony of things, of futile revolt, of fatality dominating the human being. They seem to say that all happy and brilliant life is only an illusion soon dissipated. The daily annihilation of the dream and the desire by implacable and brutal reality cannot find in the hypnoid imagination a more adequate representation, a more perfect symbol of an emotional tonality, than her royal majesty whose existence seemed made for the highest peaks of happiness and of fame—and ended on the scaffold.

SUPERNORMAL APPEARANCES

THE mediumship of Mlle. Smith is full of facts supernormal in appearance, and the question which offers itself for our solution is that of determining to what extent they are supernormal in reality.

The title of this chapter, I must assert, is not to be understood in a partisan sense. The term "appearances" is not used in its unfavorable acceptation, as meaning that they are deceptive, and that there is nothing behind them. It is taken in a frank and impartial sense, to designate simply the exterior and immediate aspect of a thing, without prejudging its real nature, in order, by the very force of this neutrality, to provoke investigation destined to separate the true from the false, the pure gold from the dross. It is precisely this investigation which constitutes my present task.

A rather difficult task, for it is always risky to touch upon a subject which is an apple of discord among psychologists, and which has even been considered the "Dreyfus case of science." The matter is complicated, too, in this particular case, by the absolute faith of Mlle. Smith and her friends in the supernormal character of her phenomena; a state of mind extremely worthy of respect, but which is not calculated to facilitate research, all desire of ordinary analysis and explanation being resented by them as an unjustifiable suspicion, interpreted as being an indication of invincible skepticism.

I. THE STUDY OF THE SUPERNORMAL

The term "supernormal" has been used for some years by the investigators of the Society for Psychical Research to take the place of the old word "supernatural," which has become impracticable on account of interloping connections, which finally caused its use to be limited to theological and philosophical environments. Mr. Meyers, to whom the credit is due, if I am not mistaken, of coining this as well as many other new terms used to-day in the psychical vocabulary, applies it to every phenomenon or faculty which passes beyond ordinary experience, and reveals either a degree of higher evolution not yet attained by the mass of humanity, or an order of transcendental things superior to the world of sense. In these two cases one finds one's self, indeed, in the presence of facts which are above the normal, but which are by no means to be taken as foreign or contrary to the true laws of human nature (as the word "supernatural" would imply).

It is to be observed that the definition of Mr. Meyers lays stress upon the character of superiority of supernormal phenomena. I shall, however, separate this character from it in the present chapter, and in spite of the etymology, and for lack of any better term, shall simply use the word "supernormal" to designate facts which come within the actual framework of the science of to-day, and the application of which would necessitate principles not yet admitted—without occupying myself, however, with endeavoring to ascertain whether these facts are messengers of a superior economy or forerunners of a future evolution rather than the survival of a condition of things which has disappeared, or whether they are purely accidental, *lusus naturae*, denuded of signification.

It goes without saying that in treating of the supernormal we must admit theoretically its possibility, or—which amounts to about the same thing— fail to believe in the infallibility and perfection of present-day science. If I consider it, *à priori*, absolutely impossible for an individual to know, some time before the arrival of a telegram containing the news, of an accident by which his brother at the antipodes has been killed, or that another can voluntarily move an object at a distance without having a string attached to it, and contrary to the laws of mechanics and physiology, it is clear that I will shrug my shoulders at every mention of telepathy, and I shall not move a step to be present at a seance of Eusapia Paladino. What an excellent means of enlarging one's horizon and of discovering something new, by being satisfied with one's ready-made science and preconceived opinion, quite convinced beforehand that the universe ends at the wall opposite, and that there is nothing to be obtained beyond that which the daily routine has accustomed us to look upon as the limit of the Real! This philosophy of the ostrich, illustrated formerly by those grotesque monuments of erudition—over whom Galileo did not know whether to laugh or weep—who refused to put their eyes to the glass for fear of seeing something that had no official right to existence; and, again, that of many brains petrified by the unseasonable reading of works of scientific vulgarization, and the unintelligent frequenting of universities—these are the two great intellectual dangers of our time.

If, on the other hand, the philosophical doubt degenerates in the presence of these scientific impossibilities into blind credulity; if it suffices that a thing be unheard of, upsetting, contrary to common-sense and to accepted truths, in order to be immediately admitted, practical existence, without speaking of other considerations, becomes unbearable. The convinced occultist ought never to allow the creaking of a piece of furniture to pass without assuring himself that it is not the desperate call of some great-grandaunt trying to enter into conversation with him; nor to complain to the police when he finds his house upset during his absence—for how is he to know that it is not some "elementals" from the world beyond who have done the deed? It is by the fortunate failure of consequences alone, and a continual forgetting of the doctrine, that one can continue to live in a universe constantly exposed to the capricious incursions of the "invisibles."

These opposite turns of the mind—the invincible fatuity of some and the silly superstition of others—inspire many people with an equal repugnance. The need of a happy medium between these opposed excesses has been felt for some time. Here are, for example, a few lines, which have lost nothing after the lapse of two centuries:

"What are we to think of magic and witchcraft [to-day we would say 'occultism' and 'spiritism']? Their theory is obscure, their principles vague, uncertain, approaching the visionary; but—they are embarrassing facts, affirmed by grave men, who have seen them, or who have heard of them from persons like themselves; to admit them all, or to deny them all, seems equally embarrassing, and I dare to assert that in this, as in all extraordinary things which depend upon customary rules, there is a happy medium to be found between credulous souls and strong minds."

It is the voice of reason itself that the sagacious author of *Les Caractères* permits us to hear. We must, however, add that this "happy medium to be found" would not consist in a theory, a doctrine, a ready-made and entire system, from the height of which, as from a tribunal of arbitration, we would judge the "embarrassing cases" which reality places in the path of the seeker; for this system—however perfect it might be—would again be one more infallibility added to all those which already encumber the road to truth. The "happy medium" dreamed of by La Bruyère can be but a "method" always perfectible in its application and prejudging in nothing the results of investigation which go against the grain of the dogmatic points of view, equally authoritative and sterile, which characterize the two extremes of the "credulous souls" and "strong minds."

To develop here this methodology of psychical research which might guide the investigator struggling with the apparent or real supernormal, would take me too far from Mlle. Smith. But I will briefly indicate its essence and general spirit, of which an excellent summary may be found in the following passage of Laplace:

"We are so far from knowing all the agents of nature and their divers modes of action that it would not be philosophical to deny phenomena solely because they are inexplicable in the actual state of our knowledge. But we ought to examine them with an attention all the more scrupulous as it appears more difficult to admit them."

In writing these words Laplace hardly thought of telepathy, of the spirits, or the movements of objects without contact, but only of animal magnetism, which represented the supernormal of his time. This passage remains none the less the rule of conduct to be followed concerning all the possible manifestations of this multiform subject. Two inseparable facts, completing each other, as the faces of a medal, may be distinguished in it; but it is advisable, in order to place them the better in the light, to formulate them separately into two propositions representing the governing principles, the axioms of all investigations of the supernormal. The one, which I shall call "PRINCIPLE OF HAMLET," may be condensed in these words: *All is possible*. The other, to which it is but just to leave the name of "PRINCIPLE OF LAPLACE," is susceptible of many forms of expression. I shall express it thus: *The weight of the evidence should be proportioned to the strangeness of the facts*.

The forgetfulness of the "Principle of Hamlet" makes the "strong minds," for whom the limits of nature would not exceed those of their system, the simpleton popes of all times and of all kinds, from the burlesque adversaries of Galileo to the poor Auguste Comte, declaring that the physical constitution of the stars would never be known, and to his noble rivals of the learned societies, denying the aërolites or condemning railroads beforehand. In its turn, the ignorance of the "Principle of Laplace" makes the "credulous souls," who have never reflected that, if all is possible to the eyes of the modest seeker, all is, however, not certain, or even equally possible, and that some evidence would yet be necessary in order to suppose that a stone falling on the floor in an occult reunion arrived there through the walls by the aid of a dematerialization, rather than to admit that it came there in the pocket of a joker.

Thanks to these axioms, the investigator will avoid the doubly signalled danger, and will advance without fear into the labyrinth of the supernormal in advance of the monsters of the occult. However fantastic and magical the things may be which will spring up before his eyes or which will fill his ears, he will never be taken unawares, but, expecting all in the name of the "Principle of Hamlet," he will not be astonished at anything, and simply say: "Be it so! Why not? We shall see." On the other hand, he will not allow the wool to be pulled over his eyes, and he will not easily be satisfied in the matter of evidence; but, firmly intrenched behind the "Principle of Laplace," he will show himself all the more exacting as to the proofs, in proportion to the degree in which the phenomena or the conclusion, which they may wish him to accept, may be extraordinary, and he will oppose a merciless *non liquet* to every demonstration which still seems suspicious or lame.

I wish to speak a word here of the inevitable rôle which the personal coefficient of the turn of mind and character plays in the concrete application of the "Principle of Laplace." This latter is of a vagueness and a deplorable elasticity which opens the door to all divergences of individual appreciation. If we could express in a precise manner and translate in ciphers, on the one hand, the *strangeness* of a fact, which makes it improbable; on the other hand, the *weight of evidence* which tends to make it admissible; and, finally, the demandable *proportion* between these two contrary factors, so that the second may counterbalance the first and secure assent—that would be perfect, and everybody would soon come to an agreement. Unhappily, the means to accomplish this result is not yet perceived.

We must pass now to the weight of the evidence. We may, up to a certain point, submit it to an objective judgment and to an impartial estimation by following the rules and methods of logic, in the broadest sense of the term. But the strangeness of the facts, or, as Laplace said, the difficulty in admitting them! Who, then, is to be the judge of them, and by what universal standard can we measure them?

We must recognize that we are here in presence of an eminently subjective and emotional factor, changeable from one individual to another.

It is necessary to take some stand. In the matter of the supernormal there are too many interior and personal factors (intellectual idiosyncrasies, aesthetic temperaments, moral and religious sentiments, metaphysical tendencies, etc.) tending to determine the quality and intensity of the characteristic of the strangeness in the facts in litigation, to enable one to flatter himself upon a disinterested, objective, and *quasi*-scientific verdict upon their degree of probability or improbability. It is only when, after the accumulation of cases and evidences of similar character, a tacit agreement shall finally have been reached by those who have studied the subject, that the problem can be said to be solved, either by the relegation of pretended supernormal phenomena to the domain of vanished illusions and abandoned superstitions, or by the recognition of new laws and forces in nature. The phenomena considered till then as supernatural will cease to be so; they will form a part of established science, they will have nothing more in them that is strange, and will be admitted by everybody. As long as this mile-post is not reached, as long as the supernormal phenomenon is discussed as such, there are but individual opinions on this subject, subjective certitudes or probabilities, verdicts in which reality is only reflected as closely welded to the personality of their authors.

Two suggestions seem to me to spring from this. First, authors who take it upon themselves to give their advice upon the extraordinary facts coming to their knowledge ought always to begin by making their confession, so that the reader may the better distinguish the intimate factors which may have influenced them. It is true that we are not always thoroughly acquainted with ourselves, but it would be something to say frankly what we believe we have discovered in ourselves as to the position involuntarily taken by us, obscure inclinations for or against the hypothesis involved in the phenomena in question. This is what I shall try to do here, by confining myself to the problems raised by the mediumship of Mlle. Smith, and without entering upon the boundless domain of "psychical research." I shall, therefore, begin each of the following paragraphs by giving my personal advice and my subjective sentiment on the point upon which Hélène's supernormal appearances touch.

It seems to me, in the second place, that the only rational position to take, concerning the supernormal, is, if not a complete suspension of judgment, which is not always psychologically possible, at least that of a wise probability, exempt from all dogmatic obstinacy. The fixed beliefs, the unshakable opinions as to the reality and the meaning of life, are certainly subjective conditions, indispensable to all properly moral conduct, to all human existence truly worthy of this name—that is to say, all that which pretends to be above the animal routine of inherited instincts and social slavery. But these firm convictions would be absolutely misplaced on the objective ground of science, and consequently also that of supernormal facts, which, though still situated outside of the scientific realm, hope shortly to be received within its pale. Practical necessities make us but too often forget that our knowledge of the phenomenal world never attains absolute certitude, and as soon as one passes beyond the brutal facts of the senses, the best-established truths, as well as the most thoroughly refuted propositions, do not rise above a probability which, however great or insignificant we may suppose it to be, never equals infinity or zero. The intellectual attitude which common-sense prescribes in the supernormal consists, for very strong reasons, in never absolutely and irrevocably denying or affirming, but provisionally and by hypothesis, as it were. Even in cases when, after having examined everything scrupulously, one imagines he has finally reached certitude, it must not be forgotten that this word is but a mode of expressing one's self; because, in point of fact, one does not rise above a probable opinion, and the possibility of an unsuspected error, vitiating the most apparently evident experimental demonstration, is never mathematically excluded.

This reserve is particularly indicated in cases of phenomena like those of Mlle. Smith, which often leave much to be desired concerning accessory information, which would be necessary in order to express one's self categorically on their account. My appreciation of these phenomena, far from pretending to an infallible and definite character, demands, therefore, from the start, the right of modification under the influence of new facts which may be produced subsequently.

For the sake of clearness I shall set off again in four groups the supernormal appearances with which I shall have to occupy myself in this chapter—viz., so-called physical phenomena, telepathy, lucidity, and spirit messages. The boundaries of these three last categories are but poorly defined and might easily be fused into one. But my division is but a kind of a measure of order, and not a classification.

II. PHYSICAL PHENOMENA

This designation again covers several rather diverse categories of strange facts. I shall only speak of the two kinds of which Mlle. Smith has furnished samples (and which I have never personally witnessed)—that is to say, "apports" and "movements of objects without contact."

1. *Apports.* [1]—Besides the unknown causes presiding over their aërial transportation, the arrival of exterior objects in a closed space, often coming from a considerable distance, implies, in order that they may pass through the walls of the room, either the subterfuge of a fourth dimension of space, or the penetration of the matter—that is to say, the passage of the molecules or atoms of the object (its momentary *dematerialization*) between the molecules or atoms of the wall. All these impediments to our vulgar conception as to the stability of matter, or, what is worse, to our geometrical intuition, seem to me so hard to digest that I am tempted to apply to them the words of Laplace: "There are things that are so extraordinary that nothing can counterbalance their improbability." This is not to declare as false, *à priori*, all the stories of this kind, for we know that the true is not always the probable; but assuredly, even in the case of the good Mr. Stainton Moses, the weight of the proof does not, in my opinion, equal the strangeness of the facts.

So far as concerns the *apports* obtained at the seances of Mlle. Smith, they all took place in 1892-93, in the reunions of the N. group, where the obscurity favored the production of marvellous things in close relation with the visions and typtological messages.

I will cite from memory certain acoustic phenomena mentioned in the reports: The piano sounded several times under the touch of the favorite disincarnate spirits of the group; the same happened to a violin and to a bell; once we also heard metallic sounds that seemed to come from a small musical box, although there was none in the room. As to the *apports*, always received with delight by the members of the group, who are ever anxiously wishing for them and asking their spirit friends for them, they were frequent and varied enough. In midwinter roses showered upon the table, handfuls of violets, pinks, white lilacs, etc., also green branches; among other things there was an ivy leaf having engraved upon it in letters, as though by a punching-machine, the name of one of the principal

---

[1] By this is meant the bringing or conveying of material objects into a closed space—the passage of one solid body through another.

disincarnate spirits at play. Again, at the tropical and Chinese visions seashells were obtained that were still shining and covered with sand, Chinese coins, a little vase containing water, in which there was a superb rose, etc. These last objects were brought in a straight line from the extreme East by the spirits, in proof of which they had the honor of a public presentation at a seance of La Société d'Études Psychiques de Genève, and were placed upon the desk of the president, where all, myself included, could satisfy themselves at their leisure as to their reality.

2. *Movements of objects without contact.*—The displacing, without contact and in the absence of all known mechanical processes, of objects situated at a distance (telekinesis), is very strange. However, it only upsets physiological notions, and does not, as is the case with the *apports*, go as far as to overthrow our conceptions in regard to the constitution of matter or our spatial intuitions. It only supposes that the living being possesses forces acting at a distance, or the power of putting forth at intervals a species of invisible supernumerary prehensile organs, capable of handling objects, as our hands do (ectenic forces of Thury, ectoplasms of Richet, dynamic members of Ochorowicz, etc.). Such are the ephemeral but visible pseudopodes that the amœba puts forth in all directions.

It may be conceived that, as the atom and the molecule are the centre of a more or less radiating influence of extension, so the organized individual, isolated cell or colony of cells, is originally in possession of a sphere of action, where it concentrates at times its efforts more especially on one point, and again on others *ad libitum*. Through repetition, habit, selection, hereditary and other principles loved by biologists, certain more constant lines of force would be differentiated in this homogeneous primordial sphere, and little by little could give birth to motor organs. For example—our four members of flesh and blood, sweeping the space around us, would be but a more economic expedient invented by nature, a machine wrought in the course of better adapted evolution, to obtain at the least expense the same useful effects as this vague primitive spherical power. Thus supplanted or transformed, these powers would thereafter manifest themselves only very exceptionally, in certain states, or with abnormal individuals, as an atavic reapparition of a mode of acting long ago fallen into disuse, because it is really very imperfect and necessitates, without any advantage, an expenditure of vital energy far greater than the ordinary use of arms and limbs. Unless it is the cosmic power itself, the amoral and stupid demiurge, the unconsciousness of M. de Hartman, which comes directly into play upon contact with a deranged nervous system, and realizes its disordered dreams without passing through the regular channels of muscular movements.

But enough of these vapory metaphysical or pseudo-biological speculations to give an account of a phenomenon for which it will be time enough to find precise explanation when its authenticity shall be beyond dispute, if that time shall ever arrive.

Three groups of proofs, of a diverse nature, have gradually brought me to look upon the reality of these phenomena—in spite of the instinctive difficulty of admitting them—as an infinitely more probable hypothesis than its opposite.

First: I was first unsettled by the reading of the too-much-neglected memoir of Professor Thury, which seems to me to be a model of scientific observations, the weight of which I could only overlook by rejecting, *à priori*—in the name of their strangeness—the possibility itself of the facts in question, which would have been against the Principle of Hamlet. The conversations which it was my privilege to hold with M. Thury have greatly contributed to arouse in me a presumption in favor of these phenomena, which the book would evidently not have done in the same degree if the author had not been personally known to me.

Secondly: Once created, my idea of the probability of these facts became rather strengthened than weakened by a number of foreign works of more recent date; but I doubt whether any, or all of these combined, would have been sufficient to create it. The displacement of objects without contact being once hypothetically admitted, it seems easier to me to explain Crookes's observations on the modifications of the weight of bodies in the presence of Home by authentic phenomena of this kind (in spite of the well-deserved criticisms that Crookes's publications brought upon him) than to suppose that he was simply Home's dupe. The same is true with the cases of *Esprits tapageurs* (*Poltergeister*), published by the Society for Psychical Research, the exclusive hypothesis of the "*naughty little girl*," without the addition of any trace of telekinesis, which seems to me a less adequate and more improbable explanation than that of real phenomena, which would have tempted fraud. Naturally all depends on the preconceived opinion one may have as to the general possibility or impossibility of these facts, and my feeling in regard to the matter would certainly be different without the preceding or the following groups of evidence.

Thirdly: The probability of the movement of objects without contact has reached with me a degree practically equivalent to certitude, thanks to M. Richet, to whom I am indebted for my presence at his house last year at several seances of Eusapia Paladino, under conditions of control which gave no room for doubt—at least without challenging the combined witness of the senses of sight, hearing, and touch, as well as the average quantity of critical sense and perspicacity with which every ordinary intelligence flatters itself it is endowed; or, again, of suspecting the walls of M. Richet's study had been tampered with, and he himself, with his attending colleagues, of being impostors, in collusion with the amiable Neapolitan herself—a supposition which the most elementary sense of propriety would absolutely forbid me to entertain. From that moment I believed in telekinesis by constraint of the perception, *sensata et oculata certitudine*, to borrow the expression of Galileo, who certainly did not mean by that an unreflecting adhesion to the evidences of the senses, like that of the casual onlooker at the tricks of the prestidigitator, but rather the final crowning of an edifice having for its rational framework the reasoned analysis of the conditions of observation, and of the concrete circumstances surrounding the production of the phenomenon.

In saying that I believe in these facts, I will add that there is no question here of a conviction, in the moral, religious, or philosophical sense of the term. This belief is for me devoid of all vital importance; it does not move any essential fibre of my being, and I would not feel the least inclination to submit to the slightest martyrdom in its defence. Whether the objects move or do not move without contact is absolutely indifferent to me. Should any one some day succeed in unveiling the physical tricks or the fallacious psychological processes which have led into error the best observers of telekinesis, from M. Thury down to M. Richet, with a number of other witnesses, myself included, I would be the first to laugh at the trick that art and nature had played upon me, to applaud the perspicacity of the one who discovered it, to congratulate myself, above all, in seeing supernormal appearances returning to the ordinary course of things.

This is a disproportionally lengthy preamble to facts of which I shall have to speak here, for they are reduced to a few displacements of objects without contact (raising of tables, transporting or projecting of flowers and diverse things placed out of reach), of which Hélène and her mother were witnesses on several occasions at their house. I cannot be accused of stubborn skepticism, since I admit the reality of telekinesis. In the present case, however, all the stories which have been told me leave much to be desired from an evidential point of view. Without suspecting in any way the perfect good faith of both Mme. and Mlle. Smith, it suffices to recall the possibility of malobservation and errors of memory in the stories of supernormal events in order not to attribute a great evidential value to the absolutely sincere evidence of these ladies.

Incapacitated as I am from pronouncing judgment upon phenomena of which I was not a witness, I shall, however, put forth a fact which might militate in favor of their authenticity (their possibility having been first hypothetically admitted)—namely, that these phenomena have always been produced under exceptional conditions, at a time when Hélène was in an abnormal state and a prey to a deep emotion. On the one side, this circumstance increases the chances of malobservation, while, on the other, the day on which it shall be well established that (as divers observations cause us to think) certain abnormal and emotional states set at liberty in the organism latent forces capable of acting at a distance, it will be permitted us to suppose that perhaps something analogous has taken place in Mlle. Smith's case. Here is, as an example of these perplexing cases, a fact which happened to her during a period of general indisposition. Abridging the story, I reproduce it as Hélène sent it to me the following day:

"Last night I had a visit from M. H. I do not need to give you an analysis of my impressions; you will understand them as well as I do. He came to tell me that he had held a seance with a lady who was a stranger to me, and that this lady had seen Leopold, who had given her a remedy for the indisposition from which I was suffering. I could not refrain from telling him that Leopold had assured me that he manifested himself only to me, and that it would consequently be difficult for me to admit his alleged utterances to others." But that is not the most interesting part of the story.

"While M. H. spoke to me I felt a sharp pain in my left temple, and, perhaps two minutes afterwards, my eyes, constantly directed towards the piano, on which I had placed two oranges the evening before, were entirely fascinated with I know not what. Then, suddenly, at the moment when we least expected it—we were all three (M. H., my father, and myself) seated at a reasonable distance from the piano—one of the oranges displaced itself and rolled to my feet. My father maintained that it had no doubt been placed too near the edge of the lid, and at a certain moment had fallen in a natural way. M. H. saw immediately in this incident the intervention of some spirit. I myself dared not pass my opinion on it. Finally, I picked up the orange, and we spoke of other things.

"M. H. remained about an hour; he went away exactly at nine. I went to my mother's room to give her a few details of M. H.'s visit. I described to her the fall of the orange, and what was my surprise when, on returning to the drawing-room and stepping up to the piano to take the lamp I had placed on it, I found the famous orange no longer there. There was but one left; the one I had picked up and replaced by the side of the other had disappeared. I looked for it everywhere, but without success. I went back to my mother, and while I spoke to her we heard something fall in the vestibule. I took the lamp to see what might have fallen. I distinguished at the farthest end (towards the door of the entrance to the apartment) the much-sought-for orange!

"Then I asked myself quite frankly whether I was in presence of some spiritistic manifestation. I tried not to be frightened. I took the orange to show it to my mother. I returned to the piano to take the second orange, so as not to be frightened in a similar way. But it, in its turn, had disappeared! Then I felt a considerable sensation of trembling. I returned to my mother's room, and, while we discussed the matter, we heard again something thrown with violence, and, rushing out to see what had happened, I saw the second orange placed in exactly the same spot where the other had been, and considerably bruised. Imagine how astonished we were! I took both oranges, and, without losing an instant, went to the kitchen and put them in a cupboard, where I found them again the following morning; they had not moved. I did not go to bed without some fear, but fortunately I quickly went to sleep. My mother is sure that it is M. H. who brought some evil spirit into the house, and she is quite uneasy. . . ."

From the oral explanations of Mlle. Smith and her mother, and also from the location of the places, it follows that the oranges had been thrown at a distance of ten yards from the piano, through the wide-open parlor door leading to the vestibule, against the door of the apartment, as if to follow and strike fictitiously M. H., who a few moments before had left by this door.

One has undoubtedly always the right of discarding at the outset, as presenting too little guarantee of genuineness, the extraordinary stories of a person subject to hallucinations. In the present case, all that I know of Mlle. Smith and her parents keeps me from doing so, and persuades me that her story is thoroughly exact, which, however, does not amount to saying that there is anything of the supernormal about it. One has, in fact, the choice between two interpretations.

First: In the hypothesis of veritable telekinesis, the following is the manner in which the adventure would be summed up: the emotion due to the unexpected and unpleasant visit of M. H. had brought about a division of consciousness. The feeling of irritation, anger, and repulsion against him had condensed themselves into some secondary personality, which, in the general perturbation of the entire psychophysiological organism, had momentarily recovered the use of these primitive forces of action at a distance, entirely removed from the will, and without the participation of the ordinary self, and thus automatically accomplished outwardly the instinctive idea of bombarding this ill-bred visitor. Notice is to be taken of the painful *aura* at the temple and the fascination of gaze, which, according to Hélène's story, preceded the first signs of the phenomenon, the orange falling and rolling at her feet.

Secondly: But the most natural supposition is certainly that Mlle. Smith, by the ordinary use of her limbs, had taken and thrown these projectiles in an access of unconscious muscular automatism. It is true that this would not agree with the presence of her father, mother, or M. H., who did not see her make the supposed movements. But an absent-mindedness of even normal witnesses will seem easier to admit than the authentic production of a supernormal phenomenon.

These episodes which have happened to Mlle. Smith and her mother since I have known them are very few, amounting to half a dozen at the most, and I will not dwell longer upon this subject. Hélène is not conscious of possessing any faculty of movement at a distance, and she always attributes these phenomena to spirit intervention. Leopold, on the other hand, has never acknowledged that he is the author of them. He claims that Hélène possesses within herself supernormal powers, and that, in order to succeed, she would only have to set them to work, but that she did not wish to do so. All my suggestions and repeated entreaties with Leopold and Hélène—either awake or in a state of somnambulism—in the hope of obtaining in my presence some physical phenomenon, have been in vain up to the present time.

III. TELEPATHY

One may almost say that if telepathy did not exist one would have to invent it. I mean by this that a direct action between living beings, independent of the organs of the senses, is a matter of such conformity to all that we know of nature that it would be hard not to suppose it *à priori*, even if we had no perceptible indication of it. How is it possible to believe that the foci of chemical phenomena, as complex as the nervous centres, can be in activity without giving forth diverse undulations, x, y, or z rays, traversing the cranium as the sun traverses a pane of glass, and acting at a distance on their homologues in other craniums? It is a simple matter of intensity.

The gallop of a horse or the leap of a flea in Australia causes the terrestrial globe to rebound on its opposite side to an extent proportional to the weight of these animals compared to that of our planet. This is little, even without taking into account the fact that this infinitesimal displacement runs the risk at every moment of being neutralized by the leaps of horses and fleas on the other hemisphere, so that, on the whole, the shocks to our terrestrial globe resulting from all that moves on its surface are too feeble to prevent our sleeping. Perhaps it is the same with the innumerable waves which coming from all other living beings, shock at every moment a given brain: their efforts are counterbalanced, or their resultant too slight to be perceived. But they exist none the less in reality, and I confess I do not understand those who reproach telepathy with being strange, mystical, occult, supernormal, etc.

As to the knowledge whether this theoretical telepathy offers results open to experimental demonstration—that is to say, whether this chain of intercerebral vibrations into which we are plunged exercises any notable influence on the course of our psychic life; and whether, in certain cases, we happen to feel emotions, impulses, hallucinations, which the psychological state of one or another of our own kind exercises directly upon us, across the ether and without the ordinary intermediary of the channel of our senses—that is a question of fact arising from observation and experience. We know how much this question has actually been discussed, and how difficult it is to solve it in a decisive way, as much on account of all the sources of errors and illusions, to which one is exposed in this domain, as on account of a probably always necessary concurrence of very exceptional circumstances (which we do not as yet know how to accomplish at will), in order that the particular action of a determined *agent* should sweep away all rival influences, and betray itself in a manner sufficiently marked and distinct in the life of the *percipient*. Everything considered, I strongly lean towards the affirmative. The reality of telepathic phenomena seems to me difficult to reject in presence of the cluster of very diverse evidences, entirely independent of each other, that militate in its favor. Undoubtedly none of these evidences is absolutely convincing when taken separately; but their striking convergence towards the same result gives to their entirety a new and considerable weight, which tips the scale, in my opinion, while awaiting an inverse oscillation, which may some day destroy this convergence, or explain it by a common source of error. Besides, I understand very well why those to whom telepathy remains a mystic, and to our scientific conceptions heterogeneous, principle, should obstinately resist it. But, seeing nothing strange in it myself, I do not hesitate to admit it, not as an intangible dogma, but as a provisional hypothesis, corresponding better than any other to the condition of my certainly very incomplete knowledge of this department of psychological research.

Although predisposed in favor of telepathy, I have failed in finding striking proofs of it in Mlle. Smith, and the few experiments I have attempted with her on this subject offered nothing encouraging.

I tried several times to make an impression upon Hélène from a distance and to appear before her during the evening, when I thought she had returned to her home, which is a kilometre distant from mine. I obtained no satisfactory result. My only case of striking success, lost among a number of nonsuccesses, can be explained by mere coincidence as well, and, after taking all the accessory circumstances into consideration, does not deserve a lengthy discussion.

As to spontaneous telepathy, a few indications would make me think that Mlle. Smith sometimes involuntarily submits to my influence. The most curious is a dream (or a vision) that she had one night at a time when I had suddenly fallen ill during a stay in the country some twenty leagues distant from Geneva. She heard the ringing of a bell at her door, then saw me entering, so emaciated and apparently so tired that she could not refrain from speaking to her mother on the following morning of her uneasiness concerning me. Unfortunately these ladies took no note of the exact date of this incident, and Hélène did not speak of it to M. Lemaître until three weeks later, when he told her about my illness, the beginning of which dated back to the approximate time of the dream. The evidential value of this case is weak. On other occasions Mlle. Smith announced to me that, to judge from her dreams or vague intuition in a waking state, i was to have on a certain day an unexpected vexation, a painful preoccupation, etc. But the cases in which she was right were counterbalanced by those in which she was wrong. It does not appear that Hélène's telepathic relations with other persons are closer than with me, and among the cases known to me there is not one that deserves the trouble of being related. An exception must, however, be made on behalf of a M. Balmès (pseudonym), who was for some time employed in the same business house as Mlle. Smith, and concerning whom she had several really curious phenomena. This M. Balmès was himself "a sensitive medium" of a very nervous and vibrating nature. He was working in the story above that of Hélène, and stopped sometimes to talk concerning spiritism with her. Their relations, which they did not extend beyond the office, ended there. There never seemed to be any personal sympathy or special affinity between them, and it is not known how to account for the telepathic bond that seemed to exist between them. The following are examples:

1. One morning M. Balmès lent a newspaper to Hélène in which there was an article on spiritism. He himself had received this paper from one of his friends, M. X., a Frenchman who had been in Geneva for some three weeks only and who did not know Hélène even by name. This M. X. had marked the interesting article in red and had added on the margin an annotation in black. During her noon meal at home Hélène read the article rapidly, but for lack of time did not read the annotation marked in black. Having returned to her office she began again to work. However, at a quarter-past three her eyes fell on the annotation of the paper, and as she was taking up her pen to make some calculation in her note-book, "I do not know," she wrote to me, "either how or why I began to draw on this writing-tablet the head of a man entirely unknown to me. At the same time I heard the voice of a man, of a high, clear, and harmonious quality; but unfortunately I could not understand the words. A great desire came over me to run and show this drawing to M. Balmès. He examined it, and seemed astonished, for the head drawn in ink was no other than that of his friend who had lent him the paper marked in pencil. The voice and the French accent were, as it seems, entirely correct also. How was it that at the sight of an annotation I

found myself in communication with a stranger? M. Balmès, in presence of this curious phenomenon, hastened that very evening to his friend and learned that at the time when I drew his portrait there was a very serious discussion in progress concerning him (M. Balmès) between M. X. and other persons."

Strictly speaking, this case may be normally explained by supposing: First, that Mlle. Smith, without consciously noticing or remembering him, had seen M. X. during his short stay in Geneva, walking in the street with M. Balmès, and that the paper, which she knew had been lent to M. Balmès by one of his friends, had, by means of a subconscious induction, awakened the latent memory of the face and voice of the stranger whom she had seen with him. Secondly, that there is but a fortuitous coincidence in the fact that M. X. spoke of M. Balmès at precisely the hour when Hélène traced the face and heard the voice of the aforesaid M. X. in an access of automatism, set free at the sight of his annotation on the paper.

In the telepathic hypothesis, on the contrary, the incident would have been explained somewhat as follows: The conversation of M. X. concerning M. Balmès (which was, as it appears, of an excited nature) had telepathically impressed the latter and awakened in him subliminally the remembrance of M. X. M. Balmès, in his turn, without consciously suspecting it, had transmitted this remembrance to Mlle. Smith, who was already predisposed to suggestion on that day by the loan of the paper, and with whom the said remembrance broke forth into a graphic, auditive, and impulsive (the desire of showing her drawing to M. Balmès) automatism. The subconscious strata of M. Balmès had thus served as a link between M. X. and Mlle. Smith.

2. "Some eight days after the preceding case, being a few minutes after noon in an open streetcar, I saw before me this same M. Balmès talking to a lady in a room apparently close to the street-car. The picture was not very clear. A kind of mist seemed to extend over the whole, which was, however, not strong enough to hide from me the personages. M. Balmès, especially, was quite recognizable, and his somewhat subdued voice made me overhear these words: 'It is very curious, extraordinary.' Then I felt a sudden, violent commotion, and the picture vanished at the same time. Soon I found myself again riding in the street-car, and, according to the progress which it had made, I understood that the vision had lasted but three minutes at the most. Notice must be taken of the fact that during these few minutes I did not lose for a single moment the consciousness of my situation; I knew and felt that I was riding home, as I was in the habit of doing each day, and I felt entirely like myself, without the slightest mental disturbance.

"Two hours later I went up to M. Balmès. Approaching him frankly—yes, even a little abruptly—I said to him: 'Were you satisfied with the short visit you made a few minutes after twelve, and would it be indiscreet to ask what you found so curious, so extraordinary?' He seemed confused, astonished, pretended even to be vexed, and looked as if he wished to ask me by what right I permitted myself to control his actions. This movement of indignation passed as quickly as it came, to give way to a sentiment of the greatest curiosity. He made me tell him in detail my vision, and confessed to me that he really had gone at noon to call upon a lady, and that they had discussed the incident about the newspaper. He had really pronounced the words that I had heard: 'It is curious, extraordinary,' and, strange to say, I also learned that at the end of these words a violent ringing of the bell had been heard, and that the conversation between M. Balmès and his friend had suddenly come to an end by the arrival of a visitor. The commotion felt by me was, therefore, nothing more than the violent ringing of the bell, which, putting an end to the conversation, had also put an end to my vision."

3. At the beginning of a seance one Sunday afternoon at a quarter to four, I handed to Hélène a glass ball, of the kind used for developing clairvoyance by means of gazing into a crystal. Shortly afterwards she saw in it M. Balmès and his friend, and above their heads an isolated pistol, but which seemed to have nothing to do with them. She told me then that M. Balmès had received the day before at his office a telegram which very much upset him, and which obliged him to leave Geneva that very evening for S. She seemed to apprehend some misfortune about to befall M. Balmès, but soon fell asleep. By his digital dictations Leopold tells us that he sent her to sleep to save her some painful visions seen in the crystal, and that she, Hélène, has a mediumistic consciousness in regard to all that is passing at S., and that the pistol is connected with M. Balmès. It was impossible to learn more, and the remainder of the seance was taken up with other matters.

M. Balmès, who returned to Geneva on the following Monday, and whom I saw the same evening, was very much struck with Hélène's vision, for, on

Sunday afternoon he really took part in a scene which came near being tragic, and in the course of which his friend X. had offered him a pistol which he always carried with him. Mlle. Smith and M. Balmès did not hesitate to see in this coincidence a highly characterized supernormal phenomenon. This case offers, however, some difficulty—viz., that the incident of the pistol at S. did not take place till more than two hours after Hélène's visions, and that M. Balmès, as he affirms, had no premonition of the affair at the time when Hélène had her vision. It follows from this that there was a kind of anticipated telepathy, a premonition experienced by another than the interested principal, and this raises the great question of the supernormal knowledge of future events. I find it easier to admit that, although M. Balmès did not consciously foresee the incident of the pistol, he foresaw subconsciously the event, and that this idea passed telepathically to Hélène. Perhaps this case might be explained without having recourse to the supernormal at all. Mlle. Smith, knowing M. Balmès' character, and up to a certain point his personal circumstances, having been present the evening before when M. Balmès received the telegram, and foreseeing (as she said at the seance), the gravity of the situation, could easily imagine the intervention of a fire-arm in the affair. Besides, no detail of the vision indicates that the pistol seen in the glass ball corresponds to that of M. X.

How far the delicate sense of probabilities can go, and how often spontaneous inferences, with people of a quick imagination, are correct, one never knows. Undoubtedly we often see a supernormal connection where there is, in reality, only a striking coincidence, due to a happy divination and prevision, which is very natural. I ought to add that this manner of evicting the supernormal and reducing the vision of the pistol to a mere creation of the subliminal fantasy, seems inadmissible to Hélène, who remains absolutely certain that this was a convincing case of telepathy.

The above example, 2, which is the best of all, in my opinion, is still not irreproachable.

IV. LUCIDITY

All the facts of lucidity (clairvoyance, second-sight, etc.) which are attributed to Mlle. Smith may be explained by telepathic impressions proceeding from living persons. This means that I not only admit from the start the *possibility* of such phenomena by virtue of the " Principle of

Hamlet," but, since telepathy is not, in my opinion, anything very strange, I shall feel no subjective difficulty in accepting the reality of Hélène's supernormal intuitions, provided that they present some serious guarantee of authenticity, and do not explain themselves still more simply by normal and ordinary processes.

Leopold, who appears in almost all of these veridical messages—whether he recognizes himself as the author or whether he accompanies simply by his presence their manifestation through Hélène—has never deigned to grant me one under entirely satisfactory conditions, and he censures my insistence as vain and puerile curiosity. As to the innumerable phenomena with which others more fortunate than myself have been gratified, they have always offered this singularity: when they appeared to be really of a nature calculated to furnish a decisive and convincing proof as to their supernormal origin, I never succeeded in obtaining a written, precise, and circumstantial account, but only uncertain and incomplete tales, too intimate and too personal to be divulged by those interested in them; and, again, when my friends were quite willing to write out a detailed account and to answer to my demand for exact information, the fact reduced itself to such a small matter that it was beyond my power to see anything of the supernormal in it.

Taking everything into consideration, I am inclined to believe that Mlle. Smith, in truth, possesses real phenomena of clairvoyance, not, however, passing beyond the possible limits of telepathy; only, in order that they may be produced, it is necessary that Leopold—that is to say, the special psychic state of Hélène which is necessary for the reception and externalization of these telepathic impressions—be aided from the outside by the influence of certain favorable temperaments, more frequently met with among convinced spiritists than among persons who are normal, and that he be not impeded, on the other hand, by the paralyzing presence of hostile temperaments, such as that of a critical observer. It is greatly to be regretted that the naïve believers who inspire and succeed in obtaining magnificent phenomena of lucidity usually care so little for the desiderata of science, and, above all, refuse to submit themselves to an examination which might explain the phenomena in a natural manner; while the investigators in search of " convincing " proofs are not inspiring arid obtain almost nothing.

However it may be, I shall give a few examples of Mlle. Smith's proofs of lucidity, which are not very varied, and can be divided into the three categories of the medical prescriptions and diagnoses, of lost objects found again, and of retrocognitions of events more or less remote.

1. *Medical Consultations.*—In promising specimens of extraordinary facts of this kind I have gone too far. Many such have been told me—as, for instance, Leopold dictating an unknown and complicated recipe of a hair tonic for a gentleman living abroad, a single bottle of which was sufficient to bring forth a full growth of hair on a head which had become bald before middle age; or, again, Leopold, being consulted about the health of a lady living at a great distance from Geneva, revealing both the veridical nature of her illness, which was unknown till then to her physicians, and its origin, which was due to certain unsuspected but perfectly true incidents connected with her childhood, and, finally, the treatment, which was crowned with success. But the absence of written testimony and precise information as to the concomitant circumstances of these marvellous cures reduce them to the rank of amusing stories, the value of which cannot positively be estimated. As to better-attested episodes, it is true I have been able to obtain authentic stories, but they are those in which the probability of a supernormal element has been reduced to a minimum—imperceptible to me. I will cite but one case.

M. and Mme. G. having invited Mlle. Smith during the month of August to pass a day with them in the country, a few leagues distant from Geneva, took advantage of the visit to hold a seance in order to consult Leopold on the health of one of their children. I will tell the incident from a written account sent me by Mme. G. soon afterwards:

"Our little girl was suffering from anæmia, and fell frequently into a state of weakness, in spite of intervals of improvement. Dr. d'Espine had been recommended to us for the time of our return to Geneva. The medium [Mlle. Smith] knew nothing of this; we had taken the precaution to keep it from her." The seance begins with a few kind words from Leopold, whom M. G. then asks whether he would do well in consulting Dr. d'Espine. "*And I*," replied Leopold, "*can I do nothing for you? Ungrateful people!*" But when he was asked to indicate some treatment, he replied: "*Wait till your return to Geneva.*" Then, upon being asked whether an egg mixed with brandy would be good for the child, he replied that the egg would be good, but the brandy was not necessary in her case. Then he recommended that the child be taken for an hour's walk in the open air every day. As to the prescription relating to her food, he repeated: "*I told you to wait till your return to Geneva.*"

On their return to Geneva in the middle of September, M. and Mme. G. held a second seance. This time Leopold was more exact; he advised: "*Not too much milk, but rather a few glasses of good pure wine at each meal.*" Then he added: "*Treat the anaemia first and you will triumph over the throat trouble, which would finally weaken her too much. Her blood is so weak that the least cold, the slightest emotion, I will go so far as to say that the expectation of a pleasure even, would be sufficient to bring the angina to a crisis. You ought to have foreseen that.*" " Leopold," M. G. notes here, "has enabled us to put our finger upon such of the details as we did not know how to explain. At each sentence my wife and I looked at each other with stupefaction." Leopold ordered also many green vegetables, warm salt-water douches of three minutes' duration in the evening, and: "The principal thing now is five drops of iron in half a glass of water twice a day before the meal. Do this and you will see the result in a month." In two weeks' time the little girl was hardly recognizable.

I have cited this case because it is among those that have most struck M. and Mme. G., and upon which they build their conviction of the independent existence and supernormal knowledge of Leopold, and because it shows how little is needed to kindle the faith among spiritists. I forgot to say that the G. family was well known by Mlle. Smith, and that during the whole winter and the preceding spring she had held weekly seances at their home. There is but one thing that astonishes me, and that is, that Leopold, at the time of the first improvised consultation, should have been taken unawares up to the point of postponing his orders until later, and adhering to such commonplace things as a walk in the open air and the suppression of brandy. In the second seance one sees the effect of a month's incubation. Leopold has had time to recover in Hélène's memory the remembrance concerning the little girl who was anæmic and subject to sore throat; also the prescription which, in the given case, surely proved most efficacious, but which hardly denotes a supernormal knowledge. One does not even need here telepathy to explain messages which are amply accounted for by the subconscious functions of Mlle. Smith's ordinary faculties.

Examples of this kind, drawn from Mlle. Smith's mediumship, might be almost indefinitely multiplied; but *cui bono?* Once more, I do not claim that Leopold has never given any medical consultation surpassing Hélène's latent knowledge and implying supernormal powers of clairvoyance. I only say that I have not yet succeeded in finding a single case where the proofs reached the height of that conclusion.

2. *Objects Recovered.*—I do not know any case in which Mlle. Smith has indicated the situation of an object which had been hidden, and as to the location of which she could have had no information through natural channels. All her discoveries consist, so far as I have been able to judge, in the return, under a spiritistic and with a dramatic aspect, of memories either simply forgotten or properly subliminal, which depended upon the incidents concerned having first belonged to the ordinary consciousness, or their having always escaped it and having been from their origin registered in the subconsciousness.

These are facts of cryptomnesia pure and simple—*i.e.*, explicable by a normal psychological process very common in its essence, while the picturesque embellishments added by the mediumistic imagination give to these teleological automatisms a certain mysterious and supernormal appearance which in other surroundings would certainly create for Hélène—or rather for Leopold—a place alongside St. Anthony of Padua. I confine myself to two examples. Mlle. Smith being charged with the duty of making ready the merchandise sent out from her department, was handed a telegram one day from a customer who asked that four yards of No. 13,459 be despatched to him immediately. "This brief order," said Hélène, "was not calculated to hasten the forwarding of the goods. How could I readily find this No. 13,459, in the midst of six or seven thousand others in the store? Pondering, telegram in hand, I was wondering how I could find it, when a voice outside of but very near me said to me: '*Not there, but here*,' and involuntarily I turned round, without knowing why, and my hand laid itself mechanically on a piece of goods which I drew towards me, and which actually bore the No. 13,459."

It is not necessary to be a medium to know by experience these happy reminiscences or inspirations which sometimes come to free us from embarrassment by shining forth like a light at an opportune moment; but that which in the case of ordinary persons remains in the feeble condition of an idea or internal image, among mediumistic temperaments assumes readily the fixed and vivid form of an hallucination. Instead of simply "suddenly recollecting" in the case of the No. 13,459, as would have happened to any one else, Hélène hears an exterior voice, and perceives her hand moving involuntarily in a given direction. It is noted that this automatism assumed an auditive and motor form which is the pendant of the vocal and visual automatism which I have referred to on pp. 58-59. It is to this same class of facts, well known and almost common to-day, that the following example likewise belongs, although the subliminal imagination had surrounded it with the form of an intervention on the part of Leopold.

One Sunday evening, on returning home, Mlle. Smith noticed that she had lost a small breastpin which had been fastened to her corsage, and which she greatly valued as a souvenir. The following day she returned to look for it where she had been the evening before, but in vain, and a notice which she caused to be inserted in the "lost" columns of a daily newspaper gave no result. Here I leave the narration of the story to her: "Persuaded that my pin was really lost, I did my best to think no more about it, but this was a difficult matter, since one night I was awakened suddenly by three raps struck against my bed. Somewhat frightened, I looked around, but saw nothing. I tried to go to sleep, but again many raps were struck, this time near my head. I seated myself on my bed (I was agitated), trying to discover what was happening, and hardly had I seated myself when I saw a hand shaking my lost breastpin before my eyes. This vision lasted only a minute, but that was long enough for it to make a deep impression upon me."

The following Tuesday evening (ten days after the loss of the trinket) Hélène held a seance at the house of M. Cuendet, at which two other persons were also present. She told of the loss of her pin and the curious vision above described; then all seated themselves at the table. After a typtological dictation upon an altogether different subject, the following incident occurred, the account of which I have borrowed from notes taken by M. Cuendet (it was in 1894, and I only knew Mlle. Smith by reputation at the time):

"We notice that from the beginning of the seance Mlle. Smith describes to us our familiar spirit [Leopold] as holding a lantern in his hand. Why? The table is shaken anew, about to tell us something. The following is then dictated to us by it: *'Arise. Take a lantern. Extend your walk to the Municipal Building. Take the path which crosses the meadow, and which ends at the Street of the Baths. In the middle of the path, to the left, a few yards distant, a block of white stone will be found. Starting from the block of stone, only one yard away from it, towards the setting sun, the pin so much sought for will be found. Go, I accompany you.*'

"I copy *verbatim* this communication, which was obtained letter by letter. I add nothing, take nothing from it. General stupefaction! We hesitate! Finally, we all four rise, we light a lantern and set out. It was twenty minutes to ten o'clock.

"We walk slowly; we arrive at the Municipal Building, and take the path which leads from it to the Street of the Baths. In the middle, to the left, some yards distant, we, in fact, find the block of stone indicated. We search for a moment without result, and begin to fear we shall find nothing. Finally, towards the setting sun, a yard from the block of stone, I find buried in the grass, covered with sand, and consequently badly soiled, the pin indicated.

"Some one had evidently stepped on it, as it was slightly bent. Mlle. Smith uttered an exclamation of surprise, and we all four returned to the house, to recover from our very natural emotion."

This case has remained in the eyes of Mlle. Smith and her spiritistic friends as one of the most striking and irrefragable proofs of the objective and independent reality of Leopold. For the psychologist it constitutes a very beautiful and interesting example of cryptomnesia, well worthy to figure among the very instructive cases collected by Mr. Myers, in which the memory of a subliminal perception (*i.e.*, registered immediately without striking the normal personality) appears as a revelation in a dream of ordinary sleep, or under some other equivalent form of automatism. Here is "Leopold"—the subconsciousness of Hélène—who, having felt the pin fall and noticed where it rolled, first manifested himself in a passing nocturnal vision, and then took advantage of the next spiritistic gathering to restore completely her latent memories. It is not necessary to see anything intentional in this restitution, the simple play of association of ideas sufficing to explain that the memory of the situation of the pin stored up in a subliminal stratum and stimulated by a desire to recover the lost object might have mechanically reappeared at the moment of the seance, thanks to mediumistic autohypnotization, and gushed forth under the dramatic form, naturally appropriate to the environment, of an apparently supernormal piece of information furnished by Leopold.

3. *Retrocognitions.*—The apparently supernormal revelations in regard to the past, furnished at the seances of Mlle. Smith, can be divided into two groups—namely, whether they concern universal history, or deal with private interests relative to the families of the sitters.

First: The messages of the first group abound, under the form of visions accompanied by typtological explanations, in Hélène's seances of 1894, but have almost wholly come to an end since I made her acquaintance, and I have never been witness of any. According to the reports which I have seen, all these retrocognitions have reference to the history of Protestantism, or that of the French Revolution—*i.e.*, to two classes of facts which are among the best known in France to-day.

It goes without saying that the firmly convinced spiritistic group in which these messages were received have never had a doubt that the apparitions which Hélène perceived were the veritable personages they asserted themselves to be, habited as they were in the costume of the period to which they belonged, communicating by means of the table, and speaking in the first person (except when Leopold acted as showman and dictated in his own name the explanations asked for).

But as the content of these messages is always the verbatim reproduction or almost exact equivalent of information which is to be found in historical and biographical dictionaries, I cannot avoid being inclined to the impression that we here are concerned with common facts of cryptomnesia.

If the intervention of the supernormal be absolutely insisted upon in this case, it can only be manifested under the form of a telepathic transmission from the sitters to the medium. In favor of that supposition two facts may be urged: first, that Mlle. Smith passed in that group as devoid of all historical knowledge, and was very much surprised at these revelations of facts totally unknown to her; secondly, that there were regularly in attendance at these seances one or more members of the teaching body, who by their general education possessed, without any doubt whatever, either consciously or in a latent manner, all the historical knowledge, which, after all, was not very great, displayed by Leopold.

But these arguments are not of much weight in my opinion. To begin with the second: as the sitters had their hands on the table at the same time with the medium, according to the spiritistic custom, they could themselves, without any telepathy, properly speaking, and simply by their slight, unconscious muscular contractions, have directed, unknown to themselves, the movements of that piece of furniture, Mlle. Smith only augmenting these shocks proceeding from her neighbors.

As to the supposed ignorance of Mlle. Smith, it is not at all so great as has been imagined, and the historical revelations obtained at her seances do not in any degree surpass the level of that which she could have absorbed, consciously or unconsciously, at school and in her surroundings.

Moreover, the hypothesis which appears to me the most probable, and on which I rest, is that the messages come essentially from Hélène herself—I ought rather to say from her subliminal memory; that, however, does not exclude a certain amount of cooperation on the part of the sitters, whose conversation, on the one hand, and their unconscious muscular action upon the table, on the other, have often maintained and directed the course of the subconscious ideas of the medium and the automatic unfolding of her latent memories.

Secondly: Retrocognition of family events, which are exhibited in Mlle. Smith's seances, have generally the savor of the unknown for the sitters, from the fact that they concern incidents of the past which have never been printed save in the memories of certain aged persons or of a few lovers of local anecdotes.

I do not hesitate to see in these stories of other days, gushing forth in visions and in dictations by the table in course of Hélène's hemisomnambulisms, narratives heard in her childhood and long since forgotten by her ordinary personality, but which reappear by the aid of mediumistic autohypnotization, bringing the deepest strata to the surface; the simple play of association, in an entirely natural manner, then causes the memories relative to the families of the persons present at the seance to be poured forth. There is nothing whatever of the supernormal in all this, in spite of the dramatic form, the piquant and unexpected art, the amusing embellishments, of which the subliminal imagination bethinks itself—or I should rather say Leopold, in his rôle of historiographer and scene-shifter of the past.

The judgment which I have pronounced is the result of a course of inductive reasoning based on the retro-cognitions of Mlle. Smith concerning my own family. I trust it may be allowable for me to enter upon some details designed to justify my opinion.

I note first that all these retrocognitions with which Leopold honored me took place in the first six seances which I had with Hélène, after which there has not been a single one in the whole five years which have since elapsed. This argues in favor of a limited group of latent memories, which my introduction to the seances set free, a sort of subliminal sac or pocket which was emptied once for all on the first occasions of my presence.

In the second place, this knowledge only concerns outside details, susceptible of striking the attention of the gallery and of being carried from mouth to mouth. Since family histories have no great interest for the ordinary reader, I will confine myself to citing, by way of example, the vision which so astonished me at my first meeting with Hélène (p. 2), and which has already been published by M. Lemaître. I reproduce his narrative, giving real names:

"The medium [Mlle. Smith] perceives a long trail of smoke, which envelopes M. Flournoy. 'A woman!' cries the medium, and, a moment after, 'Two women . . . quite pretty, brunettes . . . both are in bridal toilet! . . . This concerns you, M. Flournoy!' [The table approves by a rap.] They remain motionless; they have white flowers in their hair and resemble each other a little; their eyes, like their hair, are black, or, at all events, very dark. The one in the corner appears under two different aspects; under both forms she is young—perhaps twenty-five years old; on the one hand she remains with the appearance already described (bridal toilet), and on the other she appears very luminous in a great space, a little more slender of visage, and surrounded by a number of pretty children, in the midst of whom she appears very happy; her happiness manifests itself by her expression, but still more in her surroundings. Both women seem ready to be married. The medium then hears a name, which at first escapes her, then returns little by little. **'An! . . . An! . . Dan . . . Ran . . . Dandi . . . Dandiran!'**

"'To which of these two women does this name belong?' demands M. Flournoy—'to the one you see under two aspects, or to the other?' Answer: 'To the one who is presented under two forms.' The medium does not see the other woman as distinctly as the first, but all at once distinguishes a tall man by her side, who only passes by, when the table dictates: 'I am his sister; we will return!' after which the scene changes and we pass to another subject."

This vision revolves altogether around the facts that my mother and her sister were married on the same day; that they were brunettes, quite pretty, and looked alike; that my father was tall; that my aunt married M. Dandiran and died while still young, without children; all matters which should have been of public notoriety in a small city like Geneva. But the same is true of all the other retrocognitions of Mlle. Smith; their content is always veridical, but at the same time is also such as could not fail to be known to a host of people. This causes me to doubt whether there is at the base of these phenomena a really supernormal faculty of retrocognition.

A third striking feature is, that all Hélène's retro-cognitions concerning me are relative to the family of my mother, and are connected with two quite precise and brief periods, the first of which is many years previous to Mlle. Smith's birth. This limitation as to times and persons seems to me significant.

To clear up the matter, if possible, I addressed myself to the last representative of the present generation of my family, Professor Dandiran, of Lausanne, and laid the case before him. He did not immediately remember whether my grandparents Claparède had any communication, nearly half a century before, with the Smith family, but on the following day he wrote me that he distinctly recalled a young woman of that name in whom his mother and aunt had been greatly interested, and who had been employed by them as a dressmaker previous to her marriage to a Hungarian.

One understands that I had a reason for not addressing myself first to Mme. Smith herself; but I must do her the justice to state that when I questioned her in turn, she very obligingly gave me all the information I desired, and which was in perfect accord with the statements of M. Dandiran.

Without entering into details wearisome to the reader, it will be sufficient for me to state that all the retrocognitions in which I was involved were connected with two periods in which Mme. Smith had relations with my mother's family, periods separated by an interval during which these relations were suspended by the fact' of M. and Mme. Smith making a sojourn of several years in a foreign country. It would have been possible for Hélène to know directly the facts of the second period, at which time she was about five or six years of age. As to the first period, which was many years prior to her birth (the time of the double marriage of my mother and her sister in 1853), it is evident that Mme. Smith has had many opportunities at a later date to narrate these facts to her daughter; and it would have been altogether natural for her to have done so.

Ab uno disce omnes. Although I am less familiar with the retrocognitions of Mlle. Smith concerning other families, everything contributes to prove to me that they are explicable in the same manner. In two cases, at least, proof has been obtained that the mother of Mlle. Smith was found to have been in direct and personal communication with the families concerned, exactly as was the case with my grandparents, and this circumstance is sufficient to account for the knowledge, very astonishing at first sight, contained in the revelations of Leopold.

To sum up—pure cryptomnesia seems to me to furnish a sufficient and adequate explanation for Hélène's retrocognitions, both as to family events as well as historic facts.

And no more in this domain of knowledge of the past than in those of recovered objects and medical consultations have I thus far succeeded in discovering in her the least serious indication of supernormal faculties.

V. INCARNATIONS AND SPIRIT MESSAGES

The time having arrived to speak of spiritism, I feel ill at ease and embarrassed by my surroundings, for divers reasons, some of which I will set forth, without, however, endeavoring to explain them at length, since my aim is simply, as has been seen above (p. 373), to indicate my subjective ideas as to the standing of that doctrine, in order that the reader may share, if he pleases, in my appreciation of the phenomena of this class presented by Mlle. Smith. I confess, in the first place, that spiritism is a subject which has the faculty of arousing my mirth, and develops a spirit of playfulness. I really do not know why this should be the case, since that which concerns the dead and the great beyond ought not to be a matter for joking. Perhaps the cause is to be found in the nature of the intermediaries, and the character of the messages with which the spirits are accustomed to favor us. However it may be, I have ordinarily much difficulty in preserving a serious countenance in the presence of manifestations of "disincarnates."

But I reproach myself bitterly with this facetious humor when I reflect that it is indulged in at the expense of conceptions and beliefs which supported the first steps of our race on its painful ascent, the survival or atavic reapparition of which is yet, even today, a source of moral strength, of happy certitude, of supreme consolation for a host of my contemporaries, many of whom I have learned to know, and who, moreover, inspire me with respect as well as admiration by their uprightness of life, their nobility of character, the purity and elevation of their sentiments.

In the second place, I have often had the deceptive experience that, when it comes to a discussion of it, spiritism possesses a great advantage for its defenders, but which is most inconvenient for those who would investigate it closely—of being fugitive and incapable of being grasped on account of the fact of its double nature—a science and religion at the same time—which never permits it to be wholly and entirely the one or the other.

When we come to analyze and criticise, according to strict scientific methods, the positive facts upon which it pretends to base its fundamental argument—the reality of communication with the spirits of the departed, through the intervention of mediums—as soon as the adepts begin to unpack for you their stock of theories (I was about to say their stock theories!) they are astonished at the lack of ideal on the part of these terrible materialist-scientists, who are intent upon searching for the "hidden rat" in the demonstrations of spiritism, instead of falling on their knees before the splendor of its revelations.

A third cause of my uneasiness whenever obliged to approach this subject is the fear of being misunderstood or misinterpreted, thanks to the naïve and simple classification which prevails in the environments which the "disincarnates" frequent.

Spiritism or materialism—these are the brutal alternatives to which one finds himself driven in spite of himself. If you do not admit that the spirits of the dead reveal themselves by raps on the table or visions of the mediums, you are, therefore, a materialist! If you do not believe that the destiny of the human personality is terminated at the grave, you are a spiritist! This mode of nomenclature and labelling is surely puerile.

Moreover, no one willingly consents to be thrust into the company of those with whom, no matter how honorable they may be, he is not in sympathy.

I also wish to state that I absolutely repudiate the above alternative. There is greater variety of choice in the cabinet of human thought. In the last century, for example, outside the spiritism of Swedenborg and the materialism of Baron d'Holbach, there was yet the criticism of one named Kant, who made some noise in the world and whose vogue is even now not absolutely extinct. I should not fear to range myself among his followers. And in our own times, if it was necessary for me to choose between Büchner and Allan Kardec, as the spiritist seems sometimes to believe, I would not hesitate to choose—in favor of M. Renouvier, or my deceased compatriot Charles Secrétan.

I hold to no other philosophy, and it suffices me, in order to repulse the whole of materialism and spiritism, to be the disciple—unworthy, but convinced—of the Nazarene, who replied to the materialists of his time, not by spiritistic evocations, but by the simple words, "God is not the God of the dead but of the living, for all live unto Him." I am not sure whether this argument convinced the Sadducees, but it pleases me by its simplicity, and I have no desire for any other.

If God exists—I should say, if the supreme reality is not the unconscious and blind force-substance of conventional monism, but that sovereign personality (or *supra* personality) which in the clear consciousness of Christ made its paternal presence to be continually felt—if God exists, it is not, apparently, in order to play the rôle of a perpetual undertaker of funereal pomp that he consents to exist, or to allow to fall forever into nothingness the poor creatures who wait upon Him.

They may disappear from before our eyes, but they do not disappear from before His; for they are dead to us, but for Him, and, consequently, in actual reality, they are living. Otherwise He would not be God. This is all I need. I see nothing clearly, it is true, as to the concrete conditions of that other existence, of which the manner even, if it were revealed to me, would probably remain a sealed book to my intelligence, hampered by the bonds of space and time. But of what importance is it? That which I am ignorant of, God knows; and while waiting for Him to call me to rejoin those who have preceded me, He is great enough for me to leave to Him the mysterious fate of our personalities. "Since all live unto Him," I ask no more than that, and as for the pretended demonstrations of spiritism, true or false, I do not care a farthing.

Or I would prefer them to be false. And if they are true, if it is actually a law of nature that during long years to come, after this terrestrial existence, we must drag ourselves miserably from table to table and medium to medium, the best of us (not to speak of the others) displaying without shame the proofs of our mental decrepitude in pitiable nonsense and wretched verses—oh, so much the worse!

It is one misery and shame the more added to all those of which this satanic world is made up, a new calamity coming to crown the physical and moral ills of a world against which the Christian continually protests as he repeats "*Thy kingdom come*," an additional scandal condemned to disappear when " His kingdom shall have come."

There is nothing in common between the empirical, spatial, and temporal survivals which spiritism pretends to establish and that "eternal life" proclaimed by the Prophet of Nazareth. These things, said Pascal, are not of the same order. That is why I am not a spiritist.

Here rises a last point, which worries me when I ought to speak my mind in regard to spiritism in the presence of spiritists. "You do not personally hold," it has been often objected to me, "to these communications of the living with those who have gone before us into the great unknown, and you cry out against spiritistic demonstrations. It is all very well for you, who are a mystic, and to whom the existence of God in Jesus Christ seems a sufficient guarantee of the destinies of human personality and its ultimate palingenesis. But every one has not the same temperament, and does not take so blithely his ignorance of the kind of life which awaits him beyond the tomb. To believe in God, and to abandon to Him with closed eyes the fate of those who leave us, carrying away with them the best portions of our being, is all very well, but it is very difficult. The times of the psalmist who could say '*Though He slay me, yet will I trust Him*' are no more; and as for Christ, He was certainly a very remarkable medium, but His simple affirmation would scarcely be taken to-day for gospel words. The solid and the palpable are necessary to the 'fools' of our epoch. They are not capable of admitting a higher world than that of sense, unless they are enabled to touch it with their finger by means of messages and the return of the dead themselves. Whence it results that every attack, every hostile attitude towards spiritism tends directly to break down the only rampart which might henceforth be efficacious against materialism and its disastrous consequences—infidelity, egotism, vice, despair, suicide, and, finally, the destruction and annihilation of the entire social organism. On the other hand, when science at length shall recognize and consecrate spiritism officially, thereupon, simultaneously with the tangible certainty of another life, courage and strength will return to the hearts of individuals, devotion and all virtues will begin to flourish once again, and an elevated humanity will soon see heaven descend upon the earth, thanks to the connection established and daily practised between the living and the spirits of the dead."

My embarrassment is easily seen. On the one hand, I do not in any way admit the foregoing objection. I do not think that the gospel has had its day or is above the reach of "fools," since it was for them that its author designed it. I believe, on the contrary, that the Christian faith, the faith of Christ or faith in Christ, is, in its inmost essence, a psychological reality, a personal experience accessible to the most humble, a fact of consciousness which will survive when all theological systems shall have been forgotten and all the clergy shall have been abolished. That vital and regenerating power will save our civilization (if anything can save it) by means of the individuals whom it shall have regenerated, without owing anything to spiritistic theories or practices. Inversely, I do not share the optimism of those who would make of spiritism a social panacea, and who imagine that when the moral consciousness on the one side and the religious consciousness on the other have ceased to make themselves heard, the messages of the "disincarnates" will have better success. ("If they hear not Moses and the prophets, neither will they be persuaded though one rose from the dead.")

But, on the other hand, there are individual cases which are interesting and which certainly merit consideration. And for millions, and by a hundred different titles—religious belief, moral consolation, solemn and mysterious rites, old habit, etc.—spiritism is to-day the pivot around which existence turns, and also its only support; would not the destruction of it, then, be productive of more harm than good, and would it not be better to let matters take their course? Why prevent man from delighting in dreams, if he so pleases?

All things are possible, and was it not of the revenants that Hamlet was thinking in his celebrated apostrophe, from which I have taken this principle?

These are the things which perplex me: while waiting to find a way out of them, and by way of summing up, it seems to me indispensable to separate distinctly spiritism-religion, which is an assemblage of beliefs and practices dear to many, from spiritism-science, a simple hypothesis designed to explain certain phenomena arising from observation. The first tells me nothing, or rather it amuses me or repels me according to circumstances; but the more elevated sentiments, and those worthy of all respect, which it inspires in its adepts, impose upon me the duty of passing it by and ignoring it here. The second, on the contrary, does not fail to interest me, as it does all who are curious in regard to natural phenomena.

For the question, Do human or animal individualities continue to intervene in an effective manner in the physical, physiological, or psychological phenomena of this universe after the loss of their corporeal and visible organism? is not an ordinary one. If there are facts which peremptorily establish an affirmative answer, what problems will arise, what an unexpected field of investigation will it not open up to our experimental sciences! And even if the hypothesis is false, how captivating the study of the singular phenomena which have been able to give it birth, which simulate the return of the dead to our observable world! It is understood, therefore, that, even despoiled of all the emotional accessories in which it so easily wraps itself in the heart and imagination of men, the empirical question of immortality and spiritistic interventions, apparent or real, preserves its scientific importance, and merits being discussed with the calm serenity, independence, and strictness of analysis which belong to the experimental method.

It goes without saying that, *à priori*, the hypothesis of *spirits* to explain the phenomena of mediums has in it nothing of the impossible or the absurd. It does not even necessarily contradict, as is sometimes imagined, the directing principle of physiological psychology—the psychological parallelism—which demands that every mental phenomenon shall have a physical correlative. For, in spite of our habit of considering the molecular or atomic phenomena of the brain, the katabolism of the nerves, as the true concomitant of conscious processes, it may well be—it is even very probable—that these molecular movements do not constitute the ultimate physical term immediately paralleling the mental world, but that the real physical correlatives (spatial) of the (non-spatial) psychological phenomena should be sought for in the vibrations of imponderable matter, the ether, in which the ponderable atoms and molecules are plunged somewhat like grains of dust in the atmosphere, in order to make a sensible though somewhat inaccurate comparison.

The ethereal body, perispiritistic, astral, fluid, etc., of the occultists, and of many thinkers who are not believers in occultism, is only a notion scientifically absurd when it is made to be an equivocal and cloudy intermediary between the soul and the body, an un-assignable *tertium quid*, a plastic mediator of which nothing is known as to its being material or spiritual or something else. But conceived as a system of movements of the ether, it contains nothing absolutely anti- or extra-scientific in its nature; the connection between the subjective facts of consciousness and the objective, material facts, remains essentially the same whether one considers the material world under the imponderable form of ether or under the ponderable form of chemical atoms, of physical molecules, and of anatomical elements. Nothing, then, would be radically opposed, from the point of view of the natural sciences, to the existence of disincarnate spirits wandering through space.

The foregoing will doubtless please my spiritistic friends. Here are two facts which will please them less. First: I separate myself from them when they pass prematurely from mere abstract possibilities to the affirmation of actualities. Perhaps the outcome will prove them right some day; perhaps in the near future, but we have not yet reached that point. I freely admit that never have circumstances been so favorable for the spiritistic doctrines as at present. The authentic return of George Pelham and other deceased persons, through Mrs. Piper entranced, as intermediary, seems to be admitted by so many acute observers, the phenomena observed for fifteen years past in the case of this incomparable medium are at times so marvellous and surrounded with such solid scientific guarantees—the case is, in a word, so unheard of and astounding in all respects, that those who are only acquainted with it from a distance, by printed reports and oral narratives of immediate witnesses, feel themselves in a poor position for formulating their doubts and reservations upon this subject.

I fear, in the second place, for mediums and practical spiritists, that when their hypothesis shall have been scientifically demonstrated the result may be very different from that which they now imagine it will be.

It might well happen that the cult of the table, mechanical writing, seances, and all other mediumistic exercises, may receive their death-blow from the official recognition of spirits by science. Suppose, in fact, that contemporaneous researches should at last have proved clearly that messages actually come from the disincarnate; it has already followed from the same researches that in the most favorable cases the veritable messages are very difficult to distinguish from those which are not authentic. When people come to understand that this sorting of messages is almost always beyond their power, they will, perhaps, be put out of conceit with experiments in which they have ninety-nine chances against one of being dupes of themselves or others, and in which—a still more vexatious matter—if they should even be so fortunate as to light upon the hundredth chance, they would have no certain means of knowing it.

This subject, decidedly, is fatal to me. I lose myself in digressions when discussing it—very useless they are, too, since the verdict which the future will pronounce upon the theory of spirits, with or without an ethereal body, matters little as far as the actual examination of the messages furnished by Mlle. Smith is concerned. Even having become scientifically verified, spiritism will never absolve us from bringing to the analysis of the pretended communications less care and rigor than while it was only an undemonstrated hypothesis; each particular case will always demand to be scrutinized by itself, in order to make the distinction between that which in all probability only arises from many non-spiritistic causes, and the residue eventually proceeding from the disincarnate.

I ought to state at the outset that, as far as Hélène's mediumistic phenomena are concerned, their careful analysis has not revealed to me in them any evident vestige of the other world, not even of traces of a telepathic transmission on the part of the living. I have only succeeded in perceiving in them very beautiful and instructive examples of the well-known tendency of the subliminal imagination to reconstruct the deceased and to feign their presence, especially when the favorable suggestions of the surrounding environment incites them to do so. Not being infallible, and bearing in mind Hamlet's principle, I will guard myself well from affirming that these subliminal imitations and simulacra are absolutely free from any spirit collaboration; I content myself with repeating that I have not discovered any, and that it seems to me in the highest degree improbable, and with leaving it to others to demonstrate its reality, if they think they are able to do so. Some examples taken from the principal incarnations of Mlle. Smith will enable me to show after a more concrete fashion my manner of regarding them.

1. *Case of Mlle. Vignier.*—This case has no evidential value whatever, since (as has been seen, p. 411), there were formerly relations between the Vignier family and Mme. Smith which suffice to explain the veridical knowledge manifested by Hélène in this incarnation.

I give an abridged recital of it, nevertheless, for the sake of certain points of psychological interest. None of the spectators had any suspicion of these relations at the time of this scene, which was absolutely enigmatical to all of them.

In a seance at my house (on March 3, 1895, after a Hindoo vision, described p. 280), Mlle. Smith saw an unknown lady appear, of whom she gave the following description: "A nose bent and hooked like the beak of an eagle; small gray eyes, very close together; a mouth with three teeth only; a wicked smile, mocking expression; simple dress; a collar not of the fashion of to-day; she draws near to this portrait, [1] and gazes at it not ill-naturedly."

The name of this person is asked, and the table (Leopold) commences to spell: "*Mademoiselle*"—but refuses to go further, while Hélène sees the apparition laughing, "with a sly air"; as the name is insisted on, the table dictates: "*That does not concern you*," then she begins to jump and skip as though glad of an opportunity to mock us.

Presently Hélène falls asleep and enters into somnambulism; she leaves the table and moves towards the portrait in question, before which she remains fixed, completely incarnating the unknown lady of her vision. I take down the portrait and place it in its frame upon an easy-chair; immediately she kneels before it and contemplates it with affection; then, taking the frame in her right hand, while the left, very much agitated, plays with the cord, she ends, after many vain attempts, by. saying with a great stammering, "*J—j—je l'aimais b—b—beaucoup: je n'aime pas l'autre—j—j—je ne*

---

[1] A small oil-portrait of my mother.

l'ai jamais aimée l'autre—j'amais bien mon neveu—adieu!—je le vois." ("I liked it very much: I do not like the other one: I never liked the other one. I was very fond of my nephew. Adieu! I see him.)

It was impossible to obtain any explanation of this incomprehensible scene, until, having slipped a pencil and a writing-tablet into Hélène's hand, she scribbled feverishly, in a hand not her own, these two words "*Mademoiselle Vignier*"; then she fell into a cataleptic phase, from which she awakened without memory at the end of half an hour.

This name of Vignier evoked in me far-off memories and vaguely recalled to my mind the fact that Professor Dandiran (who had married, as we have seen, my mother's sister) had an ancestress of that name; was it she who returned to express to me by means of Mlle. Smith her affection for my mother, whose portrait she had so attentively regarded, and her regrets, perhaps, that her nephew had not been preferred to my aunt?

On the other hand, M. Cuendet recollected a Mlle. Vignier who had been a friend of his family, but who did not correspond at all with the description of Hélène's visions; he promised to obtain information, and, in fact, wrote me on the following day: "Dear Sir,—Here is some information on the subject of our seance of yesterday. This morning I asked my mother: Did you ever know another Mlle. Vignier than the one who was your friend?' After an instant of reflection: 'Yes,' replied she; 'I did know another. She was M. Dandiran's aunt, of Lausanne, his mother's sister. She stammered, and was not always very good-natured; she had three large teeth which projected, and a hooked nose.' It is useless to state to you that this was the first time I had heard her spoken of."

This information, coinciding with my remembrances and Hélène's vision, was later confirmed by M. Dandiran, who gave me the following information: "Your aunt, Mlle. Vignier, who died about thirty-five or forty years ago, loved her nephew very much; but she was made very angry by his marriage, and the sentence uttered before my mother's portrait could not have referred to a difference of sentiment in regard to the two sisters, for whom she always had an equal affection. This sentence, on the contrary, is wonderfully well explained by the following facts: My mother and her sister having become betrothed at the same time, oil-paintings of both, of natural size, were made by the same painter. These portraits were not of equal merit, and Mlle. Vignier, who was herself something of an artist, always considered that of my mother excellent, while the other, that of my aunt, she did not like at all. Mlle. Vignier was very lively, and M. Dandiran finds that the epithet 'sly' and the table dictating '*That does not concern you*,' very well express her character; she was, however, not at all malicious or mocking at heart, but it is true that persons who knew her slightly could easily have gained that impression of her. She had three or four prominent teeth and stammered badly. In her photograph she wears a white collar, has a nose long and arched, but the eyes are rather large and wide apart. She always wore gold eye-glasses, of which the medium did not speak."

If the reader has had patience to read these details, he will have remarked that the distinctive traits of Mlle. Vignier in the vision and her incarnation by Hélène (the stammering, the teeth, the shape of the nose, the ill-natured air) coincide with those spontaneously indicated by M. Cuendet, who had known her slightly; and that while M. Dandiran, better posted as to his aunt's character, finds the note of maliciousness or want of good-nature false, he acknowledges that people outside of her family could have been deceived concerning it. That is to say, has not the imagination of Mlle. Smith produced the exterior memory, the description according to public notoriety, as it were, which Mlle. Vignier left behind her? And if it be recalled that at the period at which the two *fiancées* were painted, Mme. Smith was in communication with my maternal grandparents through the only sister of Mlle. Vignier, there would be a probability amounting almost to a certainty that these are contemporary remembrances, narrated some time or other to Hélène by her mother, and which furnished the material for this somnambulic personification.

In this example, to which I might add several analogous ones, the apparent *spirit control* is reduced to latent memories of recitals formerly heard by Hélène.

In other cases, in which, for lack of information, it has hitherto been impossible to discover this wholly natural filiation of facts, simple analysis of the circumstances and of the content of the communications indicates that, in all probability, they proceed from reminiscences and impressions appertaining to living individuals much rather than from disincarnates. In other words, these messages and personifications too evidently reflect the point of view of the medium or other living persons for it to be permissible to regard them as due to the intervention of deceased persons, whose attitude towards them would, in all probability, be wholly different.

2. *Case of Jean the Quarryman.*—We have here to deal with a very curious spirit message concerning Mme. Mirbel, in which I cannot fail to see actual memories of the latter—transmitted I know not how (but not necessarily in a supernormal manner) to Mlle. Smith—rather than an authentic communication from a pretended disincarnate.

In a seance at which Mme. Mirbel was not present, Hélène had the hallucination of a very strong odor of sulphur; then the vision of a quarryman from the foot of Salève, in which she perceived and described in detail an unknown man, who, by the dictations of the table, was declared to be *Jean the Quarryman*, and charged the sitters with an affectionate message for Mme. Mirbel. The latter, interrogated on the following day, recognized in the very circumstantial description of this man, and under all the features of Hélène's vision, perfectly correct facts connected with her childhood, and which had passed away from the habitual circle of her ideas for more than twenty years. It concerned a workman employed in her father's quarries, and who, when she was a little girl, had always evinced a special affection for her.

Let us suppose—in the absence of all proof that Mlle. Smith had ever heard these remembrances of Mme. Mirbel's childhood mentioned—that recourse must be had to the supernormal in order to explain the case. It still would not amount to an intervention of the deceased quarryman; and M. Lemaître was perfectly right, in my opinion, in clinging to telepathy and in hazarding the idea of an etheric influence, to which Hélène was subjected by Mme. Mirbel, who at the hour of this seance happened to be half a kilometre distant from the place of the seance. Without going out of the domain of telepathy, I still would prefer the hypothesis of a previous transmission in the course of one of the seances at which Mme. Mirbel was present to that of telepathy at a great distance at the time of the seance. It is, in fact, not contrary to that which is believed to be known of mental suggestion, to admit that Hélène's subliminal, in the state of Esenale, for example, could in some way draw from Mme. Mirbel's subliminal the latent memories which there lay buried for some time before being ready to reappear at a seance at which she had some reason to think Mme. Mirbel would again be present.

Whatever the mode of its transmission may have been, the content of this vision seems to me to indicate clearly that it has its origin in the personal memories of Mme. Mirbel rather than in the posthumous memory of Jean the Quarryman. All the presumptions in this case are, to my mind, in favor of a memory of Mme. Mirbel, and not of a veritable communication from the other world. The personal aspect of the messages supposed to be dictated by the quarryman do not constitute an obstacle to my interpretation or a guarantee of spiritistic authenticity, this aspect being the form that the automatisms habitually assume among mediums.

3. *Case of the Syndic Chaumontet and of the Curé Burnier.*—The following case is the last. It is a very recent one, in which the spiritistic and the cryptomnesiac hypotheses exist face to face, apropos of signatures written by Mlle. Smith in somnambulism which do not lack similarity to the authentic signatures of the deceased persons to whom they are supposed to belong.

In a seance at my house (February 12, 1899), Mlle. Smith has a vision of a village on a height covered with vines; by a rocky road, she sees descending from it a little old man, who has the air of a quasi gentleman; he wears shoes with buckles, a large felt hat, the collar of his shirt is unstarched, and has points reaching up to his cheeks, etc. A peasant in a blouse, whom he meets, makes reverences to him, as to an important personage; they speak a patois which Hélène-does not understand She has the impression of being familiar with the village, but vainly searches her memory to discover where she has seen it. Presently the landscape fades away, and the little old man, now clothed in white and in a luminous space (*i.e.*, in his actual reality of a disincarnate), appears to draw near to her. At this moment, as she leans her right arm upon the table, Leopold dictates by the index-finger: "*Kiss her arm.*" I execute the order; Hélène's arm at first resists strenuously, then yields suddenly. She seizes a pencil, and in the midst of the customary struggle relative to the manner of holding it (see p. 100), "*You are holding my hand too tightly*," says she to the imaginary little old man, who, according to Leopold, wishes to make use of it in order to write. "*You hurt me very badly; do not hold it so firmly. . . . What difference does it make whether it is a pencil or a pen?*" At these words she throws away the pencil and takes up a pen, and, holding it between the thumb and index-finger, slowly traces in an unknown hand: "*Chaumontet, syndic*" (see Fig. 44).

Then the vision of the village returns; at our desire to know the name of it she ultimately perceives a sign-post on which she spells "*Chessenaz,*" a name which is unknown to us. Then, having by my advice asked the little old man, whom she still sees, at what period he was syndic, she hears him answer, "1839."

It is impossible to learn more; the vision vanishes and gives way to a total incarnation of Leopold, who, in his deep Italian voice, speaks to us at length of various matters. I take advantage of it in order to question him upon the incident of the unknown village and syndic; his replies, interrupted by long digressions, may be summed up about as follows: "I am searching. . . . I traverse in thought the ascent of this great mountain pierced through at its foot by something, the name of which I do not know; I see the name of Chessenaz, a village on a height, and a road which ascends to it. Search in this village; you will certainly find the name (Chaumontet); seek to examine his signature; this proof you will find there; you will find that the handwriting was that of this man.

To my question whether he sees this in Hélène's memories and whether she has ever been at Chessenaz, he replies in the negative as to the first point and evasively as to the second: "Ask her; she has a good memory for everything. I have not followed her in all her wanderings."

Awakened, Hélène could not furnish us any information. But the following day I found on the map a little village called Chessenaz, in the Department of Haute-Savoie, twenty-six kilometres, in a straight line, from Geneva, and not far from the Crédo. As the Chaumontets are not rare in Savoy, there was nothing unlikely in the fact of a person of that name having been syndic there in 1839.

Two weeks 'later I made a visit to Mme. and Mlle. Smith—there was no seance held—when Hélène suddenly assumed the voice and accent of Leopold, without being aware of the change, and believing me to be joking when I sought to cause her to notice it. Presently the hemisomnambulism becomes accentuated; Hélène sees the vision of the other day, the village and then the little old man (the syndic) reappear, but the latter is accompanied this time by a *curé* with whom he seemed on good terms and whom he called (which she repeats to me all the while with Leopold's Italian accent), "*My dear friend Burnier.*" As I ask whether this *curé* could not write his name with Hélène's hand, Leopold promised me by a digital dictation that I should have that satisfaction at the next seance; then he begins to talk to me of something else by Hélène's mouth, she being now entirely entranced.

At the following seance at my house (the 19th of March), I remind Leopold of his promise. He answers at first by the finger: "*Do you very much desire that signature?*" and it is only upon my insisting that he consents. Hélène then is not long in again seeing the village and the *curé*, who after divers incidents takes hold of her hand as the syndic had done, and traces very slowly with the pen these words, "*Burnier greets you*" (Fig. 44); then she passes into other somnambulisms. The moment had arrived to clear up the matter. I wrote at hazard to the mayor's office at Chessenaz. The mayor, M. Saussier, had the kindness to answer without delay: "During the years 1838-39," stated he to me, "the syndic of Chessenaz was a Chaumontet, Jean, whose signature I find attached to divers documents of that period. We also had as *curé* M. Burnier, André, from November, 1824, up to February, 1841; during this period all the certificates of births, marriages, and deaths bear his signature. . . . But I have discovered in our archives a document bearing both signatures, that of the syndic Chaumontet and that of the *curé* Burnier. It is an order for the payment of money. I take pleasure in transmitting it to you." I have caused to be reproduced in the middle of Fig. 44 the fragment of this original document (dated July 29, 1838), bearing the names of these two personages; the reader can thus judge for himself in regard to the quite remarkable similarity which there exists between these authentic signatures and those automatically traced by the hand of Mlle. Smith.

My first idea was, as may be supposed, that Mlle. Smith must some time or other have seen some certificates or documents signed by the syndic or by the *curé* of Chessenaz, and that it was these forgotten visual flashes, reappearing in somnambulism, which had served her as inner models when her entranced hand retraced these signatures. One may likewise imagine how angry such a supposition would make Hélène, who has no recollection whatever of having ever heard the name of Chessenaz nor of any of its inhabitants, past or present. I only half regret my imprudent supposition, since it has availed to furnish us a new and more explicit manifestation of the *curé*, who, again taking hold of Mlle. Smith's arm at a later seance (May 21st, at M. Lemaître's) comes to certify to us as to his identity by the attestation, in due and proper form, of Fig. 43. As is there seen, he makes it twice; being deceived as to the signature, he incontinently, with disgust, crosses out that which he had so carefully written, and recommences on another sheet; this second draft, in which he has omitted the word "*soussigné*" ("undersigned") of the first, took him seven minutes to trace, but leaves nothing to be desired as to precision and legibility. This painstaking calligraphy is very like that of a country *curé* of sixty years ago, and in default of another specimen for comparison, it presents an undeniable analogy of hand with the authentic receipt of the order for payment of money of Fig. 44.

Neither Mlle. Smith nor her mother had the least notion in regard to the *curé* or the syndic of Chessenaz. They nevertheless informed me that their family formerly had some relatives and connections in that part of Savoy, and that they are still in communication with a cousin who lives at Frangy, an

Fig. 43. Certificates written (May 21, 1899) by Mlle. Smith while in a trance. The one above was feverishly crossed out in finishing the faulty signature. The one below was afterwards written in seven minutes. Natural size. [From the collection of M. Lemaitre.]

important town nearest the little village of Chessenaz. Hélène herself made only a short excursion in that region, some dozen years ago; and if, in following the road from Seyssel to Frangy, she traversed some parts of the country corresponding well to certain details of her vision of the 12th of February (which she had the feeling of recognizing, as we have seen, p. 432), she has not, on the other hand, any idea of having been at Chessenaz itself, nor of having heard it mentioned. "Moreover," says she, "for those who can suppose that I could have been at Chessenaz without remembering it, I would affirm that even had I gone there I would not have been apt to consult the archives in order to learn that a syndic Chaumontet and a *curé* Burnier had existed there at a period more or less remote. I have a good memory, and I positively affirm that no one of the persons around me during those few days while I was away from my family ever showed me any certificate, paper—anything, in a word—which could have stored away in my brain any such memory. My mother, at the age of fourteen or fifteen, made a trip into Savoy, but nothing in her remembrances recalls her ever having heard these two names uttered."

The facts are now presented, and I leave to the reader the privilege of drawing such conclusion from them as shall please him.

This case seemed to me worthy to crown my rapid examination of the supernormal appearances which embellish the mediumship of Mlle. Smith, because it sums up and puts excellently in relief the irreconcilable

Fig. 44. Comparison of the signatures of the syndic Chaumontet and of the curate Burnier, with their pretended signatures as disincarnates given by Mlle. Smith in somnambulism. In the middle of the figure, reproduction of a fragment of an order for payment of money of 1838. Above and below, the signatures furnished by the hand of Hélène. Natural size.

and hostile respective positions of the spiritistic circles and mediums on the one side, perfectly sincere but too easily satisfied—and investigators somewhat psychological on the other, always pursued by the sacrosanct terror of taking dross for gold. To the first class, the least curious phenomenon—an unexpected vision of the past, some dictation of the table or the finger, an access of somnambulism, a resemblance of handwriting—

suffices to give the sensation of contact with the unknown and to prove the actual presence of the disincarnate world. They never ask themselves what proportion there could well be between these premises, however striking they may be, and that formidable conclusion. Why and how, for example, should the dead, returning at the end of a half-century to sign by the hand of another person in flesh and blood, have the same hand-writing as when alive?

The same people who find this altogether natural, although they have never seen any absolutely certain cases of it, fall from the clouds when the possibility of latent memories is invoked before them, of which the present life furnishes them, moreover, daily examples—which they have not, it is true, ever taken the trouble to observe.

The psychologists, on the contrary, have the evil one in them in going to look behind the scenes of the memory and the imagination, and when the obscurity prevents them from seeing anything, they have the folly to imagine that they will end by finding that which they are seeking—if only a light could be had.

Between these two classes of temperaments so unlike, it will, I fear, be very difficult ever to arrive at any satisfactory and lasting understanding.

CONCLUSION

THIS volume reminds me of the mountain which gave birth to a mouse. Its length would be excusable if only it marked a step in advance in the field of psychology or physiology, or as to the question of the supernormal. As such is not the case, it is unpardonable, and nothing more is left me to do except to make clear its deficiencies in this triple aspect.

First: From the physiological point of view, it is apparent that Mlle. Smith, as is doubtless true of all mediums, presents during her visions and somnambulisms a plenitude of disturbances of motility and sensibility, from which she seems entirely free in her normal state.

But these trifling observations do not suffice to solve the neuropathological problem of mediumship, and the question still remains open as to whether that term corresponds to a special category of manifestations and to a distinct syndrome, or whether it merely constitutes a happy euphemism for various scientific denominations already in use.

To endeavor to fix the connections of mediumship with other functional affections of the nervous system, it would first be necessary to possess exact intelligence on a number of important points still enveloped in obscurity. In regard to some of these, such as the phenomena of periodicity, of meteorological and seasonal influences, of impulses, and of fatigue, etc., we have only very vague and incomplete hints. And we know almost nothing of other still more essential questions, such as the relations of equivalence and substitution between the various modalities of automatism (nocturnal visions, crepuscular states, complete trances, etc.), the effect of spiritistic exercises, and especially of that of the seances upon nutrition or denutrition (variations of temperature, of urotoxicity, etc.), which would permit the comparison of spontaneous seizures and those excited by mediumship with those of the more serious nervous affections, the phenomena of heredity, similar or reversed, etc.

Let us hope that a near future will establish some good mediums and their observers in practical conditions favorable to the elucidation of these various problems, and that the day will come when the true place of mediumship in the framework of nosology will be discovered.

Secondly: Front the psychological point of view, the case of Mlle. Smith, although too complex to be reduced to a single formula, is explicable *grosso modo* by some recognized principle, the successive or concurrent action of which has engendered her multiple phenomena. There is, in the first place, the influence, so often verified, of emotional shocks and of certain psychic traumatisms upon mental dissociation. By means of these the birth of hypnoid states may become the germ either of secondary personalities more or less strongly marked (we have seen that the first manifestations of Leopold in the childhood of Hélène are attributable to this cause) or of somnambulistic romances, which hold the same relation towards the normal state as does that exaggeration of stories and indulgence in reveries to which so many are addicted—perhaps all of us.

We must also take into consideration the enormous suggestibility and auto-suggestibility of mediums, which render them so sensitive to all the influences of spiritistic reunions, and are so favorable to the play of those brilliant subliminal creations in which, occasionally, the doctrinal ideas of the surrounding environment are reflected together with the latent emotional tendencies of the medium herself. The development of the personality of Leopold-Cagliostro, starting from the moment at which Mlle. Smith began her seances, is easily explained in this manner, as well as the Martian dream and the previous existences of the Hindoo princess and the queen of France.

And, finally, we must note the phenomena of cryptomnesia, the awakening and setting to work of forgotten memories, which easily account for the elements of truth contained in the great preceding constructions and in the incarnations or casual visions of Mlle. Smith in the course of her seances.

But besides this general explanation how many points of detail there are which remain obscure! For example, the precise origin of Hélène's Sanscrit, and many of her retrocognitions, for want of information concerning the thousand facts of her daily life whence the ideas which nourish her somnambulism may have been drawn! And how difficult it is to gain a correct idea of her case as a whole, on account of the crudity of our actual notions as to the constitution and organization of the human being, of our almost total ignorance of psychological ontogeny!

Without mentioning Hélène's ephemeral incarnations (in which I have shown there is no reason far seeing anything beyond the imitations due to autosuggestion), the divers more stable personalities which manifest themselves in her hypnoid life—Leopold, Esenale, and the actors of the Martian romance, Simandini, Marie Antoinette, etc.—are only, in my opinion, as I have hinted on many occasions, the varied psychological states of Mlle. Smith herself—allotropic modifications, as it were, or phenomena of polymorphism of her personality. For no one of these personalities corresponds sufficiently with her ordinary personality by intellectual faculties, the moral character, separation of memories, to justify the hypothesis of a foreign *possession*.

But the theory of psychic polymorphism is still very imperfect, and inadequate to explain the embryological shades which shine forth in Hélène's subliminal products—the retrograde perspective which they open as to the different stages or periods of her evolution. The Martian cycle, with its unknown language, evidently betrays an eminently puerile origin and the display of an hereditary linguistic aptitude, buried under Hélène's ordinary self; whereas the Hindoo romance denotes a more advanced age, and that of Marie Antoinette seems to have sprung from still more recent strata, contemporaneous with the actual normal personality of Mlle. Smith. The primitive nature and different ages of the various hypnoid lucubrations of Mlle. Smith seem to me to constitute the most interesting psychological fact of her mediumship. It tends to show that the secondary personalities are probably, in their origin, as the idea has been sometimes suggested, phenomena of reversion of the ordinary actual personality, or of momentary returns of inferior phases, long since passed, and which normally should have been absorbed in the development of the individuality, instead of breaking forth again in strange proliferations.

Thirdly: As to the supernormal, I believe I have actually found a little telekinesis and telepathy. As to lucidity and spiritistic messages, I have only encountered some brilliant reconstructions, which the hypnoid imagination, aided by latent memory, excels in fabricating in the case of mediums. I do not complain of this, since for psychology, which is not specially enamoured of the marvellous, these admirably successful imitations are also interesting and instructive on account of the light which they throw upon the inward workings of our faculties.

Of course Mlle. Smith and her friends see things in a very different light. With Hélène everything, or almost everything, is supernormal, from the reminiscences of her lives as Marie Antoinette and Simandini, to the Martian and the incarnations of Cagliostro, of Mlle. Vignier, or of the *curé* of Chessenaz.

And now let us admit, hypothetically, that I have not been able to see the supernormal, which was plainly before my eyes, and that it is this blindness of mine alone which has prevented me from recognizing the real presence of Joseph Balsamo, my own mother, the Hindoo princess, etc.—or, at all events, the presence of real, disincarnate, independent spirits. It is, of course, to be regretted, but then it is I alone who will be in disgrace on the day when the truth shall be made manifest.

For, as to progress in our knowledge of things, everything is to be feared from easy credulity and obstinate dogmatism, but that progress will not be arrested or seriously retarded by possible errors, committed in good faith, through an exaggerated severity of application and a too strict observance of the principles themselves of all experimental investigation: while, on the contrary, the obstacles and the difficulties which the necessities of the method multiply along its path have always been a strong stimulant, producing new movements forward and more durable conquests based on better demonstrations.

It is better, then, to follow my advice—in the well-understood interest of and for the advancement of science, in a domain where superstition is always ready to give itself free play—it is better to err through excess of caution and strictness of method than to run the risk of being sometimes deceived; it is better to allow some interesting fact to escape for the moment, rather than to open the door to the follies of the imagination by a relaxation of necessary caution.

As to Mlle. Hélène Smith, supposing that I have failed to recognize in her phenomena which are really supernormal (which, in that case, will some day be better set forth by other observers), she will, nevertheless, accomplish more in the way of discovering the real truth, whatever it may be, in submitting herself disinterestedly to my free criticisms, than by doing as so many useless mediums have done, who, afraid of the light, in their foolish eagerness for the triumph of a cause very dear to their hearts, have shunned close investigation, and would have us rely upon their word alone. They forget the saying of Bacon, which is ever being confirmed: "*Truth is the daughter of time, not of authority.*"

www.ingramcontent.com/pod-product-compliance
Lightning Source LLC
Chambersburg PA
CBHW051543010526
44118CB00022B/2558